Local Health and Welfare
Is Partnership Possible?

A Study of the Dinnington Project

Michael Bayley,
Rosalind Seyd and
Alan Tennant

Gower
Aldershot · Brookfield USA · Hong Kong · Singapore · Sydney

Published by
Gower Publishing Company Limited
Gower House
Croft Road
Aldershot
Hants GU11 3HR
England

Gower Publishing Company
Old Post Road
Brookfield
Vermont 05036
USA

British Library Cataloguing in Publication Data

Bayley, Michael, *1936 –*
   Local health and welfare : is partnership
   possible?
   1. Community health services — Great
   Britain — Case studies
   I. Title II. Seyd, Rosalind
   III. Tennant, Alan, *1947 –*
   362.1'0425   RA 485

Library of Congress Cataloguing-in-Publication Data

Bayley, Michael.
   Local health and welfare.
   Bibliography: p.
   Includes index.
   1. Community health services — England — Dinnington
(Rotherham) 2. Social service — England — Dinnington
(Rotherham) I. Title II. Seyd, Rosalind, 1943 –
III. Tennant, Alan, 1947 –   . III. Title.
RA488.D56B39 1988   362.1'09428'23   87–21082

ISBN 0 566 053691

Printed in Great Britain by Billing & Sons Ltd, Worcester

LOCAL HEALTH AND WELFARE:
IS PARTNERSHIP POSSIBLE?

For Jill, Robin, Andrew and Emma
Benjamin, Dan and Rachel
Matthew, Luke and Peter

Contents

List of tables and figures   vi
Foreword   vii
Preface   x

1 Introduction   1
2 Informal care: the context of the project 4
3 Setting up the project   21
4 Introducing Dinnington   31
5 A model for the development of community practice 51
6 Formal care before the project   56
7 Four important influences on the action 78
8 The health service   83
9 The social workers   94
10 Other local authority services 123
11 A real partnership?   147
12 Discussion and implications 164

Bibliography   183
Index   190

Tables and Figures

Tables

4.1 Care given by relatives, and by friends and neighbours,
to 187 patients or clients of health and welfare services,
1980   35

4.2 Average number of visits made by relatives, and by
friends and neighbours, to 187 patients or clients of
health and welfare services, 1980   37

4.3 Frequency of visiting by relatives, and by friends and
neighbours, to187 patients or clients of health and
welfare services, 1980   37

4.4 Type of care reported as being received by 187
patients and clients of health and welfare services,
1980   43

4.5 Relationship of care giver and type of care reported by
187 patients and clients of health and welfare services,
1980   46

5.1 Development of community practice   53

8.1 Persons consulting a general practitioner, by sex and
age, 1980-2   84

9.1 Principal characteristics of community social work
practice: long-, medium- and short-term cases, 1979
and 1981   100

9.2 Referrals made to project office, 1980 and 1982   109

9.3 Source of referrals to the social work service, 1980 and
1982   110

10.1 Home help service provision, 1979 and 1982   125

Figures

3.1 Dinnington research programme   29

8.1 District nursing practice, 1980 and 1982   92

9.1 Community social work/locally-based work matrix 121

Foreword

Community care has been talked about for well over 20 years. It has been a declared policy of successive governments to promote and foster community care, particularly for elderly, mentally ill, mentally handicapped and disabled people. Despite this long standing policy and a broad acceptance by society at large that providing care in the community is better than providing it in institutions, progress has been patchy to say the least.

In recent years interest has again grown in community care, perhaps unsurprisingly, since some £6bn is spent annually in public funds providing long term care and support for people in the community; millions of people receive such care and millions are involved in delivering it. The only surprise is that community care has taken so long to come to the forefront of policy concerns. The 1986 report of the Audit Commission 'Making a Reality of Community Care' identified major drawbacks in the current provision of community care services, focusing specifically on the effect of funding policies on the provision of care and the organization of services to provide that care in the most effective and efficient manner. This report in turn spurred the government to ask me to review the way in which public funds are used to support community care policy. My report 'Community Care: Agenda for Action' was published in March 1988. It is against the background of these reports that this study will inevitably be read. But it is important to remember that the project described here began life in 1980 and has been concerned with turning the existing community care policy into reality. The Dinnington Project, chronicled here in such sharp detail by Dr Michael Bayley and his colleagues, serves to illustrate both the potential and pitfalls of a number of recommendations contained in the two reports, in particular, the development of packages of care; the need for effective co-operation (at global level); and the need for inter-professional working to ensure delivery of effective services.

When Dr Bayley approached me to write the foreword to this book and described the project to me I was irresistibly drawn to it as the community he describes is very close to the small mining community where I grew up. That village, like Dinnington, had a strong sense of identity and we looked after our own. The Dinnington 'Hut' served as the catalyst which enabled that community once more to assert its identity and to express it more fully through its caring services. T.S. Eliot wrote 'Where there is no temple there shall be no homes, though you have shelters and institutions'. In small communities a sense of belonging is often strongly expressed, or never far from the surface. In larger communities that sense of identity, of ownership, is more difficult to find but imaginative projects will often find themselves tapping into rich veins of community feeling and can serve as a new focus for that identity.

While I was engaged on drawing up my report I made many visits around the country to see the process of community care in action. One of the enduring memories I have is of the sheer diversity of need and the complexities involved in meeting those needs. I was left with the very strong impression that no one agency could hope within its own resources to meet successfully all those needs. Clearly, then, if we are not to abandon hope entirely of ever delivering good quality services to those in the community who need them, then partnership must not only be possible but it must be recognized as necessary and made commonplace. To achieve this is not easy but, as this study shows, it is not impossible. Clear goals, shared objectives, a common language and clear responsibilities are the key elements needed for co-operative projects to succeed. One version of the process of making that co-operation a reality is clearly evidenced here.

This study begins with people and their need for care. The cases it draws on illustrate clearly the range of those needs and equally the range of responses which are possible to meet those needs. It also looks at how best to enable those needs to be met, both immediately and at the organizational level, getting right down to the practicalities of confronting and overcoming the various roadblocks to care which, inevitably, exist at present.

Dr Bayley and his team have tackled that most difficult of management processes, the translation of ideas into actions. In doing so they have shown that, although the road may be difficult, the provision of good quality community care is not impossible if it is built on individual needs, if it involves the individual user of services and their carers and if it is sensitive to what they have to say about services. This study also proves, if proof were needed, that there is a great deal to be achieved in the community without waiting for government to act to initiate reviews or to undertake re-organization. Such central action takes time. Local initiative can go a long way towards improving things now and smoothing the path for when central action is taken to develop care services.

The Dinnington Project demonstrates what can be achieved with relatively little in the way of additional resources. The local nature of the project led quickly to the involvement of the local community, users and carers, it afforded easy access and fostered a spirit of ownership. This in turn led to an increased responsiveness in the project offices and when combined with initiative and flair produced many instances of effective service co-ordination and delivery.

The authors of this report are not however deceived into regarding all their achievements in a rosy light. The project is subject to careful analysis and its shortcomings are recognized.

This project, while unique in the particular solutions developed to meet the particular challenges encountered, has valuable lessons in terms of approach which can be usefully studied by those involved in the difficult, complex, and rewarding business of delivering services to people. I commend this report to all those interested in translating the rhetoric of community care into action. I hope that many will learn the lessons that this project teaches and that others are fired with the message it conveys.

Sir Roy Griffiths
October 1988

Preface

When the first ideas for this research were mooted in 1975, patchwork or locally-based work was an idea in the minds of a few and the practice of even fewer. Now the idea is fashionable, the practice quite widespread and the terminology confusing. We had problems with the terminology.

Patch, patchwork, community social work, community-orientated work, community practice, locally-based work and other variations are all in use. The term 'patch' or 'patchwork' had, we felt, become too much of a rallying cry and we wanted as objective a term as possible. Eventually we decided on 'locally-based work' as the term we would use generally. This is partly because it is descriptive and does not carry connotations in the way some of the other phrases do. However, it is not entirely adequate because the approach we are considering in the book is not just locally based but also community-orientated and probably the least inaccurate phrase we could have used would have been 'locally-based community-orientated work'. This is too clumsy but when we say 'locally-based', 'community-orientated' is implied as well. Just occasionally we use this full phrase as a reminder.

Another advantage of the term 'locally-based work' for us was that it could apply equally well to all types of worker, and this is particularly important as the Dinnington project covered a wide range of agencies within both local authority and health authority. Only in Chapter 9 on social work do we use a term, 'community social work', that is specific to one department (because it is relevant to that setting).

We also use the phrase 'community practice' when we are mainly concerned with the workers' overall approach. Thus, for example, in Chapter 5 we refer to a model for the development of community practice. This also acknowledges that there are some aspects of community practice which may not necessarily be locally based, although in Dinnington all the services were based in the village.

The debate about locally-based work is often conducted more on the basis of personal conviction, for or against, than on the basis of evidence. This study adds to the evidence that is slowly accumulating and we hope that it will assist constructive debate, encourage imaginative practice and point to where further research is needed.

The research side of the project was funded jointly by Rotherham Metropolitan Borough Council, with support from Urban Aid, and the

Department of Health and Social Security. Evaluation of the project was undertaken by a research team in the Department of Sociological Studies in the University of Sheffield under the direction of Michael Bayley.

We acknowledge gratefully the initiative and determination of those members and officers of Rotherham Local Authority and Area Health Authority who contributed to the development of the project. In addition, we would like to thank the fieldworkers and the people in Dinnington, who co-operated unstintingly in providing research data, ideas and encouragement. The fieldworkers in particular showed great patience in filling up innumerable research forms.

We wish to thank the National Westminster Bank and Lloyds Bank for grants which carried us over difficult gaps in our funding.

Many people have helped and advised us. We would like to acknowledge the help of the members of the research advisory group: Eric Sainsbury, John Westergaard, John Knowelden, Jack Barnes, I.F. Ralph. Hazel Qureshi, Peter Marsh, Roger Hadley and Phoebe Hall made invaluable comments on drafts of various papers. Hazel Canter, our liaison officer at the DHSS, has given consistent support and much helpful advice, and Tilda Goldberg gave invaluable guidance, especially in the early stages of the project.

We acknowledge the part played by our interviewers, headed by Margaret Fall, our secretaries Brigitte Byart and Margaret Jaram, who have been key members of the research team, and Janice Hart, who has been a tireless assistant with innumerable administrative tasks.

Finally we acknowledge our debt to two former colleagues in the research team who have been co-authors of some of the earlier articles and reports, Paul Parker and Ken Simons, who succeeded him. Paul's energy and enthusiasm played a vital part in launching and sustaining the project, especially in its difficult early stages.

Michael Bayley
Rosalind Seyd
Alan Tennant

January 1987

1 Introduction

On the face of it life was not very bright for Mrs Fenton. She lived in a semi-detached house on one of the less desirable council estates in Sheffield with her daughter, Joyce. Her husband had been killed in the 1939–45 war and her son, her only other child, had been killed in a car accident two years previously. Joyce was severely handicapped, mentally and physically. She could not talk at all, though she was able to communicate a little by noises, and physically she could do nothing for herself. She was in bed permanently: she could not feed herself or even hold her head up. At the time of the visit for the research interview Joyce was in her mid-twenties. How, one might ask, had her mother managed to cope with the pressure of caring for Joyce for that long?

In fact she had coped very well, not just because she was a competent and resolute woman, but also she received a great deal of support from other members of her family. She had two sisters and two brothers. This quotation from the interview gives some idea about how the family functioned.

> The eldest lives quite close. She is the one whose caravan I go to stay in when I go on holiday. I see her every Tuesday and Friday. They come up ... and while they're here my sister and sister-in-law, that helps to bath Joyce, they'll do my mother's ironing because she can't stand. This sister-in-law comes in on Monday, Tuesday and Friday. Monday she comes to help bath Joyce, on Tuesday she is here with my elder sister. Sister-in-law's husband, my brother, is on turns. When he is on nights he pops over before he goes to bed, and if he's over and Joyce is still in bed, he'll go up and carry her down.
>
> Then I've another sister who lives quite close, that's the one whose husband took us up into Yorkshire Dales, and it's their girl what sits with Joyce, and boyfriend.
>
> *Interviewer*: Is this mostly at weekends, that they sit in with her?
>
> Well Thursday, if her dad can't get up she'll get up in place of her dad, and then me and her mother have an hour at tombola.
>
> *Interviewer*: So you see all the members of the family quite frequently?
>
> Oh yes, we all sort of live in a circle.

This case example is taken from previous research conducted by one of the authors (Michael Bayley) from 1967–72 on community care for people with mental handicaps. That research had been founded on the belief that informal care by family, friends and neighbours was the basic care on which all other care, voluntary and statutory, needed to be based, and the research gave ample evidence to support this view (Bayley 1973). Joyce's family was an outstanding example of that. Not many families could match the extent of support given by her family but, though there were some families who received very little support, overall the amount of care and support given was impressive.

That earlier research not only found remarkably extensive informal care, help and support for people with mental handicaps, but also considerable expertise. Many of the parents were highly skilled in the way they cared for their handicapped sons and daughters. For example, Judith was also very severely disabled. She looked as though she could only sit in a wheelchair. When her mother was asked if she could move around herself, she explained how she had taught Judith to walk and then she had encountered another problem.

> She didn't know a door from a space when I started her walking. She knew that she went through this door, but I think she thought it were permanently open, but her brain didn't tell her it was closed and she used to go smash into it like a budgie out of a cage when it goes blind. We got four steps, we got marvellous right up to this door, and I knew she hadn't the sense to know it was a space. Anyway we started putting her hand on the handle and pushing it, and she used to cry, but we did it, week in and week out, she could open a door you know in six months.

These findings, which showed the extent and importance of informal care and the great competence of many carers, seemed to have a wider relevance than just the care of people with mental handicaps. Indeed the study had been undertaken in the first place as a case study of what was meant by community care and especially the part that 'the community', that is ordinary people, played in it. All this suggested that it would be valuable to set up a project which would test the findings of the mental handicap study in a wider context. Central to such a study would be the importance of informal care and how it was possible for statutory care to link in more efficiently and sensitively with it. One major clue about how that might be done was provided by this earlier research. It was apparent that the most effective informal care was generally provided by someone who lived near at hand. Thus it seemed that nearness might well be an important element in an effective service and that in turn meant that it would need to be locally based. This also seemed to be a requirement if the workers were going to *know* enough about informal care to be able to link in with and support its complex patterns.

This was the main premise behind testing the idea in a wider context – that a pattern and style needed to be found to enable the statutory bodies to offer their services so that they could fit in with local patterns of informal care rather than the other way round. There was an important supplementary premise. People have both welfare needs and health needs. We cannot divide people into separate health and welfare parts but, of course, that is precisely how the services are divided. Thus the supplementary premise was the simple one that far closer co-operation was needed between health and welfare (mostly local authority) services.

These two premises put the issue in a rather mechanical way as though it is just a question of getting the organization right and the ideal service will follow. There is obviously far more to it than that. Underlying the two premises is the conviction that well-being, welfare and health are not technical matters for the experts but are rooted in the life, experience and competence of ordinary people and that responsibility for them is something to be shared in a partnership with professionals, not handed over to them. Indeed the extent to which it is possible to achieve a genuine partnership is likely to be the acid test of any such project. To put the matter another way, the underlying assumption behind the project was that life in society, not just in the realms of health and welfare, is not a matter of people becoming as independent as they can, nor of allowing themselves to become dependent (though sometimes that is appropriate) but of acknowledging that all members of society are interdependent and that includes relationships with the formal agencies we have created to help cater for our health, welfare and other needs.

It is one thing to have the idea that a more widely-based project is desirable: it is quite another to have the opportunity to try it out in practice, especially if it is to embrace not just local authority welfare services but also health services. It was fortunate that Rotherham MDC approached Sheffield University in 1976 to help them develop the work of their social services department. This invitation happened to be passed down to Michael Bayley and the eventual result was the Dinnington Project.

This account of the project shows how these ideas did or did not work out in the reality of everyday practice. First, we shall consider the social, political and professional background to the project.

2 Informal Care: The Context of the Project

The 1970s were years of considerable change in the health and welfare services, which we call collectively the welfare state. This was largely due to organizational changes which began in 1971 with the reorganization of social services following the Seebohm Report (1968), continued with the reorganization of local government and the health service in 1974, spilling over into the 1980s with a further reorganization of the health services in 1982. These changes were brought about by both political and professional interests, which may be seen as two forces for change that can be followed through the 1970s, sometimes overlapping but mostly separate. Together they form the backdrop to the Dinnington Project and as such it is important that we are aware of their general characteristics. Their crucial importance, however, lies in the fact that towards the end of the 1970s, these two forces came together to give rise to a quite extraordinary interest in informal care.

Informal care, that is care given by family, friends and neighbours, makes up the largest part of what is often referred to as the informal sector, which also subsumes those aspects of the voluntary sector associated with the individual volunteer, or small voluntary group, as well as other aspects of lay care such as self-help groups. It does not, however, include large-scale voluntary agencies which often mimic the state-run agencies, not only in organizational terms, but also in the fact that some of them are predominantly funded by the state. The informal sector, of course, predates and dwarfs the welfare state in all but the latter's most sophisticated aspects. That it has been 'discovered' in the 1970s is a remarkable story, not because of its discovery *per se,* but rather because of the strange alliance of forces which have contributed to the emphasis that is being placed on it. The Dinnington Project has been an integral part of the growth of this alliance. As a background to the project we shall look back to see what we can discover about these political and professional forces for change, and set the scene for one small experiment in health and welfare care in a northern mining community.

Professional interest in informal care

We begin with this as its roots are more obvious. We are not attempting a systematic synthesis of professional and political developments, although undoubtedly one has influenced the other throughout the period. We would argue that professional interest preceded the political in becoming aware of the informal sector, and so we begin our account with a look at the development of the notion of community care and some related concepts and developments.

Community care and the growth of understanding of the importance of informal care

If we consider the change that has taken place in the official understanding of that much-abused term 'community care', we can see that, for all the reservations that must be made, it has turned from being simply a reaction to the damage that institutions can do to their residents, especially long-term residents, to being a policy which has at least some understanding of the positive role that 'the community' can play. An important part of the development of that understanding has been the appreciation of the central role of informal care as well as the importance of volunteers. This development can be traced through the Seebohm Report (1968), the Aves Report (1969), the Wolfenden Report (1978), the *Care in the Community* document (DHSS 1981a) and the Barclay Report (1982). The effect of these reports has been to place a steadily greater emphasis on the need for a community orientation in the formal services. They both reflect and reinforce the growing awareness of the importance of informal care.

Along with this growing appreciation of the importance of informal care has gone the notion of interweaving. This was implicit in the Seebohm Report. In the chapter on 'the Community', it spoke about the importance of community development and in the course of this it said (para. 483):

> Just as we have argued that the family often needs assistance and encourage-ment to perform many of its mutual aid and caring functions, so too the wider groups to which people belong need help in developing these attributes. We are not suggesting that 'welfare through community' is an alternative to the social services but that it is complementary and inextricably interwoven.

This idea was taken up by one of the authors (Bayley 1973; 1978). It is important to be clear about the case that is being argued. Bayley (1973) considered in his introductory chapter three prepositions which could come between 'community' and 'care': care *out of* the community, exemplified by the large institutions; care *in* the community, for example large hostels for mentally handicapped people which have little or no contact with the people living in the neighbourhood in which they are built; and care *by* the community, which refers to the whole mass of informal care given by family, friends and neighbours. This has some-times been read as if Bayley was supporting the view put forward by

Patrick Jenkin when he was Secretary of State for Social Services, which appears in the White Paper *Growing Older* (DHSS 1981b, p.3), that 'care *in* the community, must increasingly mean care *by* the community'. Such an interpretation implies a policy approach to the role of informal care which ignores the vital importance of the notion of the interweaving of formal and informal care. In his final prescriptive chapter, as opposed to his introductory descriptive chapter, Bayley (1973, p.343) outlines the notion of interweaving and what he thinks the relationship between formal and informal care should be:

> The simile of the interweaving of the informal help and caring process active throughout society, and the contribution of the social services, is a sound one. It takes one beyond the stage of care *in* the community at home but living in isolation from those round about. It takes one beyond care *in* the community *in* institutions, even small ones, which have little involvement or share in the community. It takes one beyond care *by* the community, if by that one is suggesting that members of the community, untrained and unaided, should be left to get on with it. It takes one to the point where a partnership of the community at large and the social services is seen as essential to both. The caring done by families, friends, neighbours or larger, more organized groups of people is seen, recognised and acknowledged. An attempt is made to see both particular needs, and the strengths and limitations of the informal resources available. The social services seek to interweave their help so as to use and strengthen the help already given, make good the limitations and meet the needs. It is not a question of the social services plugging the gaps but rather of their working with *society* to enable *society* to close the gaps.

Such an understanding of the relationship between formal, informal and voluntary care requires a far more dynamic approach than is implied in such a passive word as 'care' (one of the many disadvantages of the phrase 'community care'). Something of that dynamic can be seen in the growing importance attached to participation.

Participation
The last two decades have witnessed increasing demands for the rights of those affected by the decisions of official bodies to have some say in those decisions. The publication of the Skeffington Report in 1969 marked a change in the theory of how planning departments should proceed, even if the practice has lagged behind. Local action groups on housing and social issues have become increasingly effective and the *principle* of participation is established firmly, though large bureaucracies still find it difficult to put it into practice.

Self-help groups, mutual help groups, pressure groups and parents' groups are another manifestation of the growing expectation that the users of services should be able to participate in decisions about those services. They have made impressive progress in persuading the authorities that they must be consulted when policies are being decided. Again it is true that much remains to be done, but it is interesting to note that in the *Report of the All-Wales Working Party on Services for Mentally Handicapped People* (Welsh Office 1982) considerable emphasis is put on the need to involve the voluntary bodies, such as MENCAP, in the whole of the planning process. In practice, consultation is being made a requirement by the Welsh Office before the authorities receive the cash to develop the services.

The influence of community work was evident in the Community Development Projects. These showed the potential of some forms of locally-based action and development, but they also laid bare the broader social and economic issues that must be taken into account. Community work has continued to exercise its influence on the development of locally-based work, though in a less spectacular way, and has helped to keep the issue of genuine participation alive and make people aware of the power issues that are involved.

Beresford (1981), for example, has argued strongly for local *control* of social services departments and has been very critical of patch schemes which do not give an adequate say to local people, a theme which Beresford and Croft (1986) have developed subsequently.

Developments in social service departments

Another factor which has contributed to the development of the locally-based approach is a negative one, that is the widespread but often ill-defined unease with the style of service delivery of many social service departments. The part played by the Seebohm Report in the developments which have led to this state of affairs is curiously ambiguous. We referred to the Seebohm Report above as a report which had contributed to the development of the understanding of the role that the community at large has to play in welfare. That is quite correct, but, as Hadley and McGrath (1981) point out:

> The Seebohm re-organisation can be seen as having offered two different directions for development. One was towards greater specialisation and professionalism, as conventionally understood. The other was towards greater community involvement. While both developments were advocated in the Seebohm Report, the Committee did not seem to appreciate that they were likely to prove incompatible, at least with foreseeable levels of staffing. In practice, by coming down in favour of large area teams on the grounds of the needs of the social workers, rather than much smaller areas related to the requirements of the community, the Report effectively favoured the professional-specialist model of organisation. Most, but not all, local authorities followed this lead.

A succession of reports in recent years have painted a reasonably consistent picture of social workers and social service departments (for example, Stevenson and Parsloe 1978; Parsloe 1981; Sainsbury *et al.* 1982; Black *et al.* 1983). That picture is one of the dominance of one-to-one casework, little teamwork, poor relationships between workers and managers, poor and sporadic contacts with workers from other disciplines and domiciliary workers, little contact with the wider social networks of clients, few contacts with or adaptation to the localities in which work was being carried out, a narrow departmentally-limited approach, and a management system and professional orientation which reinforced this. It is a disturbing picture. In the conclusion of their study of clients' and social workers' perceptions in long-term social work Sainsbury *et al.* (1982, p.178) write:

> The study drew our attention also to the serious limitations of the 'encapsulated case-load' model of work-organisation – a model which was implicitly endorsed and perpetuated by the use of the one-to-one style of supervision and by the traditional procedures of case-allocation following intake. The limitations of this model were illustrated in several ways: cases were rarely shared with other workers (inside or outside the agency), even when the social worker felt seriously at a loss and when a family's circumstances were in serious decline; although both workers and clients stressed the need for more time, the use of volunteers (initially at below 1:10 of families) declined over time; within the team-structures, little use was made of some available expertise (for example from home helps or community workers). Not surprisingly, therefore, collaboration with other services owed less to a broad conception of family needs than to the onset of particular crises or to the personal interests of individual workers. This collaboration was ad hoc, spasmodic and structurally underdeveloped. Clients were, in effect, dependent on the limited expertise and vision of an individual worker, with little access to other help (save on their own initiative), and with virtually no appeal against inefficient service.

Parsloe (1981, p.23f.) has a most helpful observation on both the reason and the impact of allocating work by the case:

> This method of work allocation was based originally upon a particular ideology ... no longer widely accepted, which saw all problems as rooted in the family and which paid little attention to the structural causes of social problems ... Given this ideological base the development of allocation by case is understandable. It is, however, surprising that the Seebohm Committee, which was equally attracted by notions of community participation and support, did not see how allocation by case maintains an individual approach to people in difficulties which is, in many ways, at variance with a community approach ... It may no longer have strong ideological support but it is now central to the way many teams manage their work, their relationships within the team and with their hierarchy.

Later on she notes some of the consequences of this: 'Few of the respondents in our study seemed to be aware, either individually or as a group, of the social needs of local communities or areas' (ibid., p.27) and 'Teams which consciously considered their own work in more than individual terms were ... the exception (ibid., p.29).

The views of Parsloe and Sainsbury found strong support in the Black *et al.* (1983) study of social service teams in very rural North Wales, rural Norfolk and central Birmingham. 'Social workers did not only reject as legitimate a community work role and fail to collaborate with voluntary agencies but they were also disinclined to hold working partnerships with either volunteers or informal carers' (ibid., p.208). They point out the impact of accountability to the agency: 'All three teams were constantly reminded about their overriding responsibility to the agency' (ibid., p.208).

Their particular contribution is to show that the separation of resource planning from practice led to a feeling of powerlessness among the workers (also reported by Parsloe (1981, pp.98–100). This in turn meant that the workers derived as much job satisfaction as they could from the professional authority they were able to exercise in their privatized work. The effect was to reinforce a professional approach which was narrowly based

> to escape the undoubted stresses associated with the formal rules and regulations of their centralised administrations. (Such an approach) militated against the development of what might be termed resource creation activity in relation to informal carers, volunteers and voluntary bodies and it also severely affected the flexibility and diversity of response to presenting client needs. (Black *et al.* 1983, p. 210).

This tends to undermine any sort of teamwork or collaboration with other workers and agencies (*ibid.*, p. 212). Sinclair *et al.* (1984), who were looking at informal care, services and social work for elderly clients living alone in a London borough, show how this approach also leads the workers to view a client's needs in terms of what the department could provide.

> Perhaps the most important failures stemmed from the predominant 'service orientation' of most of the workers. They did not find it easy to look beyond the problem for which the client was referred and the service that had been prescribed, such as residential care or day care ... Clients would then get assessed in terms of a need for a telephone, a home help, a bath aid, a lunch club (ibid., p. 202).

In addition Sinclair *et al.* (1984, p. 202) found that 'the question of clients' quality of life was generally ignored along with their particular interests, past hobbies and occupation'. They, too, noticed the workers' limited perspective of what contacts needed to be made.

With some exceptions, workers were too remote from key carers, including home helps, either to use them as co-assessors or to understand sufficiently the carers' need for support. They also lacked sufficient contact with occupational therapists, GPs, district nurses and geriatricians for adequate joint assessments of some of the clients with complex medical problems (*ibid.*).

The overall impression of these studies is of a pattern of organization, a brand of professionalism, a type of accountability and an approach to the job, which, between them, made for a cramped approach to social work practice which isolated it from the client's social world, contacts with workers in other agencies and even from other workers in the social service department. Notable among these was the almost invariably poor liaison with home helps. The studies above recognized this as a serious defect and we will consider the place of home helps in some detail later on.

This may seem an unduly gloomy picture. However, it is not to deny that much good work is being done. Goldberg and Warburton (1979), in a study of an area office in 'Seatown', show how the vast majority of the clients were satisfied with the service they received. But the evidence does suggest that the picture we have painted above is a fair reflection of the bulk of social work as it was being practised in the UK in the mid-1980s. This is not to deny that there are exciting developments, but the norm appears to be the rather cramped approach we have outlined.

Developments in the health service
Health authorities have been subject to similar pressures to those experienced by the local authorities, which have led to larger, more centralized units. It is true that the 1974 reorganization did include the creation of community health councils, but despite this the overall effect of the reorganization has been to create larger units which are less amenable to influence from users of the services and the community at large, and more subject to the influence of professionals working within the service, especially doctors. However, there have been some developments in the opposite direction, for example, the development of the nursing process (Kratz 1979) which seeks to introduce a wider perspective into nursing. It originated in the hospital setting, but it is highly relevant in a community setting.

The nursing process seeks to re-emphasize the wider links with family, friends, neighbours, and so on, that a patient may have. We say 're-emphasize' because this has always been part of good health visiting and district nursing theory, if not always its practice. The nursing process does not normally have as strong a community orientation as a thoroughgoing locally-based approach in a social services setting, but it has the potential to head in the same direction.

The development of the nursing process is itself a reflection of the increasing realization of the importance of an holistic approach to medical care. The repeated exhortations for greater co-operation between local authorities and health authorities show an administrative recognition of the need to address the wider context in order to understand health and sickness. This has been backed up by the provision of joint financing money by central government which has allowed the development of some imaginative schemes, and has given local authorities and health authorities some encouragement to develop joint plans. Given the scale of the challenges facing the health service and the local authorities (for example the rundown of the big mental illness and mental handicap hospitals), progress so far leaves much to be desired, but some progress has been made and some patterns of co-operation established (Glennerster 1982).

This could hardly be described as a *pressure* towards better integrated, locally-based work but it does indicate a climate of opinion which is likely to be more receptive to it. There are more unequivocal examples of moves in a community-orientated direction: the growth of patient associations in general practice (Pritchard 1981); the involvement of general practitioners in neighbourhood care schemes (Allibone and Coles 1982); schemes to provide help for families with terminally ill people at home and the development of hospital-at-home schemes (Wells 1980). The Riverside Child Health Project in Newcastle is an encouraging example of an interdisciplinary approach at the local level which is working hard at involving mothers, children and other local people in the development of its work (Riverside Child Health Project 1983). The Milson Road Project had a different focus. The central feature of this project was the appointment of a full-time volunteer organizer who was based in a comprehensive health centre in Hammersmith (Mocroft 1981). The number of people affected by these schemes is tiny and the impact of the large-scale, centralized approach is dominant in the health service; nevertheless such schemes do break new ground and make it easier for others to follow.

The most recent development arises from the report on neighbourhood nursing services (DHSS 1986a). This advocates a whole-hearted shift on the part of domiciliary nursing to a local base:

> The cornerstone of our report ... is a recommendation that in each District neighbourhood nursing services should be established. Health visitors, district nurses and school nurses, with their support staff would thus provide a strong, closely integrated, locally managed service near to the consumer. We suggest that such neighbourhoods should comprise between 10,000 and 25,000 people.

If the recommendations of this report are accepted, it would increase the chances of effective co-operation at the local level between health and social services. Insufficient attention is paid in the report to how those links could be made effectively and there would always be the danger of areas not being co-terminous (the report is over-optimistic about the ease with which neighbourhoods can be chosen). The report also considers that the link with general practice should be maintained but does not deal in sufficient detail with the problem of the geographical spread of patients on general practitioners' lists. However, overall it does offer exciting possibilities for building up effective co-operation at the level where it is needed most – the local area where the client or patient lives.

Developments providing care in domestic settings

As long ago as 1964 Tizard advocated populations of 100 000 as the basis for planning services for mentally handicapped people. This was developed further by Kushlick (for example, Kushlick 1970), and such services have been set up quite extensively in Wessex. In 1974 this approach was applied to the elderly. Kushlick and Blunden put forward a scheme which would provide for the needs of elderly people based on a population of 10000. It entailed a joint approach by both health and social services and advocated a local hospital unit within the population of 10 0 00 for elderly people not in need of acute hospital care. It pointed out that in a population of that size it would be possible for all the paid workers, including groups like home helps, to know one another by name. Over ten years after its publication it still has much to say about joint, locally-based local authority/health authority work.

The scheme relates to the ideas put forward in support of hospital-at-home schemes, mentioned briefly above, such as the undesirable consequences of removing old people from their familiar environment and the desirability of treating and caring for them at home if at all possible. This approach has also been adopted in the Kent community care scheme for old people who might otherwise have been admitted to a local authority old people's home. In this scheme a special team of social workers may spend up to two-thirds of the cost of a place in an old people's home to put together a package of care to enable the old person to stay at home, if that is what the old person wants. The results have been very encouraging (Challis and Davies 1980) and the scheme has been replicated in Anglesey (Dimond 1984) and Gateshead (Challis 1983). In most cases the money is spent mainly to pay people, often those who live nearby, to fulfil certain caring or simple nursing tasks for the old people.

The Kent scheme differs from Kushlick and Blunden's suggestions in that it is a purely local authority scheme and it is not necessarily locally based. The old people for whom the service is provided live over quite a wide area, but it and its related schemes do provide powerful evidence of the potential for interweaving formal and informal care with a reasonable sum of money to help it along. The Anglesey study found that a large proportion of the carers lived within a mile of those for whom they cared. This was in a rural area with a scattered population.

The Elderly Persons' Support Unit which is being started in Sheffield (MacDonald *et al.* 1984) is also locally based. The support unit covers all elderly people within a well-defined area and has a new category of worker, the community support worker, who has a more flexible role combining home help tasks and basic care tasks. The aim is to provide the flexible package of services the client needs rather than trying to fit the client into existing services.

> Underlying the concept of support units ... is the belief that care for elderly people who are frail or have a disability can be provided more effectively by placing specially deployed resources in the centre of an area, rather than by waiting for disability to increase and then removing individuals to an establishment providing total care (ibid., p. 28).

The current emphasis on enabling people with mental handicaps to live in ordinary houses in the community (for example, Ridgwick 1981) is one further example of a trend in the development of services, which puts greater emphasis on the relationships between formal and informal care and has implications for the development of locally-based work.

Developments specific to social work practice
There have also been developments in social work thinking, the most important of which has probably been the gradual appreciation of the relevance of the unitary approach to the locally-based approach. The best known exponents of this are Pincus and Minahan (1973). The impact that their theory could have on a team trying to develop a broader approach to their work is illustrated by Holder and Wardle (1981, p.1). 'The team did not set out with that goal (to produce a unitary approach to social problems) – their initial task was to develop an intensive family casework service and a community work service within a council housing estate in south west Durham.' They began with what they called the 'multi-method phase'.

> The skills of the team at that time meant that we could use casework, group-work or community work methods. We saw each method as distinct, therefore we did not try to apply different methods to the same situations, indeed we invested time in keeping them separate (ibid., p. 30).

They went through a stage which they called the 'integrating methods' phase when they were trying to use more than one method in a situation. Finally came the stage when they were applying the unitary approach. They discovered the work of Pincus and Minahan only in 1976, via a student on placement with them, and the theoretical concepts 'closely paralleled the assumptions to which their (that is, the team members) practice was pointing. The later stages of the work were influenced, in part, by the work of these theorists' (ibid., p. 1).

Holder and Wardle's book is an honest and most illuminating account of the upheavals that social workers with a background in traditional one-to-one casework have to go through to adopt a community-orientated approach. People who do not have that background may find these contortions difficult to understand, but part of the value of the book is to make clear the extent of the change in basic orientation that is required. The team of which they were members was a Family Services Unit team, not a social services one, and they do not link their work with the locally-based approach, though they were based on and working in an estate of about 6000 population. Their concern is with the unitary method.

On the other hand, there are no explicit references to Pincus and Minahan in Hadley and McGrath (1980), or in Brake and Bailey (1980), the latter including several chapters relevant to the locally-based approach including one by Bennett. The first people who appear to have made the link explicit are Currie and Parrott (1981), whose book has the subtitle 'An analysis of a patch system and team approach within a unitary framework in a social services department'. They show the relevance of the unitary model to locally-based work very convincingly but this has not been pursued by other writers. Anne Vickery wrote an article 'Settling into patch ways', which appeared in *Community Care* in January 1982 and drew on the insights of the unitary approach, but apart from that few, if any, explicit links have been made.

However, despite the limited explicit use of the unitary approach to develop the theoretical framework of locally-based work, it seems likely that it has increased workers' sensitivity to the possible relevance of the locally-based approach because it encourages them to work with a much wider range of systems.

The study by Sinclair *et al.* (1984) mentioned earlier can perhaps be viewed best as an evaluation of the effect of consultants in the unitary method on two teams of social workers. The development workers who provided the orientation were Anne Vickery (referred to just above) and Margaret Richards. Few of the normal conditions for locally-based work were met. The workers were still based in their area offices; there was no concentration of social workers' cases in a small section of the area; there was no reorganization of the home help service; there was no change in duty allocation or referral systems; and the project was affected by a series of hideous organizational and management problems which made any change in organization or management virtually impossible. Despite these formidable handicaps, the project did show some useful changes in a more community-orientated direction. In particular, the number of contacts that the workers made to workers in other disciplines and services increased, as did contacts to relatives, friends and neighbours (Sinclair *et al.* 1984, p. 247). They report that the teams concerned knew more about the areas in which they worked by the end of the project and they make the interesting comment that both teams: 'became aware of how much their normal working patterns distanced them from the community' (ibid. p. 236). They also give some excellent examples of good practice involving a range of people working together with a client to produce a result which they could not have managed working separately. In addition to these good examples of the unitary method, they give details of much less satisfactory practices, some of which have been mentioned above, in which the workers showed little awareness of the importance of, for example, family, neighbours or home helps.

The examples of good practice show clearly the relevance of the unitary approach to improving much current social work practice, but one could argue, as we would, that the unitary approach would have been a great deal easier to apply if the workers had been based more locally than at the area office. (The populations of the two areas were 31 500 and 33 500 respectively.) This study is particularly interesting in showing what change in workers' orientation can do (for example, the workers made an attempt to get to know their neighbourhoods and they contacted a wide range of people and agencies in them) *without* a change in organization. The change was limited but, given the problems, not insignificant. It makes us ask what would have happened if not just the attitudes of (some of) the workers had changed but also their location and the management and organization of the teams.

Developments in thinking about natural helping networks
Another major influence contributing to ideas about informal care is Pancoast and Collins (1976). They pointed to the considerable caring capacities of many members of the community. They paid special attention to those they called 'natural neighbours' and they outlined ways in which professionals could discover who were the 'natural neighbours' and how professionals could offer consultation to them to support them in the work they were doing. This work involved gaining a detailed knowledge of people's networks which they elaborated in a later paper (Collins and Pancoast 1977). Further work has been done in this area by people based at Portland State University (Froland *et al.* 1981) who have also produced a handbook for working with natural helpers (Crawford *et al.* 1978). Much of the other influential work in this field has also come from the USA (Warren 1981; Gottlieb 1981; Fischer 1982; Whittaker and Garbarino 1983). More recently some attention has been given to

informal networks in the UK and we shall review this when we look at informal care in more detail.

The 'natural helping network' approach appears to have had more impact than the unitary method. This may be because it is not limited to social work in its application. The unitary method never seems to have got beyond social work, while Pancoast and Collins always saw their approach as relevant to a wide range of workers. It may be that the work of Pancoast and Collins linked in more obviously with the growing interest in and awareness of informal care.

Demographic developments
All these influences would probably have had much less effect if managers had not been aware of the increasing pressure to which the services will be subject due to the increasing number of elderly people, especially those over the age of 75. Between 1983 and 1988 the number of people aged over 75 was expected to rise by 10.6 per cent and those aged over 85 by 22 per cent. If we look at the longer term, 1983–2021, the number of over 75s is expected to increase by 30 per cent and those aged over 85 to increase by 90 per cent (Henwood and Wicks 1984).

In the light of these figures the level of concern of those responsible for the health and welfare services, particularly when linked with the increasingly severe restrictions on public expenditure, is not surprising. It is also easy to understand why those responsible for balancing their departmental budgets have seen closer links between formal and informal care as one way of easing their problems.

The combination of these two factors appears to have been a major influence in encouraging locally-based work but it has also complicated the issue and highlighted the political dimension. It is proper and inevitable that the development of the health and welfare services should be a matter of political concern but in this case the political passions which locally-based work arouses have made careful discussion of the issues difficult.

One purpose of this introduction is to make it clear that interest in informal care and ways in which the statutory services could link in with and support it (the professional interest), came a long time before any substantial political interest in the subject. Thus, from a professional perspective, it is a question of how political interest in the approach is managed.

We have been looking at the influences which have contributed to professional developments and have led to the increase in the number of locally-based schemes. We have also highlighted the growing number of old people and the restraints on public expenditure. This last point raises the larger political question and we now turn our attention to this.

Political interest in informal care

It will be clear from the last section that the political context of all locally-based schemes is likely to be delicate. The Dinnington Project was no exception and it must be considered in its wider political context. A major part of that context is provided by the serious problems the welfare state has encountered in achieving its central objectives. This has led to a reappraisal of its role by the major political parties and a breakdown of the consensus that has characterized much post-war thinking from Beveridge onwards. The reappraisal has been more marked on the political right than the left.

The Conservative Party has always advocated individual self-reliance and personal responsibility, but has enacted policies of interventionism in the economy and paternalism in welfare. However since 1975 the doctrines of the liberal market economy have become central to Conservative Party policy. Reduction in public sector spending, control of the money supply, and limiting the role of government to the maintenance of conditions under which markets can function properly have been central to this government's policy. The logical relationship between an economic system dominated by free market forces and a theory of welfare, where state involvement should be similarly minimal and restricted to the provision of a safety net for certain vulnerable groups and individuals, is clear. The classical liberal values of freedom, individualism and inequality are the dominant ones of the free market system and these values are increasingly reflected in statements about welfare. For example, Margaret Thatcher has said: 'my kind of Tory party would make no secret of its belief in individual freedom and individual prosperity ... in the wider distribution of private property, in reward for energy and skill and thrift' (see *Daily Telegraph*, 30 January 1975). In stressing the role of the statutory services in underpinning other sources of care in the community she said (Thatcher 1981): 'They are vital in sorting out the logistics, but the army in the field is overwhelmingly made up of volunteers.'

This is typical of the sentiment that has been expressed by the key members of the Conservative Party during the past ten years. Patrick Jenkin argued at the Conservative Conference in 1977:

The family is not just mum, dad, and kids – a sort of snap, crackle and pop. It is very much more besides. What sort of encouragement do we give to families to look after their elderly relations? Yet the family must be the front-line defence when Gran needs help. Rightly we argue that the best of social work is helping people to help themselves.

Over the years there has been an increasing emphasis by the Conservative Party on the importance of the non-state sector in care in general, particularly with regard to the elderly.

In response to this the left has been forced into a defence of the existing principles and institutions of the welfare state, while at the same time experiencing considerable doubts about its practice. For the left, active government intervention in economic and social relations has been demanded in order to bring about an egalitarian society. The belief in the necessity of state provision of welfare is linked to the principles of universality and equity. Current disillusion over the failure of the welfare state to live up to the expectations of the left is reflected in several areas of unease. There are anxieties that the principle of wage-related contributions merely perpetuates existing inequalities; there is unease about the extent to which universality sometimes discriminates against those with greatest need; there is unease about state-administered welfare that is paternalistic and insensitive to individual requirements. Advocacy of state provision is tempered for some by the knowledge that the state is not a neutral arbiter of conflicts, but an instrument of the predominant social class. The left, therefore, is defending a welfare state about which it has considerable anxieties.

The position of the political left is one where the inherent conflict between the welfare ethic of co-operation and communal responsibility, and the economic ethic of competition and individual responsibility is maximized. Economic recession merely heightens the underlying difficulty of superimposing a socially directed goal onto an economic infrastructure directed towards goals of achievement and profit. Some leaders on the political left have argued that paying more attention to what happens at the local level may offer a way out of the impasse. Thus David Blunkett, formerly Labour leader of Sheffield City Council, sees great potential in developing services, and not just social services, at the local level. Area-based management for housing has been introduced in Sheffield and there is a commitment to locally-based social services as well. Greater democratization is part of that commitment.

Thus, despite a wide divergence in political philosophy, there is a remarkable degree of consensus about the value of a locally-based approach. As Peter Baldock (1983, p. 38) remarks:

> There is something at once impressive and confusing in the fact that an enthusiasm for patch systems is shared by people of such widely differing political viewpoints. It is not immediately clear why the same institutional reform should be advocated with equal fervour by a Conservative minister, such as Patrick Jenkin, a theorist of the political centre, such as Roger Hadley, and a grassroots socialist leader such as David Blunkett .... In particular, it is worth asking why a cause whose national spokesmen in the political and academic worlds are mainly of the centre right should find support within social services departments from many basic grade staff who would describe themselves as radicals.

The support across the political spectrum is significant, but we should recognize that inevitably the right and the left have rather different expectations of what may result from supporting locally-based schemes. This has been explained in an interesting way by Hughes (1986) who links the patch/decentralization debate with the two main responses to the industrial revolution, that is, on the one hand, the utilitarian, individualistic, centralist tradition stemming from the work of Mill and Bentham and followed by such people as Chadwick, Joseph Chamberlain, the Webbs and the Fabians and Beveridge; and, on the other hand, the romantic, pastoral, community, decentralist tradition of such people as Cobbett, Coleridge, Carlysle, Ruskin, Morris, the Guild Socialists and, from the Catholic Christian stream, Belloc and Chesterton. The important point is that neither tradition can be equated with the political right or left and Hughes suggests that a more useful focus for the political background to the locally-based work debate is the utilitarian, centralist/romantic, decentralist divide.

This also helps to explain the wide range of political support that locally-based work commands but Hughes goes further and shows how, largely as a result of the two world wars and the intervening depression, the centralist tradition has been predominant for most of this century. In particular the success of central planning during the Second World War in responding to the extreme demands of wartime conditions produced a post-war consensus about state planning and welfare provision that the decentralist tradition did not challenge.

But with the end of the period of full employment and expansion and the onset of the depression in the mid-1970s this tradition started to re-emerge. In the case of the right the liberal market economy has become dominant and this has linked itself not so much with a decentralist approach (in practice the Thatcher government has strengthened the power of the centre – for example, through rate-capping – despite its rhetoric) but with elements of the romantic/community tradition especially concerned with the centrality of the family, of the key role of women within the family, of the importance of self-help and voluntary organizations.

By contrast, as we have seen above, the left is in a more ambiguous position. In part this is due to its greater historical attachment to the centralist tradition. Although we have also seen that the decentralist/community tradition also has its place in the history of the left, it has been much more difficult for the left to express this; first because the right have taken the initiative and have set the terms of the debate: second, they have not succeeded in making a strong link between the positive elements of their centralist and decentralist/community tradition. The aspect of the locally-based/decentralization issue which concerns the left most deeply is the question of genuine participation and devolution of power.

Thus the support across the political spectrum does not involve a betrayal of traditional concerns by either left or right and the romantic, community, pastoral, decentralist tradition they share means that in some respects there can be genuine agreement, but in others their approaches, assumptions and priorities are likely to be different.

If we are aware of the wide range of influences and traditions which have come together to push the locally-based/decentralization debate to the front of the stage, we will be able to be discriminating about the assumptions we make about any one supporter of the locally-based approach. It is unhelpful to the debate to assume that, for example, anyone who supports the locally-based approach is also in favour of cutting and privatizing services. This is something that Beresford and Croft (1986, pp. 134, 139) come perilously near to doing due to their failure to discuss the different political traditions that lie behind the locally-based approach. As Hughes (1986, p. 45) concludes his essay: 'The appeal to community and pastoral, latent as it is in the industrial age, can ... be equally used to justify policies of the ideological left or right.'

We have looked in some detail at the context of the Dinnington Project and the development of locally-based work, of which it is part. We have traced some of the significant features of the professional and political concerns through the 1970s and 1980s. It is time now to look at the project itself. The following chapter gives an outline of the early development of the project.

3 Setting up the Project

The Dinnington Project is a story of change and resistance to change. It is about the way people in organizations reacted to suggestions and plans for a new style of delivery for the health and welfare services in a mining village in South Yorkshire. The central focus of the project derived from a belief in the importance of interweaving formal services with informal care as we discussed in the first chapter.

The organizations concerned were Rotherham Local Authority, especially the Social Services and Housing Departments, and the Rotherham (Area, later District) Health Authority. In the beginning it was not easy for these agencies to respond to the ideas behind the project because the changes required of them could be outlined only in general terms. Yet the project was to involve both attitudinal and organizational changes that were quite significant. Thus a basic requirement was a change in the relationship between the services, their personnel and the community at large. The way in which this was expressed in an early planning paper was: 'The involvement of members of the community, not just professionals, will be a fundamental aspect of the approach adopted'.

The other major change was 'the *joint* involvement of various departments of the local authority and health authority'. This called for a level of co-operation and a crossing of departmental and authority boundaries far greater than that to which they were accustomed. In practice this change was more radical than it might appear at first sight.

If these two principles were to be taken seriously, they would, at the very least, put a question mark against the established practice of workers and management in both authorities. One might expect that it would be viewed with considerable suspicion. This proved to be the case. A major feature of the project was the way it gained and sustained momentum fitfully and gradually in the face of the inertia which is characteristic of any large organization.

Origins, exploration and non-engagement, 1976 and 1977
From the time Rotherham Metropolitan District Council was first formed at the time of local government reorganization in 1974 there was evidence of a desire to consider the current basis and future direction of authority policy. The Chief Executive was involved centrally in this move, though there was evidence of similar thinking within the social services department. In 1975 a working party was set up to take a broad look at the social

services department.

It was decided to invite some outsiders onto the working party and as a result Michael Bayley from Sheffield University attended a meeting in April 1976. He presented some ideas to the meeting about possible lines of development. He referred to the rapidly increasing number of 'old' old people, the importance of informal care and the potential of a locally-based approach. These ideas interested the Chief Executive in particular and Rotherham MDC provided money for a research assistant to work with Bayley to develop these ideas. As a result of this it was agreed that:

> The overall aim of the project is to develop a new pattern of service, probably for the elderly, which will have three main characteristics:
> (a) the involvement of members of the community, not just profession-als;
> (b) the *joint* involvement of various departments of the local authority and health authority;
> (c) particular attention to the relationship between residential care and domiciliary care with special emphasis on involving carers (that is family, friends, neighbours and so on).

In January 1977 the university research team produced a project proposal called 'The Rotherham Project: a scheme for a corporate approach to meeting individual need'. It placed great emphasis on the 'from-the-bottom-up' approach, and proposed that four areas each with a population of about 1500 people should be chosen. The basic scheme proposed that contacts be established with representatives of the statutory services active in each area who would be asked to identify a number (perhaps six) of old or chronically handicapped people who posed problems, particu-larly problems which concerned more than one of the authorities providing services. The professionals concerned would form the basis of a 'Combined Care Team' which representatives of those involved in voluntary or informal care would be asked to join. Before long it was anticipated that the work of this team would grow to the point at which 'the servicing of the scheme should be taken on by a ... Care Co-ordinator who would need to be paid, either on a full-time or a part-time basis'.

The scheme is interesting as a thoroughgoing attempt to build things up from below so that the service could suit the users rather than the users being expected to fit the existing services. It is equally single-minded in its preoccupation with developing a new pattern of *service*. Whether the scheme was really practical is an open question. The proposal certainly understated the problem when it said: 'the scheme will need to be flexible, since we are treading on new ground'. However there were some useful ideas which could have been moulded into a pilot scheme, if the proposal had been seen as a starting point for discussions.

But these discussions did not take place. Various meetings proposed that the scheme should go forward but nothing came of them. The main feature of this period was that there was no effective engagement between the university and either the local authority or the health authority. The research team had no named person within either authority who had a particular responsibility to liaise with them. The researchers did make some progress both in developing their ideas and in understanding how the local authority and health authority worked, but in the autumn of 1977 the research assistant left and the project appeared to be stillborn.

Revival, 1978
In November 1977 Bayley contacted the Chief Executive to see if there was still any interest in the project. In response the Chief Executive convened a meeting later in the month of chief officers of the local authority and health authority. They agreed that the project should be undertaken and that the method of approach would be:

(a) to establish the needs of a small area of the Borough;
(b) to discuss with professionals the adequacy of existing patterns of service;
(c) to suggest alternative means of meeting the need;
(d) to have regard to demographic changes.

They also suggested that the project should be based in Dinnington. The social services department viewed Dinnington as one area that made considerable demands on the department. In addition it had the advantage of being served by just one general practice of eight doctors. Bayley accepted the revised plan put forward by the chief officers, although he had some reservations, the most serious of which was that the method of building the project 'from-the-bottom-up' with the full involvement of users of the services and those caring for them had been abandoned. It was the professionals who were to be consulted and the emphasis on community involvement was seriously undermined. The scheme which had been put forward in January 1977 would undoubtedly have been difficult to put into operation but so would any scheme which involved genuine user involvement in how the service was to develop. It is sad that no discussion with the local authority and the health authority took place about how the scheme might be implemented and what changes might be needed. It seems that it was too radical and too far removed from their experience. This grave weakening of the user/local community involvement in the thinking, planning and development of the project had serious consequences, as we shall see. At the same time, it should be recognized that given the political realities there was little likelihood that a scheme on the lines of the original proposal would have been adopted.

Money was provided for Bayley to employ a research assistant again. Paul Parker was appointed and started work on 1 January 1978. His first task was to undertake a survey of all the active cases of the district nurses, education welfare officer, health visitors, home helps, home wardens and social workers in one part of Dinnington (population of about 1800). A record was kept also of all home visits by general practitioners to patients in the chosen area over a three-month period, as well as some other basic information about admissions to hospitals, local authority old people's homes, children's homes, domiciliary chiropody, and so on. In order to produce a report as soon as possible the survey was limited to interviews with workers. The main findings of the report were that:

(a) collectively the statutory services had a substantial knowledge of the needs in the area;

(b) the relationships between the services were often haphazard, being left largely to the individual efforts of those involved without systematic encouragement from management;

(c) links between local voluntary groups and the statutory services were minimal;

(d) fieldworkers reported a high degree of support being given to the elderly by family, friends and neighbours – wardens and home helps were particularly well informed of this;

(e) the contact that social workers and even social work assistants had with the elderly was very limited;

(f) the home helps and wardens, especially the wardens, were isolated from the other workers;

(g) the home helps and the wardens played a central role – the main recommendation was 'that a practical project be undertaken to give greater support to home helps and wardens to improve and extend the service they offer and to integrate their work with local authority social workers. This could involve the appointment of an additional warden supervisor and the allocation to the project of a social worker and a member of the home help service'.

The report was completed in June 1978 and went to the local authority and health authority. There were responses, some favourable, some unfavourable, from the local authority but none from the health authority. One factor which may have affected this was that, although the report discussed the health services and reported on the activities of the district nurses, health visitors and general practitioners, the emphasis was much more on the local authority services and the main recommendation was concerned exclusively with the local authority services. In retrospect it can be seen that this may have been a tactical error because it did not give the health authority a major investment in the project. Yet the report proved to be critical for the development of the project. It was local to Rotherham, specific in its findings and had a clear recommendation for action. As such it provided those who were keen that the project should go ahead with a clearer aim and more definite purpose and it enabled the momentum of the project to be built up and sustained. It was also important for the research team. It made them more aware of the centrality of the role played by the home helps and wardens in the community. The evidence contained in the report provided a good empirical base for the project they proposed.

The autumn of 1978 saw a flurry of activity. A series of meetings of chief officers of the local authority was held at the instigation of the Chief Executive. These created the administrative machinery for setting up and, in due course, managing the project. The senior body was the Neighbourhood Services Unit consisting of chief officers of the local authority and chaired by the Chief Executive. Working with it was a working party of middle managers from social services, housing and education chaired by the assistant to the Chief Executive. The university was represented on both bodies by Bayley and Parker. These organizational decisions were critical to the development of the project and marked a decisive stage in the project. It is clear that the report of June 1978 had a great deal to do with it. The Neighbourhood Services Unit gave the project a power base and the working party provided sufficient resources of time for the detailed planning to be done.

By the autumn of 1978 the project had become established and for the first time gained a real momentum of its own apart from the efforts put into it by the tiny University research team. However, there had been one major cost. The officers of the health authority were not present at these critical meetings. They were invited but were unable to attend. The Chief Executive was keen to get the project under way and so decided to go ahead without them. This was the source of some resentment later on, making the full participation of the health authority hard to achieve.

The momentum the project had gained was maintained by the working party. Its first task was to prepare an application for Urban Aid. In the application the purposes of the project were set out as follows:

    (a) to develop a system of caring that will use the resources known to exist within the community to their fullest potential;

    (b) to assist those residents with special needs, such as the elderly, the handicapped and the chronically sick, to remain in their homes as far as is possible and desirable;

    (c) to strengthen the relationship between the community and the various departments which serve it;

    (d) to provide a more cost-effective service to the public;

    (e) to strengthen co-ordination between departments, and also between the local authority, other statutory agencies, and the local voluntary agencies, in relation to these purposes.

The main development to be noted is the move away from the emphasis on the elderly which had been evident in the 1976 discussions, although there was still special mention of the chronically sick and handicapped.

The working party also decided that the action team of the project should consist of two social workers and a housing assistant. Subsequently this was called the core team. Urban Aid funding would be sought for the senior of the two social work posts (called social worker/ co-ordinator) and the housing assistant, and the second social worker was to be seconded from the area office. The working party decided that an office should be provided in the centre of the village and that the assistant home help organizer responsible for Dinnington should also have desk space in the office, thus making possible easier liaison between the home help service, the social workers and the warden service.

The post of housing assistant was created with the particular aim of developing contact with informal networks through the wardens, one of the main goals of the project. The housing assistant would upgrade and extend the wardens' role by developing contacts with other statutory workers on their behalf, by helping individual clients when needed, and by establishing meetings amongst the wardens where they could develop a sense of professional identity. She would establish and develop co-operation between wardens and other fieldworkers in such a way that the wardens' extensive knowledge of community needs and resources could be utilized. It was anticipated that the assistant home help organizer would play a similar role with the home helps and that this would be done in close collaboration with the housing assistant. In this way it would be possible to identify those situations which might develop into crises and prevent this happening by early intervention.

The Chief Executive's support ensured that the project was top of the local authority's list of Urban Aid bids to the Department of the Environment. As a result the bid was successful and by spring 1979 the working party had turned its attention to the details of how the project was to be set up.

Preparation for action: the detailed planning, 1979

Nineteen seventy-nine was almost wholly taken up with the detailed preparations for the launching of the project. The start was delayed by a number of difficulties including finding premises and a dispute within the local authority about the grading of social workers. The focus throughout the year was on the working party, whose membership was widened to include a nursing officer and a principal education welfare officer.

By the end of the year a portable classroom had been obtained to provide a base for the core team in Dinnington; the grading of the posts advertised and the appointments made to start early in 1980; the health authority had become involved in the project once again both at working party level and at the level of the Neighbourhood Services Unit (the Chief Officers' meeting).

The working party had also spent some time discussing the management of the project. In November Parker produced a draft management model for the project which the working party adopted. It put forward a three-tier managerial structure related to fieldworker, middle management and senior management levels. In organizational terms this meant a fortnightly meeting of fieldworkers to develop close local interdisciplinary co-operation, a Project Management Team, based on the existing working party, and the Neighbourhood Services Unit (the Chief Officers' meeting) with overall responsibility.

The Project Management Team was to be 'responsible for maintaining the broad objectives of the project [and] providing a link between the project and individual departmental managements...'. This points to what was to be a major problem in the project, namely the split accountability of the workers. They were responsible to their departments for professional and departmental matters and to the Project Management Team for project matters and project development. The Project Management Team was to be the main instrument in resolving the difficulties which, it was anticipated, were bound to arise. Unfortunately there was a further complication as the senior body, the Neighbourhood Services Unit, never discussed or agreed to these terms of reference. Thus the project entered the action phase with the serious potential problem of the split accountability of the workers, and no agreement from the senior body on the terms of reference of the committee which carried particular responsibility for resolving the problem.

The research programme
The successful Urban Aid bid included provision for one research worker and this covered Parker's salary. It had always been understood, however, that an application would be made for further research funds so that the project could be researched more thoroughly, and in May 1979 an application was submitted to DHSS for funds to cover the cost of two full-time research workers, part-time secretary, interviewers, and so on. In August the DHSS agreed to fund the research and two research workers, Rosalind Seyd and Alan Tennant, were appointed and took up their posts at the beginning of 1980. The induction period for new workers began on 28 January and the project became operational at the beginning of March. This gave very little time for the detailed planning of the evaluation. Though the overall design of the research programme and the interrela-

tionship of the studies were set out in the DHSS application a considerable amount of work was needed to prepare sets of questionnaires. Some of this work had been done by Bayley and Parker, but the main part of their energies had been taken up with the start of the action side of the project.

The evaluation programme was based upon a before and after design that focused on the impact of the project on both formal and informal care in the community, to collect information about those using the services, those caring for them and the local fieldworkers. Figure 3.1 shows how the different studies relate to one another. The main studies were as follows.

The caseload study

This study, together with the referral study, was designed to provide a detailed understanding of the nature and extent of statutory provision in the project area. The study used a self-completed questionnaire to record the caseload of workers on one particular day and concerned all the statutory workers involved with the project, except the general practitioners. These were social workers, social work assistants, wardens, home helps, health visitors, district nurses and the educational welfare officer. Demographic, diagnostic and action information was recorded for each of their patients and clients. The only exception to this was the health visitor whose routine child-care cases were omitted as they were considered to be outside the main concern of the project. The first caseload study was run in the summer of 1979, six months before the project commenced. Subsequent annual studies were run until the summer of 1982.

The referral study

This was designed to give an understanding of the nature and extent of referrals made to the statutory agencies during a five-week period at the beginning of each year. Workers used a self-completed questionnaire to record demographic information, the nature of the referral and action taken for every referral received during the five-week period. The study was run annually in January–February from 1980 to 1982.

The general practitioner study

This study was designed to provide similar information to that from the caseload and referral studies. The Dinnington general practice, serving about 18 000 people in the village and neighbouring communities, responded to requests for services rather than carrying a caseload as such. In view of this a separate biannual study was designed to record basic demographic, diagnostic and action information for all consultations given in a seven-day period to those people from the project area (about half the practice list). It took place over one week in January and July

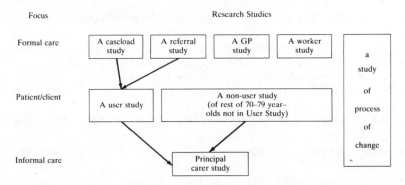

Figure 3.1 Dinnington research programme

between 1980 and early 1982.

The GP study, like the others, took the form of a self-completed questionnaire. The practice receptionists completed the basic demographic information and passed the form to the doctors for diagnostic and other details. Five of the eight doctors agreed to participate, but in practice holidays and sickness meant that the number who did so varied from three to five. Therefore, while a complete picture was gained for the demographic characteristics of consultations, this was not so for diagnostic details.

The user study

This interview-based study was focused on the attitudes and experience of users of the services in the project area. It was one of three studies (with the carer and non-user studies) which were central to the identification of the nature and extent of natural helping networks. It also looked at the interaction between formal and informal care givers and whether users had any sense of care being consciously shared between the two. The study population was derived from the caseload and referral Studies and was run each summer from 1980 to 1982.

The principal carer study

The carer study was designed to provide a clearer understanding of the extent and nature of care given by the informal sector to those receiving statutory care. Carers were identified by the users themselves and for this study each person identified as visiting the user on three or more occasions per week formed the population. We refer to them as 'principal carers'. The notion of care in both the user and carer studies was broad. Calling in for a chat was considered to be as much a caring activity as doing a specific task. This is discussed in some detail in the next chapter. A major aspect of the study was the interaction of statutory, voluntary and informal care and the extent to which care related to socio-demographic characteristics. The study ran each summer from 1980 to 1982 immediately after the user study from which its population was drawn.

The non-user study
All the research studies outlined so far have been concerned with those people receiving statutory care, but it was evident that to understand community care adequately, it would be necessary to approach those who were not patients or clients of the services. The non-user study examined the nature and extent of informal care for those not receiving statutory support. There is evidence to suggest that demand for services increases at around the age of 75 and so we interviewed all those between the ages of 70 and 79. This study was carried out in the summers of 1981 and 1982.

The worker study
Other studies offered clients and carers the opportunity to discuss their circumstances in depth; this study provided the same opportunity to those statutory workers central to the project. The study included those doctors who were fully involved in the GP study, together with the full-time receptionists and the practice nurse. It asked about the working methods, job satisfaction and interaction between agencies and informal networks. The study was run twice, in late 1980 and during 1982.

The study of process
The collection and use of such a range of data would be a mechanistic exercise if it were not set within a framework that offered some structure and explanation of what we were observing. The qualitative data derived from observation of meetings; discussions, such as conversations, comments and telephone calls; analysis of records; and less formal sources provided this framework. We believe that the process by which change is introduced and the resistance to such change is one of the more important aspects of this and any other evaluation and so we draw extensively on this qualitative material to understand how, from an initial starting point, we arrived at our end-point.

Summary
We have described the history and development of the planning of the project and outlined the evaluation programme. It is now time to introduce Dinnington itself and to describe the patterns of informal care we found there.

4 Introducing Dinnington

Characteristics of the village

Dinnington is a mining village of just over 7000 people eight miles south of Rotherham – an urban village. Work by John Craig (1985) based upon the 1981 Census shows the Rotherham area to be classified under what he calls 'the family of mixed, town and country, areas with some industry'. This 'family', one of ten he identifies, contained a greater share of the 1981 Census population (22.4 per cent) than any other. Most 'families' have subsets or clusters, and Rotherham is cited as the most typical district in the 'More Industrial Areas' cluster, the cluster itself containing 8.7 per cent of the 1981 population. According to information provided for us by the Office of Population, Census and Surveys, based on the earlier work of Richard Webb and John Craig (1978) Dinnington is typical of settlements throughout northern and north-eastern England.

Dinnington is a stable community. For example, the average time spent living in Dinnington for a cohort of female 70–79-year-olds we interviewed in 1982 was 59 years, and they had averaged over 22 years in their current dwellings. The village grew up round the pit which traditionally provided the main source of employment and originally attracted immigration into the area, particularly from Poland. More recently, people have moved into other forms of employment, travelling to Rotherham or Sheffield to work in the steel industry, and light industry has been developing to the west of the village. It is an area with a high number of skilled manual workers, though unemployment figures rose rapidly through the life of the project, being quoted as 29 per cent in the local paper in November 1982.

It is quite distinct geographically, except to the south where it adjoins the neighbouring village of North Anston. In comparison with this village, Dinnington has little new housing, though a private estate has been completed recently. Most of its housing stock is pre-war, and it has an above-average stock of publicly-owned dwellings. Of particular relevance to the question of informal care is the fact that the village has a low number of married women in paid employment. This may reflect the cultural assignment of gender roles in mining communities, or it may reflect constraints upon women entering the labour market because of their caring roles within the family, a restriction noted by Hunt (1978) in her national survey of the elderly at home. Two other statistics, related to health, reflect the industrial character of Dinnington. Both the death

31

rate and the incidence of chronic ill health are high – legacies of the coal-mining and steel-making industries.

Most of Dinnington's health and welfare services are located in the village. One general practice of eight doctors covers almost the entire population, and a health clinic, from which the health visitors and domiciliary nurses work, is situated just off the southern end of the main street. Educational resources are locally based too. Both primary and secondary schools lie within the village, as does the local college of further education, which runs a variety of day and evening courses. Administratively Dinnington is part of Rotherham District Council, Rotherham being part of one of the six metropolitan counties created in the local government reorganization of 1974, and abolished in 1986. It is Labour-controlled, though not a Labour authority that is characterized by a commitment to high levels of public spending and the maintenance of welfare services, in contrast to neighbouring Sheffield. The Labour group's majority on the Council must be one of the largest in the country. At the local elections in May 1986, 63 out of 66 seats were Labour, two were Conservative and one went to the Liberal– SDP Alliance.

As a village then, Dinnington may be described as a stable and close-knit community, with distinct geographical boundaries and with locally-based health and welfare provision. Socially it is relatively homogeneous, though there is a 'top end' to the village, characterized by large owner-occupied housing and the new Wimpey estate. Overall though, it is a working-class area. It is socially lively, providing extensive shopping facilities for neighbouring villages, and having a variety of working men's clubs and miners' institutes that are typical of northern urban life.

This book is concerned with particular kinds of social relationship, namely the pattern of practical and social support exchanged between people within the community. But what is known of such informal care and how extensive are caring networks in Dinnington? The remainder of this chapter sets out what was learnt from our studies of support networks, relating the information, where appropriate, to other similar work.

Characteristics of informal care

Terms such as informal care, community care, helping networks, and neighbourhoodism are used frequently, both in the academic literature and in the media. They have also, as we have shown, become part of the political debate about the future of health and welfare institutions and the respective roles and obligations of the family and the state in providing care. In the late 1970s when attention started to be focused on these issues, there was limited empirical evidence either to sustain or to refute the claims that were made. Since then various research studies have tackled this deficiency. Currently there are two types of research evidence. On the one hand, there is the earlier well-established sociological tradition of community studies which examine, for example, the changing nature of community life, or the consequences of family dispersal for elderly people who are themselves becoming more dependent (for example, those discussed by Frankenberg 1966, and Townsend 1963). On the other hand, there is a growing collection of recent studies which attempt to examine informal care. These can be highly focused, such as those which quantify the time given and the social costs incurred by relatives caring for highly dependent people in their own homes (for example, Bristow 1981; Nissel and Bonnerjea 1982; Equal Opportunities Commission 1982). These studies describe and analyse the patterns of the most demanding forms of care given in the community. Alternatively they can be more general, looking at community-wide patterns of in-formal care (Wenger 1984).

There are, however, still few studies which give empirical information about the presence or absence of personal caring networks in particular localities. There is also limited knowledge about the day-to-day supportive interaction between people that comes between individual needs and the demands that may be placed on the services. There is little understanding of whether workers and carers act independently or whether they co-operate, or of what factors might influence that relationship. Though there are sociological studies of family and friendship networks, they do not focus on the relationship between these networks and interventions made by formal agencies.

Several books and articles written during the time of the Dinnington Project raised questions, not only about the nature of informal care, but about whether or not it existed. Knight and Hayes (1981) suggest that, in those inner London areas which they studied, community support networks appeared to be very weak. Similarly, Barker (1980) wrote that 'The caring community is arguably becoming something that is to be found only in *Gemeinschaft* settings such as rural or urban villages'. Philip Abrams (1978) suggested that community care is a romantic concept, bearing little relation to the realities of contemporary society. 'In the typical social settings of contemporary British society care is typically volatile, spasmodic and unreliable; very much *not* a social fact.' Areas that display significant levels of informal care are either 'a relic of a fast disappearing agrarian social system', or immigrant communities whose support pattern

> seems to be directly related to the high degrees of enclosure and isolation (to say nothing of poverty and extreme economic insecurity) which these communities also experience ... . The evidence we have of the actual existence of bases for community care in contemporary Britain is almost entirely about types of community which are either doomed to disappear or which for other reasons we should strongly hope will disappear (ibid., p. 84).

However, other studies have found evidence of active informal care, in both urban and rural environments (Hunt 1978; Wenger 1984). Hunt's national study of the elderly, in particular, suggests that the incidence of informal care that we discuss below is not atypical. Confirmation of the importance of informal care was found in the 1980 General Household Survey (OPCS 1982), which reported about six out of every seven elderly informants seeing relatives or friends at least once a week, and almost a third seeing them every day or nearly every day. Only three per cent said they did not see relatives or friends at all nowadays. Four-fifths said they talked to a neighbour at least once a week and only one-tenth said that they did not see a neighbour to talk to at all. Similarly Wenger (1984) found that three-quarters of the elderly had support networks of five or more persons and 85 per cent of those in her study visited others.

Extent and source of care
In Dinnington we found that informal care existed, that it existed in quantity, but that it was highly variable. Only 29 respondents (16 per cent) out of 187 health and welfare service patients and clients interviewed in 1980 (in the user study) had no contact with kin. This was due to either inactive or non-existent kinship networks. Nearly one-half (49 per cent) identified friends who gave help. In all, only 17 (9 per cent) out of all 187 respondents were without support from either family or friends (Table 4.1). However, there were important variations amongst the support given to different types of household. For example, a substantial minority of respondents in the family group (that is households with at least one adult plus children under 16) were without visits from either relatives or friends. Nearly one-quarter (24 per cent) of this group received no visits at all. Just over one-third (34 per cent) said they had visits from friends, compared with the overall average, given above, of just under one-half. In contrast to this, those elderly aged 75 or more and living alone were almost all supported by informal caring networks, with nine out of every ten being supported by kin and more than six out of ten by friends.

If we separate practical help and social support the distinction between these groups becomes even more obvious. Only 11 out of 80 (14 per cent) very elderly people living alone received no help with tasks, while over half (55 per cent) of the family group received no such help. This is not surprising considering the respective needs and problems of these two groups, but nevertheless it highlights the role of social support for the family group: a high proportion of the visits they received were purely social. Overall, nearly three-quarters (73 per cent) of respondents were supported by relatives or friends who gave them practical help. Relatives played a bigger role than friends: twice as many people were given practical help by relatives (63 per cent) as by friends (31 per cent)(Table

Table 4.1 Care given by relatives, and by friends and neighbours, to 187 patients or clients of health and welfare services, 1980

	Social and task care		Task care only	
Help received from	No	(%)	No.	(%)
No-one	17	9	51	27
Relatives only	78	42	78	42
Friends only	12	6	19	10
Relatives and friends	80	43	39	21
Total	187	100	187	100

4.1). This predominance of relative support for tasks can be put another way by saying that when we looked at all forms of care the most common source of help was a combination of relatives and friends, but when we looked at practical care people were far more likely to be helped by their relatives.

Similar conclusions were reached by Marjorie Cantor (1975), reporting the results of a large cross-cultural study of the elderly in New York. She commented on the role of 'neighbours-friends' during emergencies, due to their proximity. She stressed that help given was usually short-term or sporadic: the longer-term care of the more seriously or chronically ill was assumed by kin.

Frequency of visiting
The frequency with which the 187 patients/clients in our 1980 study received visitors varied widely. On average they received nine visits a week from carers but this ranged from those who received no visits to those who received 66 visits a week.

When we distinguished between visits made by relatives and by friends we found that relatives made nearly twice as many visits as friends (Table 4.2). Respondents were visited on average nearly six times a week by relatives, compared with just over three times a week by friends. When we looked at elderly people living alone we found that the friends played a larger part. A possible explanation of this is that they were substituting for relatives who were either absent or non-supportive. Those elderly living alone still received more visits from relatives than they did from friends, but they received a lot of visits from both family *and* friends.

We have seen that there were differences in the amount of care given by relatives and that given by friends. Eight-and-a-half people out of every ten received care from relatives while only five out of every ten received care from friends or neighbours. When visits are grouped according to frequency – daily (that is seven visits a week); at least once a week; less than weekly; and none at all – we found that although nine per cent of patients and clients reported no visits from informal carers, it was evident that, where relatives and friends were visiting respondents, they were doing so on a regular basis (Table 4.3). Nearly half (49 per cent) of all respondents had daily care and only four per cent reported that visits were made less than once a week.

At the most intensive level of support there was little overlap between relatives and friends. Thirty-four per cent of respondents received daily care from relatives and 20 per cent from friends and neighbours, an overlap of only five per cent (from the 49 per cent receiving daily care from any source) in support. At this level of daily care, either relatives or friends were providing help; it was not being shared between them.

Nearly four out of five respondents received at least weekly care from relatives and nearly half received weekly care from friends. This does not lend initial support to the argument of those who claim that families are unwilling to accept responsibilities towards their relatives, and that local communities no longer generate and sustain supportive relations among those who live there. Other research into the caring networks of elderly people has also reported frequent visiting. The Johnson *et al.* (1981) study of the meals-on-wheels service in Leeds found that 60 per cent of visits by clients' children took place on a daily or weekly basis, and 34 per cent of other relatives were seen at least weekly, while 69 per cent of friends also visited weekly. Butcher and Crosbie's (1977) Cleator Moor study reported that almost half those interviewed had received a visit from a family member within the previous 24 hours. Mark Abrams' (1978) study of a group of elderly people aged 75 and over found that 42 per cent were visited by family and friends more than once a week, 31 per cent once a week, and 27 per cent less frequently, or not at all. So, nearly three-quarters of all his respondents received visits at least once a week. Finally, Hunt (1978) reported that 90 per cent of respondents were visited by relatives and 71 per cent by friends. If we look at all the elderly patients or clients in our 1980 study, we find that 88 per cent of the 141 respondents were supported by relatives and 53 per cent by friends.

Table 4.2 Average number of visits made by relatives, and by friends and neighbours, to 187 patients or clients of health and welfare services, 1980

Type of household of respondent	Average visits each week by			
	Relatives	Friends	Together	No.
Alone 60 – 74	5.3	4.2	9.5	29
Alone 75 +	6.9	4.1	11.0	80
Family	4.2	2.6	6.8	29
Other	5.6	1.9	7.5	49
Total	5.9	3.3	9.3	187

Table 4.3 Frequency of visiting by relatives, and by friends and neighbours, to 187 patients or clients of health and welfare services, 1980, expressed as percentage of source and type of care given

% receiving	Frequency of visits			
	At least daily	At least weekly	Less than weekly	None at all
Any form of care by relatives	34	45	5	16
Just task care by relatives	23	35	5	37
Any form of care by friends	20	29	0	51
Just task care by friends	10	20	1	69
Just task care	32	37	4	27
Any form of care	49	38	4	9

Responsiveness to need
It has been suggested that carers make positive responses to need. In their study of the meals-on-wheels service in Leeds, Johnson *et al.,* (1981)

argued that caring arrangements were responsive to increasing levels of disability, pointing out that carers gave more help to those people who reported the widest range of problems in managing household tasks. The meals-on-wheels group were more ill, more disabled and less able to perform everyday tasks than either a group attending a luncheon club or a comparison group. Johnson reported that when considering all tasks people in the first group were given 25 per cent more help than those in the other two. When domestic tasks only were included in the calculation the meals-on-wheels group were shown to be receiving twice as much informal care as the other two.

When we examined the relationship of informal care to need we found that it did also respond to need. This was shown most clearly for relatives, where we found the number of visits made was in direct response to need (expressed as a composite of Activities of Daily Living (ADL) scales and self-reported health status). The relationship was particularly strong for visits by relatives to give practical help: they made an average of 5.3 visits a week to people with high levels of need compared with only 2.5 to those with low needs. Social visiting by relatives did not follow this pattern and support by friends and neighbours also was less clearly related to the degree of disability and ill health of the client.

The response of carers is clearest with the elderly. Visits made by relatives to provide practical care to those at the highest level of need were approximately twice those at the lowest level of need. Once again visits by friends and neighbours for purposes of practical care do not reflect levels of need. There was also little difference between informal care given to the elderly who lived alone and those who lived with others, although there were more than three times as many of the former receiving care from the health and welfare services.

Making visits

So far we have considered support networks in the context of inward visits made to the respondent, but contact with networks may be sustained equally by making outward visits to the homes of relatives, friends and neighbours. Information on levels of inward visiting therefore, needs to be complemented by analysis of the range of contacts between respondents and their networks maintained through outward visiting. Other studies have shown a relationship between both age and household composition and outward visit levels. The General Household Survey (OPCS 1982), in its analysis of elderly informants, reported that they were more likely to receive visits than to make them: two-thirds of the elderly received visits at least once a week, whereas about one-half made visits as often as this. The frequency of visits received varied little with age, but the frequency with which outward visits were made to relatives and friends varied considerably with age. The proportion of elderly people who said they did not visit at all rose from nine per cent of the 65–69 age cohort to 42 per cent of those aged 85 and over. The GHS reported that contact with neighbours also declined with age.

The survey pointed to the importance of contact with relatives and friends outside the household for elderly people living alone. They were more likely than were those living in other types of household to see friends and relatives daily or nearly every day; they were likely both to make and to receive visits with this frequency.

In our 1980 study we found a little over half (53 per cent) of all respondents reported making visits to the house of a relative or friend. They made an average of slightly more than six visits a week, more frequently to relatives than to friends, though there were large variations in these frequencies. Age was related to outward visiting. Those aged 60–74 visited their networks more frequently than those aged 75 years and over. They averaged nine visits a week compared with 5.6 visits a week made by the older group. However, this masks variation within groups. Those respondents aged 75 and over and who lived alone made more outward visits than those of the same age living with other elderly people, closely following the findings from the other studies quoted above. Over half (54 per cent) of those living alone made visits, compared with one-third of those living with others.

Size of network

Implicit in the foregoing discussion on overall contact with networks is the importance of the presence or absence of such networks and of their size. How many people are actively engaged in helping this group of patients and clients? As a measure of the strength or vulnerability of support, size of network is a crude indicator since, by implication, it assumes that the burdens are shared between different members of the network – so if one member is unable to help, another will take their place. In other words, it assumes that large networks are strong because responsibility is shared between a variety of members, who are prepared and able to substitute for each other. Conversely, fragile or vulnerable networks are small, with few people either to share the burdens or to substitute for one another. This assumption is open to qualification because it is not possible to predict that role substitution will take place. This is particularly so in the case of basic nursing care. One cannot assume, for example, that another member of a family will substitute for the help given by a daughter towards the personal care needs of an old person. Nor can it be assumed that if one neighbour ceases to collect the weekly pension of an elderly person another neighbour will take over this task.

In spite of this reservation, size of networks is a variable that other studies have focused upon to indicate levels of vulnerability in caring arrangements.

Wenger's (1984) study of the rural elderly, based on a sample of elderly households in a cross-section of rural communities in North Wales, found that three-quarters of the elderly had support networks of five or more. She noted that active networks increased in size for both men and women after the age of 85 as a reflection of increasing dependency and that there seemed to be some relationship between network size and loneliness.

> No-one with a large network claims to be often lonely, and more than twice as many with small networks as those with average networks say they feel lonely often. It should be stressed, however, that those who claim to experience loneliness are in a minority whatever the size of their network. (ibid., p.140).

In our work in Dinnington we took the view that the ability to give help is clearly affected by proximity and that it would be unreasonable to classify someone whose relatives lived a considerable distance away as having an unsupportive family on the grounds that they did not visit. On the other hand, family who live far away may have their elderly relatives to stay or may visit them in the summer or over public holidays, and when this happened we recorded it. We chose to use the locality of Sheffield, Rotherham, and Worksop as the geographical area over which a visiting network might be expected to operate. If nobody visited but a named relative or friend lived in the Sheffield/Rotherham area, the network was classified as passive. If nobody either visited or lived within that area we considered there to be no network. If a named relative or friend lived in that area and visited, they were classified as being part of the active network.

The question of proximity is important since, as we shall suggest, the willingness and ability to give help seems to be tied to small geographical areas. As Wenger (1984, p.11) comments:

> The frequent inference that elderly people have families who do not take care of them does not seem to be supported by the current data. Sometimes there is no family to care simply because there is no close family.

Analysis of the networks of the Dinnington patients and clients in 1980 showed that respondents identified networks ranging in size from zero to eleven people, the most frequently mentioned being three, although 47 per cent identified networks of five people or more. Only four respondents (two per cent) failed to identify any relatives or friends (local or otherwise), a further 13 identifying networks of various sizes where nobody visited. For example, of the 27 people who named five people in their networks, two said they did not receive visits from any of them.

If the belief about the vulnerability of small networks is valid, then the

35 households (19 per cent) that identified only one or two people in their networks were potentially vulnerable. As well as this group, 17 households were without support from local relatives or friends. Nine out of the 17 failed to identify any relatives or friends living in the area; the remaining eight households had passive networks; that is they identified local relatives and/or friends, but were not visited by them.

Another of our evaluative studies gave similar findings. This was the non-user study in which all people in the village aged 70-79 but not covered by the user study were interviewed in the summer of 1981. We have reported these findings elsewhere (Tennant and Bayley 1985). Fifty-two (21 per cent) of 242 respondents reported *local* networks of less than three people. A further 69 (29 per cent) respondents reported local networks of seven or more people. A principal difference between those with small local networks, as opposed to those with larger networks, was that almost all (94 per cent) of the members of small networks were visiting or being visited at least weekly, compared to just over three-quarters (76 per cent) of the members of large networks. There was little difference in the levels of ill-health or disability reported by respondents with different size networks, but the formal services, notably the warden and home help, were making twice as many visits to those with small networks.

Roles of relatives and friends/neighbours

We have shown that most of the patients and clients we interviewed in the summer of 1980 were supported by relatives, and that nearly half of them reported help by friends or neighbours. What was the nature of that help and was there any difference in the caring activities undertaken by friends and relatives?

We deliberately sought information about what help was given during visits by asking a straight question rather than by showing a prompt card that listed a range of possible helping activities. This gave us the benefit of spontaneous response and a more accurate and comprehensive picture of the care being given to people. However, it presented us with the problem of classifying these tasks for analysis. The most striking feature of the mass of activities that were described to us was the difference in the level of demand which they put upon those giving the help. At one end of the scale a few carers were making several visits a day to supply meals, dress, wash and generally care for a highly dependent person, while at the other end of the scale there was a lot of neighbourly support in the form of short checking visits or 'popping in and out'. In order to represent this pattern while at the same time minimizing our subjective interpretation of information we developed a fourfold hierarchical classification. This is not a sophisticated model, but rather one that is based on a combination of several factors such as the amount of time involved in certain activities, whether they take place in the user's home, and the level of responsibility they place on the carer. For example, bathing an elderly parent is obviously a task quite different from doing the same person's garden.

Our hierarchy ranges from basic nursing care, through household care, and general care, to social care. Basic nursing care was defined as washing, bathing, dressing and undressing the respondent; household care was defined as cooking, doing housework, laundering clothes; general care was collecting prescriptions, shopping, gardening, odd household jobs and providing transport. The fourth category we have called social since it represents all those visits made purely for social purposes. Although, as we have said, social visiting represents the base of our hierarchy, its importance should not be under-estimated since social support, particularly for elderly and disabled people, has an important function to play in maintaining their well-being and in checking on their day-to-day health. As Cantor (1975) says:

> Visiting, sitting and talking, and eating with neighbours are some of the many social support tasks assumed under the rubric of socialisation. They are essential to sound mental health and must frequently be carried out on a day-to-day basis by friends and neighbours.

The mere fact of visiting enhances social interaction and has the potential to reduce loneliness; this should not go unrecognized as 58 per cent of the patients and clients in the 1980 study lived alone.

We recorded the activities of individual carers at the level of the most demanding task they mentioned. This does not mean that we assumed that a daughter giving basic nursing care would also be undertaking those household caring acts such as laundering the clothes, though in practice she invariably was. It seemed more accurate to record the most demanding task mentioned and to think of this model as a pyramid or hierarchy.

The number of people who received basic nursing care was low, less than five per cent of the 187 respondents in our 1980 study (Table 4.4). The proportion of people receiving other forms of care was much higher, increasing as one moves along the spectrum towards the less demanding tasks. Two-thirds of respondents, therefore, received visits from members of their informal network for purely social purposes, although some of these people also received other visits to help with particular tasks.

Considerable variation exists in the types of care being given to different groups. Five of the nine people being given basic nursing care were aged 75 years and over and living alone. This represents a small proportion of the 80 respondents in this group, nevertheless, a considerably higher proportion of these lone very elderly people received household care than did people in other groups.

As we have observed, the level of basic nursing care was low, account-ing for only a small proportion of the total informal care given to respondents. When we examined the help given with such tasks as bathing, dressing and undressing both from carers living within the household (who were excluded from Table 4.4) and from those living outside, we identified eight people who had help from outside only, seven people with help from within the household only, and one person with help from both sources. In all, therefore, only 16 people (nine per cent) were

Table 4.4 *Type of care reported as being received by 187 patients and clients of health and welfare services, 1980*

Type of household of respondent	Type of care (% received)					
	Nursing	Household	General	Social	None	No.
Alone 60–74	3	38	52	72	10	29
Alone 75+	6	63	53	66	3	80
Family	0	14	45	66	24	29
Other	6	31	51	65	10	49
Total	5	43	51	67	9	187

Note: More than one carer giving different types of care means rows add up to more than 100.

given the kind of intensive care reported in the study by Nissel and Bonnerjea (1982). Likewise, in our 1981 study of 70–79-year-olds, we found only 16 per cent of respondents receiving basic nursing care, and no overlap between in and out of house care. The information from Dinnington sets these other studies within the community-wide context. Though basic nursing care may be the most intensive and demanding, it only accounts for a small proportion of all informal care being given.

When we differentiated between relatives and friends as a source of care, we found the more demanding the care, the more likely it was to be provided by relatives rather than by friends. Though the numbers are small, almost four times as many respondents in our 1980 study received nursing care from relatives (four per cent) as from friends (one per cent). The predominance of relative support for tasks like cooking meals, doing laundry and housework was even more marked. More than five times as many people received this household care from relatives (37 per cent) as from friends (seven per cent). It is only when we come to the level of less personal and less demanding tasks that the gap is narrowed. At the level of general care relatives (37 per cent) were supporting 1.5 people for every one supported by friends (24 per cent) and at the level of visits made for purely social purposes, relatives (56 per cent) were supporting two people for every one supported by a friend (28 per cent).

The difference in the type of support given by relatives and by friends and neighbours is suggested in other work. Litwak and Szelenyi (1969) report that people turn to kin, neighbours and friends for different services. They argue that people rely on their neighbours for aid in emergencies and everyday exchanges, so that reliance on the neighbourhood as a source of help is more likely to occur in situations requiring short-term or emergency aid, like looking after a child for an hour or taking someone to the hospital, rather than in situations requiring long-term help.

If people turn to various parts of their personal network for different kinds of help, what happens when a specialized source of help is either temporarily or permanently unavailable? What is the extent of substitutability between different sources of help? Cartwright *et al.* (1973), studying the care provided to people in their last year of life, suggested that friends do often substitute for relatives when care from kin is not available, even though they generally give a less intimate type of care. They concluded that single people received much more help from friends than did any other category, concluding that 'for them ties of friendship and neighbourliness seem to compensate for their lack of immediate family' (ibid, p. 145). Cantor's (1980, p. 138) 'hierarchial compensatory model' suggested that people seek help from kin, substituting neighbours only when kin are unavailable.

We tested the question of substitutability between different sources of help, looking particularly to see whether there was any evidence that friends and neighbours give help when relatives live within the area, but do not visit. At the general level we found no evidence to support this. Overall friends and neighbours were just as likely to be involved in visiting whether the respondent had active supportive relatives or not.

Sex roles in caring

We have gone some way towards answering the claim that informal care is family care, showing that in Dinnington relatives did provide the bulk of the more demanding care, but friends and neighbours gave social support as well as general tasks such as shopping, decorating and gardening. A second and related claim is that within the family the main burden of care-giving falls on women. Walker (1982, p. 23) in his introduction to a book of essays on community care, argues that 'Care is socially divided between the state and the family and between family members. In practice "community care" is overwhelmingly care by kin, and especially female kin, not the community'.

There is now considerable evidence to support the argument that the care of elderly and handicapped dependants is predominantly undertaken by women. Over 20 years ago Townsend's (1963) study of the family life of old people showed that the family system of care was organized around female relatives, particularly daughters. More recent evidence is provided by the Equal Opportunities Commission (1980) survey, conducted in 1978, which reported that three times as many women as men were looking after elderly or handicapped relatives. Similarly, the Crossroads study (Bristow 1981) found that daughters, mothers, wives, sisters and daughters-in-law made up the great majority of carers. Hunt (1978, p. 63) found 'further evidence that the burden of caring for sick or elderly relatives most often falls on women and makes it impossible for them to work'.

In their small-scale study of 22 families involved in caring for the handicapped elderly, Nissel and Bonnerjea (1982, p. 20) analysed the hours spent on care activities each day and reported that

> well over half the husbands played no direct part in caring for the dependent relative, whereas over half of the women spent over three hours. Seven out of the 22 dependent relatives were mothers of the husband, and six out of the eight husbands who spent time on care, were helping to look after their own mothers.

However, a study of gender and the care of dependent elderly people (Durie and Wilkin 1982) reported that the relationship may not be as clear-cut as earlier work has suggested and that a variety of more complex caring experiences were apparent in the population they studied. They reported that though the burden of caring fell more heavily on women than on men, there was a substantial minority of male carers who appeared to be coping with similar problems of dependency to their female counterparts. 'Where the carer is not a spouse there appears to be a tendency towards a matching of the sex of carer and elderly person' (ibid p. 8). Seventy-one per cent of men were cared for by their sons or nephews and 73 per cent of women by their daughters or nieces. However, male carers tended to receive substantially more help from other sources than female carers, especially for domestic tasks like housework. Gender appeared to influence the willingness of others to give help to carers. 'It is expected that women should be able to cope alone, whilst men require extra help to enable them to cope (ibid.).

Our 1980 study of clients and patients gave us information about the distribution of caring tasks among relatives and showed to what extent the gender factor was predominant. Nearly two-fifths (39 per cent) of visits made to all respondents were by daughters, who gave more visits than any other relative (Table 4.5). Sons gave the second highest number of visits per week (21 per cent). However, if we add the contribution made by other female relatives we find that women provided almost two-thirds of the total. The predominance of care by daughters is even greater when visits are class-ified according to the type of care given. Though, as we have seen, relatives gave basic nursing care to around only four per cent of respondents, almost all (88 per cent) of these visits were made by daughters. Daughters also provided nearly half (49 per cent) of the visits involving household care and over one-third (34 per cent) of those for social support.

As we move down the hierarchy, away from the demands of nursing care, more relatives gave support. For example, over one-quarter (28 per cent) of the visits to give general care came from sons, who gave more of this sort of care than any other relative. The general caring tasks which sons undertook included gardening, shopping, odd household jobs and providing transport.

Table 4.5   Relationship of care giver and type of care reported by 187 patients and clients of health and welfare services, 1980

Relation-ship to respondent	% of all visits each week by relatives	% of visits giving at least			
		Nursing care	Household care	General care	Social care
Daughter	39	88	49	16	34
Son	21		23	28	20
Mother	3			8	2
Father				1	1
Sister	7		5	3	13
Brother	5			2	12
Other female	16	2	15	27	14
Other male	9	9	8	16	5
Total	100	100	100	100	100
No. of visits made each week	1110	85	363	264	398

These findings are not unexpected. They confirm one's own observations and experiences that social expectations of the caring roles of men and women are markedly different. The point is clear, and consistent with other research findings that though some men bear the major responsibilities for parent care, in the main they are more likely to experience the effects of caring through the stress it may place on their wives, sisters and daughters. There are a variety of sources of active kin care, but those tasks which are the most demanding fall heavily on daughters. They are involved in caring activities for people whom Isaacs and Neville (1976) categorize as having potential need or disability of 'short interval' or even 'critical interval' types. These categories relate to the interval which elapses between necessary episodes of help. People with short or critical interval needs of necessity make particularly heavy demands on carers.

The high level of responsibility that is carried by these daughters who are dressing, feeding, doing housework and laundry for their mothers is markedly different from the responsibility of digging the garden or doing odd household jobs. The second activity may well affect the quality of life for the user and its value should not go unrecognized, but the first activity may be the crucial factor that enables an elderly person to remain in a familiar environment rather than to enter an old people's home.

There is considerable evidence, both from our own work and in the literature we have referred to, of the primacy of the family in providing care for dependants, and, within the family, of the sexual division of labour in giving care. This situation is legitimized by the state through the ideological assumptions that it is 'natural' and 'normal' for care to be provided in this way. Hence it is possible for the state to maintain the illusion that the family is a private domain into which the state would not intrude, lest it undermine the role of the family (Land, 1978; Wilson 1982).

However, demographic and social changes are occurring that make the continuation of this relationship between the family and the state less likely in future. Roy Parker (1981, p. 21) has drawn attention to the growth in need for what he calls tending, that is paralleled by 'trends which are certain to affect the resources available for that tending'. The effect of changes in fertility rates and in family structure during the same period as the projected large increases in the number of very elderly people will lead to higher levels of need, yet reduced family caring resources. In addition, changing employment patterns and increased mobility mean that many elderly people will not be able to call on the resources of family in their immediate neighbourhood, although it is as yet uncertain how high levels of long-term unemployment will affect this situation. As Parker (1981) has commented, the social organization of tending is becoming a major issue in social policy, and rightly so. The ideological justifications for relying on female family care are beginning to be questioned, which in turn threatens the consensus regarding the respective roles of state and family in providing community care.

Geographical factors

One basic assumption of the Dinnington Project was that members of active informal networks will tend to live nearby. Other work suggests the limited geographical area over which networks operate. Thirty-four per cent of the elderly studied by Butcher and Crosbie (1977) lived within ten minutes' walk of a child and 24 per cent of the British sample in Shanas *et al.* (1968) lived this distance from their nearest child. The General Household Survey (OPCS 1982) reported that 26 per cent of elderly men and 30 per cent of elderly women living alone had a relative nearby. One-quarter of the children of the elderly people studied in Johnson *et al.* (1981) lived within a mile of their parents, and a further quarter lived between one and five miles away. Other relatives lived similar distances away and well over half the old people's friends lived within a mile. Wenger (1984) reported that in most rural communities approximately one-half of the elderly had children living within five miles.

This information tells us about the possibility of local support but not about whether help is actually given. Butcher and Crosbie's study found that within the 'past 24 hours' almost half the sample had received a visit from a family member, and of those over half lived within the same district (that is the immediate vicinity), but he does not specify the nature of the visit or whether help with specific tasks took place.

We found in general the premise that informal care is locally based holds true, though more so for care given by friends than by relatives. Of all the visits made by relatives four out of five came from people living in the village, while for friends, less than 0.5 per cent of visits made by friends came from outside the village, demonstrating the extremely localized pattern of friendship networks for this group of patients and clients.

The location of family carers is more complex and requires some discussion. For all respondents in our 1980 study we found that all the visits made to give basic nursing care came from within the village, as did 84 per cent of those giving household care. But more of the visits to give general and social support were made by people living outside Dinnington. The more demanding the task the more likely it was that the carer lived in the village.

In general our findings suggest that location is a relevant factor when considering both the relationship between respondent and carer (whether the carer is family or a friend or neighbour) and the purposes of visiting. Relative support networks were more widely dispersed than friendship networks and relatives travelled further to do the less demanding tasks, but the most intensive caring was given by those living in close proximity to the user.

Finally we should note that there are various ways of giving support that were not included in our survey. Fischer's (1982) study of networks found that proximity is relevant only for the giving of certain kinds of support. Looking at non-kin networks, he concluded that respondents asked near associates for help when practical considerations demanded proximity, but were just as likely to draw upon distant as near associates for those kinds of support for which distance is not a logistical problem (for example, giving advice). Furthermore, respondents actually felt 'closer' to their distant associates than to their nearer ones, suggesting that 'just knowing that they are there if you need them' is an important component of people's perceptions of their network. The implication of these findings, he suggested, is that there is

> nothing mystical about proximity. Nearby associates are preferred when nearness is critical. When proximity is less critical ... there is little or no preference for those nearby.... In matters of minor need, people turn to neighbours, and in matters of great need they turn to intimates wherever these people live.... They are similarly consistent with other findings on neighbours, that they largely provided house care and rarely provided 'serious' assistance (ibid, p. 175).

On the other hand, he argued, proximity is important to the extent that distance is an unsupportable cost, which it is for the poor, the elderly and women with young children, all of whom are restricted to their neighbourhood. For these people local associates form a substantial portion of their networks. Similarly, Wenger (1984, p. 139) argues that 'long-distance support is more common among the middle class'.

Summary

We can begin to draw together the key characteristics of informal care found in our and other studies. It exists, sometimes in quantity, but it is also highly *variable*. It is not possible to consider, for example, that care to the 'elderly' is in any way a homogeneous entity. Care by relatives, who provide most of the basic nursing and household care, is responsive to need. Such care is predominantly given by women and there is crude evidence to suggest that some informal networks are *vulnerable*, both through being small in size, and because there are doubts about substitutability of caring – particularly basic nursing care. This type of intensive care is almost always given by local relatives, and indeed most care comes from the local neighbourhood.

Our observations also tell us that informal care can be *volatile,* in that it can change over relatively short periods. Our cross-sectional studies do not provide adequate information to support this, though some aspects of social work practice described in Chapter 6 suggest the volatility of informal care. In the meantime we must wait for the results of longitudinal studies such as those being carried out by Wenger and her colleagues at Bangor.

These three key characteristics – variability, vulnerability and volatility – provide the background to everyday practice for the health and welfare services. Some of those working for these services will have considerable knowledge of informal networks but, as we will show in Chapter 6, they are less likely to be professionals than ancillary workers, who both live and work in the locality.

5 A Model for the Development of Community Practice

In this brief chapter we set the scene for understanding the outcomes of the project. We shall argue that most of the statutory work we studied in Dinnington before the project displayed a style and method of work that we have labelled as working 'outside the community'. We shall argue that there is an intermediate stage through which some, but not all, of the workers passed during the course of the project, which we have called working 'alongside the community'. Finally, there is a third stage which we have called working 'within the community', which some of the workers reached some of the time. We shall outline the main characteristics of each stage, before going on in the following chapter to outline the health and welfare practice before the project started, which will include brief descriptions of the position of the various services, most of which could be described as working 'outside the community' at that time.

Several points should be made clear at the outset. We did not have in mind this model of changing practice when we began our evaluation. Certainly we had several hypotheses and assumptions about the changes that would occur in workers' practice. Some of these have been borne out, others have not and, since this was an evaluative programme, we have measured the extent to which goals were met. But there is no sense in which our research programme was organized to fit the demands of a preconceived model of how locally-based work would develop. Rather, four years of observing management and fieldwork practice enabled us to build up a picture of the processes involved in decentralizing to locally-based work. This has been refined and reassessed constantly in the light of our developing understanding. In seeking to make sense of the complex data in front of us we felt that the best overall explanation of what we observed was a model that illustrated the processes or stages of changed practice, against which we could set the successes or failures of the project in meeting its declared objectives. The model is, therefore, very much an explanatory device that emerged out of empirical material as we sought to interpret and put together various sets of information.

Throughout this book we argue that both organizational and attitudinal changes must occur for community-orientated work to develop fully. It is necessary and proper to separate the two but it must be recognized that they interact very closely. For example, in Dinnington the social services department agreed to one major organizational change, namely decentralization of two social workers to Dinnington. However, at the time, this organizational change was not accompanied by the necessary attitudinal change on the part of management. This lack of attitudinal change was manifested in the failure to make a whole series of lesser organizational changes in managerial procedures such as more flexible hours of working, record-keeping, exercise of powers, categorization of workload. This inhibited and restricted change at the worker level. There were two aspects to this. First, these procedures blocked experimentation in professional practice. Second, the stimulus to change attitudes that could have been given by changed managerial procedures was absent.

Attitude change at the worker level is clearly vital. Table 5.1 outlines the stages of the workers' development towards a fully community-orientated approach to their work. It also shows how both the organization and the attitude of the workers affects the pattern of demand and the response to it. None of the stages of development is completely self-contained since change occurs incrementally.

Working 'outside the community'

Stage One of community practice we have called working 'outside the community'. Organizationally it is characterized by centralized, hier-archic and large-scale institutions. This can be seen at its purest form in, for example, the traditional area-based approach to social services or the provision of ante-natal health care service.

In the former, demand is filtered through a referral system that processes requests for help via receptionists, duty officers, intake teams, and so on. The main organizational unit is the departmental team within the area office. Fieldworkers at Stage One see little or no community dimension to their role, working within a conventional individual case framework. The inaccessibility of the centralized office to the public restricts demand, which tends to be made late in the development of a problem. Hence the department's role is reactive, rather than preventive. The response of fieldworkers is to focus on individual clients or patients, mainly in a one-to-one situation and to use predominantly the resources of their own department. Use of resources from other departments or agencies tends to be on a one-off basis rather than as part of regular, co-ordinated work. Even where services are based locally, as was the case in Dinnington for all workers except the social workers, the style of service remains essentially the same, focusing on individual clients, with little systematic reference to other workers or other resources in the locality. In its own way, ante-natal health care practice is similar. Centred in the main on hospitals (98 per cent of babies are now born in hospital), emphasis is given to a highly technical and highly centralized operation. Little emphasis is given to anything but the patient-health service interaction.

Table 5.1 *Development of community practice*

	Organization	Attitude	Demand	Response
Stage One Outside the community	Large-scale, centralized. Filtering system. Departmental team.	No community dimension.	Restricted and made at later stage of problem therefore reactive service.	Focus on client. Departmental resources mainly Sometimes client as household or family.
Stage Two Alongside the community	Small-scale, decentralized. Open access. Regular sustained liaison with local workers.	Community orientation as extra to main stream casework.	Immediate increase and made at earlier stage of problem.	Focus on client in network. Expanding range of formal resources.
Stage Three Within the community	Small-scale, decentralized. Open access. Locality team.	Community orientation is integral to ordinary work.	Sustained higher level therefore moves towards preventive service.	Focus on client in network and community. Wide range of community re-sources.

Working 'alongside the community'

Stage Two, working 'alongside the community', indicates some shift in attitude and may require some organizational change. Certainly this would be a requirement for the traditional area-based social services provision, though less so for primary health care teams. Stage Two units of organization are small-scale and localized, with open access to the relevant fieldworkers. Relationships between locally-based workers are characterized by regular rather than sporadic contact and by the beginnings of a sense of identity as an inter-agency locality team. Demand on the service is high with the greater accessibility of the agency, and workers are able to intervene at an earlier stage in the development of problems. Their response is to focus increasingly on the client's network and to call upon a wide range of formal resources, linking up with other statutory workers and bringing in the occasional volunteer to support hard-pressed carers. Attitudinally, workers are thinking about work of a preventive nature in the community, but this is seen as an adjunct to their mainstream work with clients; the community dimension remains something extra to normal work.

Working 'within the community'

At Stage Three, working 'within the community', local fieldworkers display the characteristics of what Payne (1982) calls the matrix team, that is one where the members have a dual responsibility, both to their department and to their team, often one where members are drawn from different departments or even different authorities. They have internalized the community orientation to the extent that it has become integral to their everyday work, rather than something extra and different. The level of demand remains high and preventive work is given greater priority. Knowledge of the area enables workers to organize resources in ways that prevent or at least lessen the development of problems in the future. Thus, working 'within the community' means that workers do not just focus on clients and their networks, but also on particular groups or streets within their area. They now call upon a range of community-based resources, from workers in other agencies, to self-help groups, individual volunteers and voluntary groups.

Our understanding of work 'within the community' is very close to the Barclay Report's (1982, paras 13.25–13.26, 13.43) description of 'community social work':

> Community social work demands that the people who form a client's environment are seen for what they are or may be – an essential component of the client's welfare.
>
> Social workers have already moved from a focus upon individuals, or mothers and children, to seeing people as members of families. What

community social work demands is that the area of vision is extended to include those who form, or might form, a social network into which the client is meshed.

Community social work requires of the social worker an attitude of partnership. Clients, relations, neighbours and volunteers become partners with the social worker in developing and providing social care networks ... The function of social workers is to enable, empower, support and encourage, but not usually to take over from, social networks.

The stages of development towards the style of community practice outlined above are only distillations of a range of organizational practice features that characterize modern health and welfare systems. Being selective and brief they are necessarily crude oversimplifications of the real world, but they serve as benchmarks against which to examine changed practice. They have the additional value of being sufficiently general to apply to the range of departments associated with the project so that we are able to compare both management response and the development of fieldwork practice between departments, as well as comparing management and workers' behaviour within a specific department.

6　Formal Care before the Project

Before we look at the organizational changes which were introduced by the project, and the extent to which workers changed their practice as a result, we must look at the position from which they started. We outlined our model of community practice in the last chapter and would maintain that health and welfare practice in Dinnington in 1979 was mostly 'outside the community', and only occasionally what we have described as 'alongside the community'. We shall substantiate this claim by examining the principal agencies involved with the project, by means of information gained from three of the evaluation programme's research studies. These are the caseload and referral studies and the GP study.

The general practitioners
Arguably the hub of the primary health care team in the community is the general practice. In 1980 the General Household Survey (OPCS 1982) reported that 11 per cent of males and 15 per cent of females had consulted a NHS general practitioner in the 14 days before interview. In Dinnington one general practice of eight doctors, six full-time and two part-time, covered 90–95 per cent of the population. There was also a local health clinic from which health visitors and domiciliary nurses worked. So most of the practice's patients had easy (physical) access to their doctor, which is consistent with a report (OPCS 1981, p. 21) on access to primary health care which stated that: 'About half the informants lived within one mile of their doctors' surgeries and three-quarters lived within two miles. Only five per cent had to travel five miles or more.'

The involvement of almost the whole community with one general practice offered an advantage compared with other areas. A recent study of informal care, social work and other services for elderly clients living alone in one borough in London (Sinclair *et al.* 1984, p. 15) found a very different situation. 'A survey of 86 elderly clients who had a social worker ... showed these people were registered with 26 different GPs.' On the assumption that the fewer involved, the easier it is to get to know one another, we must regard Dinnington as having a head start in developing a partnership between the primary health care team, other workers and the community.

Our 1980 general practitioner study found:

(a) a high consultation rate for children in the first five years of life (The 1980 figures can be seen in Table 8.1 on p. 85);

(b) a transition from consultations predominantly for acute illness to those predominantly for chronic illness at 40 years of age for females, and 50 years of age for males;
(c) a high proportion of cases where the doctors expected no further action, again related to age;
(d) a low consultation rate for the elderly;
(e) an overall consultation rate that was 81 per cent of the national level.

We were particularly concerned about the low consultation rate for the elderly. Traditionally they have been regarded as under-consulters (Williamson *et al.* 1964) although this has been questioned recently (Ford and Taylor, 1985). Whatever the overall position, consultation rates for the 65–74-year-old group in Dinnington were less than half the national level. With the project giving some emphasis to the development of an integrated system of support for elderly people, we expected to see some improvement in their consultation rates.

Developing Stott and Davis's (1979) idea of the chronology of the consultation we identified three types of consultation;

(a) *one-off* consultations, defined as those where there had been no consultation for the same symptom during the previous month, *and* where no further consultation was foreseen;
(b) *concluding* consultations, where no further consultation was foreseen but there had been a consultation for the same symptom during the previous month;
(c) *continuing* consultations, where a further consultation was foreseen, and where there may or may not have been a consultation for the same symptom during the previous month.

A four-week time period may seem rather short as some chronic symptoms require less frequent consultation. However, these would have been classified as a 'continuing' consultation as a further consultation would be seen as necessary. The classification only falls down when a concluding consultation occurred for a symptom where the previous consultation was more than a month ago. In these circumstances the consultation would be designated as one-off, but it is thought that such occurrences were rather rare.

One immediate result of this classification is an understanding that 'no further action' and 'one-off' consultations are not necessarily the same. In 1980, 14 per cent of consultations were the conclusion of a series. Only 49 per cent were 'one-off' consultations. So while two-thirds of consultations required no further action, a figure which associates closely with other findings (for example, Fry, 1977), purely one-off consultations in Dinnington were less than half the total.

Patients aged 40 and over were much more likely to be involved in a series of consultations, linked to the onset of chronic illness which we noted earlier, rather than a one-off consultation. However it is important to note that almost two in five (39 per cent) consultations associated with those aged under 40 were also part of a series.

Approximately one half of consultations were diagnosed as acute illness, with just over one quarter diagnosed as chronic illness. Other consultations were for a range of needs, for example contraception. Acute or chronic illness apparently made no difference to the extent to which the doctor called in other resources. The principal response by the doctor was to give treatment at the time of consultation (more than three in five consultations) and offer support to the patient.

The main differences that we observed in 1980 were those between continuing consultations and one-off or concluding consultations. Continuing consultations, as we might expect, were predominantly concerned with chronic illness (over half of these consultations), while both one-off and concluding consultations were predominantly concerned with acute illness (approximately two-thirds of these consultations). The major difference in the response to these groups was the importance of 'form filling' for the chronically sick. Normally we found writing a sick note was associated with the doctor thinking the consultation inappropriate. When the doctor wrote a sick note he thought 33 per cent of the consultations were inappropriate, but the proportion was only 13 per cent when no sick note was written. This was clearly not the case for continuing consultations. Two in five of these consultations involved writing a sick note, yet the doctors considered only four per cent to be inappropriate, a significant difference between continuing and other types of consultation. It seemed to signify a number of 'one-off' visits to the doctor for legitimization of short periods off work – something the doctors considered 'inappropriate'.

Our principal concern was, however, with the consultation within the context of the total health and welfare scene. Thus we were interested not only in the diagnosis and immediate action of the doctor, but also the source of referral and any resources which may have been brought to bear either immediately or as part of planned further action. It is the total context of the consultation that we seek. In order to do this we had to sacrifice aspects of the process of the consultation which others consider important (Pendleton *et al.* 1984), as well as some depth in diagnosis and response.

The principal characteristic of the pattern of consultation in 1980 was its simplicity. Ninety-six out of every 100 consultations were initiated by either the patient or the patient's family or friends. Of these consultations one-half belonged to a series of consultations. For all consultations, only one in ten involved a referral to other resources, of which the largest group

(58 per cent of those referred on) were to other health services. Only eight per cent were to social services, although we must not underestimate the number involved. This represents 806 referrals a year to health services, and 104 a year to social services. Nevertheless, the predominant characteristic of the pattern of consultation was the patient, or their relative or friend approaching the general practitioner. On average there was little involvement outside this single contact. Thus we can identify one of the principal characteristics of Stage One of our model of community practice, the emphasis upon one-to-one intervention with few resources brought in from elsewhere.

The district nurses
We found a similar pattern of care with the district nurse. The term 'district nurse' encompasses several types of qualified nurse. A division can be made between those nurses with a State Registered Nurse (SRN) qualification and those with a State Enrolled Nurse (SEN) qualification. In addition, each of these nurses may or may not have an additional district nursing qualification. The largest group identified in a survey of nurses working in the community by Dunnell and Dobbs (1982) were SRNs with a district nursing qualification. They represented 55 per cent of the nurses in the four possible combinations mentioned above (SRN with district training, SRN without, SEN with, SEN without). Generally speaking, SRNs have the responsibility for a caseload of patients from one or more general practitioners. The SEN is supervised by the SRN and may or may not have her own caseload depending upon local practice. Nursing auxiliaries, often referred to as 'the bath nurse', are also part of the district nursing team.

There are also several patterns of organization under which the district nurse works. Attachment or alignment is where community nursing staff are responsible for providing services to people on lists of specified GPs. More than four-fifths (83 per cent) of district nurses in Dunnell and Dobbs's (1982) survey were attached to general practices. These nurses could either cover the whole of the GP's area, or some parts of it, or a combination. The largest group of district nurses in the survey were those attached to the GP and covering all parts of the area (47 per cent).The nurses in Dinnington belong to this category.

One aspect which Dunnell and Dobbs did not address, and which is important in the context of the Dinnington project, is the relationship between organization of nurses and the situation of the general practice. By this we mean not only the number of practices and/or doctors that they work for, but also where the practice is situated. In Dinnington the nurses are attached to a practice which covers three or four discrete communities, the largest being Dinnington itself. Both doctors and nurses can readily identify with these small communities. This is not likely to be the case for those nurses attached to some practices in urban areas. They are much more likely to have a wider catchment area with many diverse communities to serve. We would suggest that, unless they are zoned in some way, nurses working in urban areas will find great difficulty in moving out of Stage One of our model of community practice. Stages Two and Three imply a local focus to their work, something to which the Cumberledge Report (DHSS 1986a) gives high priority.

In the summer of 1979 two SRNs, two SENs, and a nursing auxiliary were attached to the general practice serving the project and neighbouring villages. (An additional SEN had been drafted in because of high demand.) Our caseload study showed 38 patients were being cared for in the project village, and the nurses visited each of these patients on average three times a week. We found that the type of care given by district nurses to their patients was very similar to that illustrated elsewhere, for example Dunnell and Dobbs (1982) and Poulton (1977). We also discovered that there was considerable variation in the amount of care which was given to different patients. This variation has led us to examine patients according to the number of visits received each week. Using the median visit level as a guideline, we divided patients into those who received one visit a week or less (whom we shall refer to as the 'occasional' group) and those who received more than one visit a week (whom, as they often received very frequent visits, we shall refer to as the 'daily' group).

The differences between the two groups were substantial and, to a large extent, rational. Eighteen of the 38 patients fell into the 'occasional' group. Nurses visited this group on average less than once a fortnight, although there was considerable variation. The group was characterized by those patients suffering from acute illness or infection (72 per cent) with only one-third classified as having chronic illness or disability.

The response made by the nurses was primarily 'technical procedures' (to 94 per cent of patients). By this we mean injections, dressings, enemas, suppositories and so on (following Dunnell and Dobbs' categories). Two-thirds received 'other nursing care' by which we mean routine nursing care, bathing, giving medicine, supervision of patient and assessment. Over three in five (61 per cent) received advice and counselling (including advice to relatives and just social chatting), while less than three in ten (28 per cent) had 'technical tests' (for example blood samples, skin testing, audiometry, and so on). While the SRN was in attendance for all but two of these 'occasional' patients, the SEN attended half and the auxiliary just over one-quarter (28 per cent). This pattern is consistent with the SRN having a supervisory role over all patients.

Most contacts made on behalf of the patient by the nurses were to other health authority staff (for example 16 per cent to the health visitor), or to relatives living in the same household (25 per cent of cases). As the nurses were attached to the GPs (contacted in 97 per cent of cases) and they see it as part of their job to teach relatives how to care, we would expect to see a pattern of this nature. In just over one fifth of the cases nurses contacted home helps (22 per cent), and in slightly fewer cases, wardens (19 per cent). Otherwise contacts were few and far between and averaged 2.3 per patient over the previous year.

In sharp contrast, nurses were visiting the 'daily' group on average 5.4 times each week, and, for the 20 patients involved, were providing two-fifths of the total number of visits received from the project services (compared to just five per cent of visits for the 'occasional' group). Six patients who were living with spouse or sibling(s) were receiving on average over nine visits a week from the nurses. Two of these patients accounted for nearly one-third of all the visits given by the nurses to the village.

Mrs A lived with her husband in one of the three units of sheltered accommodation in the village. At the time of our first caseload study in the summer of 1979 she was 76 years old. Two months previously she had been discharged from hospital where she had been cared for after suffering a stroke. She was bedfast and had an indwelling catheter. An SRN, two SENs and an auxiliary nurse visited on average nearly three times daily, carrying out a wide range of tasks, including, initially, rearranging the furniture in the house to make caring for Mrs A much easier. The team of nurses had made contact with a large number of agencies including the aids and adaptations officer in social services, the home help organizer, the warden and the DHSS.

Mrs A was also receiving two visits a day from the warden (or her relief) and three visits a week from the home help to do general housework. In all she was receiving 35 visits each week from the statutory services in the village. Nevertheless it is interesting to note that the home help wrote 'Mrs A is the patient, and her husband looks after her'.

Mrs B, aged 77, lived with her 62-year-old sister in a large house in the village. After a car accident she was quadraplegic, bedfast and still suffering from the loss of her husband. Once again the whole team of nurses was involved in her care, visiting on average some 32 times each week. As with Mrs A, a wide range or agencies had been contacted on Mrs B's behalf, including the physiotherapist and the chiropodist.

In addition to the care given by the nurses, a team of home helps (three) were calling nearly three times a day, one of whom concentrated entirely on simple nursing care such as washing the client and putting her back to bed. A peripatetic warden also called daily. In all Mrs B received on average 51 visits each week from the statutory services in the village.

Both these patients, according to our classification, received nursing care, technical procedures, technical tests and advice and counselling. It is noticeable that the 'daily' group as a whole received much more care and that this related to a much higher proportion suffering from chronic illness or disability (65 per cent) with one-quarter being bedfast. Most of the care was given by the SRN with the SEN, and, in contrast to those patients in the 'occasional' group, it was only with those living with another elderly person, such as the two case examples above, that the auxiliary played any part.

As might be expected, nurses made more contacts for these patients than for those in the 'occasional' group. On average four contacts were made for each patient, but still to the same groups of people as were contacted for the 'occasional' group. Thus in the 'daily' group home helps were contacted in over one-third of cases (34 per cent), relatives living outside the household in over two-fifths of cases (43 per cent). Contacts to social workers of any kind were noticeable by their rarity.

The 1980 Referral Study showed us the equivalent of 71 annual referrals for each 1000 population cared for. This was the highest level of demand placed upon any of the project services in the village. Given the pattern of work of the nurses, it is not surprising that 58 per cent of their referrals originated with the general practice and a further 26 per cent from other parts of the health sector. This left just 16 per cent of referrals originating outside the health sector, mostly with patients or their informal networks (13 per cent).

This way of working, with its emphasis largely within the health sector, is confirmed when we examine the response made by nurses to those referrals. On average the nurses made only 0.8 contacts for each referral, three-quarters of which were within the health sector. Only five (14 per cent) referrals were made to statutory services outside the health service. All were to the social services.

When we examined the case load of nurses in the following summer of 1980, we found a substantial drop in both the number of patients on their books at the time (from 38 to 26, a fall of 32 per cent) and in the average level of visits they gave to their patients – from three to 2.3 (a fall of 23 per cent). This fall was concentrated in the 'daily' group whose numbers had fallen from 20 in 1979 to 12 in 1980. Furthermore, the average number of weekly visits to this group had fallen from 5.4 to 4.6. In 1979 the nurses had five bedfast clients, but in 1980 (according to their definition) there were none. The fall in the level of care was also matched by a fall in the average number of contacts made on behalf of patients, from 3.4 in 1979 to 2.4 in 1980.

Certain key characteristics stand out in the pattern of care we have examined. In the first instance demand is clearly very volatile. The discharge of a handful of patients from hospital over a short period of time can place great pressure on local nursing resources. This was very much the situation in the summer of 1979. The second point is that there were two distinct groups of patients in the community: those who required infrequent visits from the nurses, either for a routine injection, or for bathing; and those who required almost daily care, a few of whom, as we have seen, required very intensive care. In most of the more demanding cases nurses were part of a much larger team of health and welfare services caring for the patient in the community. Although in a few of these cases contacts were made to a wide variety of agencies, generally speaking the nurses worked within the framework of the health services. There was no evidence to suggest any co-ordinated approach to the health care of patients, although co-operation clearly existed between nurses and others with some of the more demanding patients.

It is this understanding of the nature and extent of care in 1979 and 1980 which leads us to believe that, despite its local base, district nursing practice was firmly embedded at Stage One of our model of community practice – working 'outside the community'. Only for those patients in extreme need did nurses display some characteristics of Stage Two – working 'alongside the community'.

The health visitor

In early 1979, in the preliminary discussions about the involvement of various workers with the evaluation programme of the project, a critical decision was taken about how the health visitor's work was to be recorded. As the health visitor argued that all 400 children under five living in the village were on her caseload, it was considered an inappropriate imposition on her time (particularly as she was the only health visitor in post) to fill in forms for all her patients. It was decided that she would complete forms only for 'non-routine' patients. With hindsight, this was an error. We have since realized that working 'within the community' means bringing a new perspective to traditional practice. We should have taken a sample from her total routine caseload, as well as all her non-routine cases. As it is, we were unable to measure accurately the impact of project ideas upon health visiting practice. All we have is quantitative information from non-routine cases, together with qualitative material gathered for our study of process. However, we hope that this limited material will enable readers to grasp the essential aspects of health visiting practice as the project developed.

In the summer of 1979 the health visitor cared for 23 patients whom she classified as 'non-routine'. Family problems were most common with these patients, although over one-fifth suffered from some form of physical disability. Almost invariably the health visitor responded with 'friendly support' (in 87 per cent of cases) and also some counselling (35 per cent). She visited her patients approximately once a month. Her most frequent contacts on behalf of the patient were to the social worker (48 per cent) and to the general practitioner (30 per cent). On average, she made 1.7 contacts for the non-routine cases. In nearly four out of five (78 per cent) non-routine cases the health visitor was the only project worker involved with the patient.

In early 1980, just before the project began, the health visitor received six non-routine referrals in our five-week referral study. This represented an annual rate of 38 'non-routine' referrals per 1000 children under 16 years of age. Four of these referrals were followed up in the study period and contacts were made on behalf of three of them, two to others in the primary health care team, and one to a social worker.

By the beginning of the project we can see that, at least in her non-routine cases, the health visitor displayed characteristics of practice which placed her at the boundary of Stages One and Two of our model of community practice. She was locally based and in touch with other workers, particularly social workers from the area office. However, there was no evidence of sustained co-ordination with other workers, a fact which would have clearly placed her within the second stage – working 'alongside the community'.

The social workers
This style of work is maintained when we turn our attention to the welfare services. The social services office serving Dinnington was situated at Maltby, a town five miles away. In contrast housing, health and educational welfare all had offices in the village. Dinnington was served by one of the two teams in the South area of Rotherham social services. In 1979, ten social workers with six welfare assistants and other service and clerical support served a population of around 60 000 in the South area.

As well as being inaccessible to the public the area office was bureaucratized in the way of most social services departments. Gilbert Smith (1978) claims that organizational segmentation between reception, intake and allocation arrangements may help to clarify functions and responsibilities, but increases the problems of co-ordination, since so many personnel are involved. The South area did not have an intake team but used a duty officer system so that clients calling at the office were seen first by a receptionist and then a duty officer. New cases were allocated at a weekly allocation meeting, though urgent referrals would be passed from the duty officer to a social worker for immediate action.

Social work practice at Stage One of our model was characterized by individualized one-to-one casework between social worker and client, with little conception of the client as part of a wider community, school or work place network. Social work was seen as concerned principally with individuals and their immediate families. So clients' problems tended to be individualized, with the 'client' defined at most as the household or family unit, rather than as part of an extended network.This pattern prevailed in spite of the fact that many of the practical and physical problems that clients brought to the department were associated with their immediate environment, while many of the psychological problems were to do with relationships within the extended family or with their neighbours.

The social service department's response to client demand, therefore, was to allocate cases to individual workers, bearing in mind current workloads and the balance of particular skills and preferences for different areas of work within the team. There was little evidence of teamwork, of shared work with clients or of joint planning with workers from other departments. In this respect Rotherham represents a typical model of service delivery. Whilst the most common organizational pattern of social work delivery is the team, in practice social work is very individualistic.

Social work 'outside the community' is essentially reactive, a response to levels of individually presented or inferred need that become translated into demands on the department in the form of referrals. Some of these demands are filtered through the system to become the cases of professionalized workers, others are filtered through to the caseloads of welfare assistants or ancillaries, reflecting the priorities attached to certain client groups (Black *et al.* 1983). The lack of a network context in which to locate clients is paralleled by the frequent lack of a context for contact with other workers. As Bennett (1983, p.54) comments:

> Inter-agency liaisons are likely to be on an individual case basis, rendering each contact an isolated event. There is little potential here for developing a working relationship in which mutual education, shared responsibility and reciprocity can flourish.

All of the above has been documented in the social work literature, both on organizational features (Smith and Ames 1976; Stevenson 1980) and on practice (Holme and Maizels 1978; Sainsbury *et al.* 1982; Goldberg and Warburton 1979; Goldberg and Connelly 1982). We merely restate it as the starting point for social work in the village. When we examine the data on the caseload of social workers who had cases in Dinnington we can see that it illustrates these features of individual casework, lack of shared or team involvement in cases and a focus on other statutory, particularly within-agency, resources.

Two points should be made about the data. The first concerns the population bases of the study. We have used whole populations rather than samples, so the data refer to all those clients living in the village who were on the caseloads of social workers. But since Dinnington's population is only slightly over 7000 the actual number of cases in certain client groups is small. For example, the number of clients with mental handicaps, adults or children, is low; when we refer to children in care we are referring to a handful of children. This does not invalidate the findings, but it does require an element of caution when attempting to generalize from such a low base.

The second point relates to the way we have analysed the caseload data. Other studies, particularly those based on the case review system on which the 'current cases' form adopted in Dinnington was based, frequently analyse caseloads according to the length of time a case was open. Analysis based on the longevity of cases, therefore, seemed a useful starting point. Data drawn from the 1979 study were divided into four time periods: long-term cases that had been open for 12 months or more; short-term cases of three months or less; and two medium-term groups, those that had been open for between 7 and 11 months, and for between four and six months. These divisions do not represent the time from the opening of the case to its closure, but from the opening of the case to the day of the study: that is a snapshot of all cases on a particular day, not a picture of the total life history of the cases.

Qualified social workers were carrying the majority of the long-term cases (19 out of 33) but ten were being looked after by unqualified social workers, who generally had considerable experience, and four were in the hands of a social work assistant. The shorter-term cases were nearly evenly divided between qualified and unqualified workers. Social work assistants were dealing more with the shorter-term work, where, as we shall see, there was a significant number of elderly people.

In 1979 there were 67 cases from Dinnington on the caseload of the Maltby-based team that covered the village (see Table 9.1 on pp. 107–8). Of these, 33 (49 per cent) had been open for at least a year. These long-term cases were dominated by those involving family relationships, especially those with child behaviour problems and those where there was a statutory requirement on the department to provide social work support. Clients were visited on average once every three weeks, principally to offer counselling with information and advice and, in a quarter of the cases, to give financial or material aid. A wide range of contacts was made by social workers with respect to such clients, averaging slightly over four per case (in the past 12 months). Liaison took place primarily with other formal agencies concerned with families, such as health staff (school nurses), education welfare officer, school staff, DHSS staff and the department of employment. However, contact with relatives was significant also and there was some contact with friends and voluntary bodies.

The largest client group within the long-term cases was characterized by family relationships and child behaviour problems, of which there were ten cases. The overwhelming response to this group was counselling support with information-giving, the social workers visiting slightly more frequently than fortnightly. They also made extensive contacts about these clients both to formal agencies and, in three out of the ten cases, to friends and voluntary agencies. Overall they made almost seven contacts per case for these clients, who represent the intractable family stiuations that are part of most social workers' caseloads. However, even in these situations there was no evidence that there was any sense of planned inter-agency response to the multiple problems faced by such families. Contact to the health visitor regarding family X was likely to be a one-off request for any assistance that her department could offer, or an exchange of information, not an ongoing planned strategy of joint intervention.

There were 20 short-term cases from Dinnington held at the area office, half of them elderly clients. Problems associated with physical disability were given as the major area of need for 11 of the 20 short-term clients. Surprisingly none of these 20 cases involved legal obligations on the department: the non-elderly cases reflected a variety of family relation-ship issues and financial difficulties. It will be seen that the unusual situation of having no statutory cases amongst the short-term cases from Dinnington was not repeated in later years.

Social workers visited their short-term cases more frequently, almost once a fortnight on average, principally to give financial or material aid. But they liaised with other departments or individuals infrequently. Only 1.8 contacts were made per case (since the case was opened) and a high proportion of these were within the boundaries of their own department, for example to the aids officer, or other social services staff. This reflects the high proportion of elderly clients with disability problems in short-term caseloads, a feature noted in other research (Goldberg and War-burton, 1979). One may assume that the higher rate of visiting to these short-term cases was part of the initial intensive social work input required in making arrangements for residential accommodation or day care, sorting out additional domiciliary support, or tiding families over a difficult financial period by giving financial or other practical assistance.

Between the short- and long-term cases we identified two groups of medium-term clients, cases that had been open for between four and six months, and between seven and 11 months. The interesting question is whether these medium-term groups had characteristics of their own, or whether they were merely cases that were 'passing out' or 'passing through' to become long-term cases six months or so later.

A longitudinal study of a particular cohort of clients is the only satisfactory way to answer this question, but putting together information from our linked cross-sectional studies we are able to respond to it partially. The cases that had been current for at least seven months displayed characteristics of long-term cases and could be described as passing through the system. Both the presenting problems and the department's response showed greater similarity to the long-term caseload than to the short-term one. The four-to-six-months cases, on the other hand, were more akin to the short-term ones; mostly they were the tail end of the short-term caseload with, for example, social workers completing arrangements for residential care. From this we suggest that, under a conventional social work model, six months represents the cut-off point between short-term and long-term cases, with the associated characteristics that we have described above.

Once again, the overwhelming reliance on social service resources and limited contact elsewhere, particularly with short-term cases, points to a style of practice consistent with working 'outside the community'. Further evidence is provided by the study of referrals made to the area office in early 1980 just before the start of the project. This showed that most referrals were made by other formal agencies, with low numbers of referrals from the informal sector. The response of social workers was to meet requests for help within their own service and there was little evidence of a wider range of resources being brought to bear. Both the pattern of demand for social work and the response made to such demand reflect the characteristics of a service that is essentially 'outside the community'.

Referrals from Dinnington to the area social services office during a five-week period from January to February 1980 showed 16 referrals representing an annual rate of 24 referrals per 1000 people served. Warburton (1982), in a study of Cambridgeshire social services covering an area of small towns servicing dispersed villages similar to the project area, implies a rate of 20 referrals per 1000 people served, while Goldberg and Warburton's (1979) study of 'Seatown' found a rate of 25 per 1000 in this more urban community. Black *et al.* (1983) found referral rates of 17.6 per 1000 in 'Aber' (a very scattered rural population), 20.8 in Dereham (an arable farming area in Norfolk with no large centres of population) and 22.2 in Selly Oak in Birmingham (with a very high population density). It must be remembered that a contributing factor to Dinnington's being selected as the project area was that it was already placing a relatively heavy demand upon social services. One may assume that it represents the 'heavy' end of demand for Rotherham social services, thus tending towards the referral rate shown in the more urban areas. Information on the referral rates for neighbouring villages to Dinnington suggests that the demand from the village was comparatively high. In general the demand faced by Rotherham social services was fairly typical for this kind of area.

In 1980, eight referrals were made by or on behalf of elderly people, a rate of 64 per 1000 people aged 60 and over in Dinnington. Eight referrals from non-elderly people represented an annual rate of 14 per 1000 people aged 59 and under. We should note here that referrals for domiciliary services are not included in this analysis. Like 'Seatown' (Goldberg and Warburton 1979), only social work referrals are being considered at the moment. The principal sources of referral were other agencies or departments within the formal sector, particularly other local authority departments and agencies such as the police. Sixty-nine per cent of referrals came from within the formal sector and only 31 per cent from either clients or members of their networks. Referrals received by phone and by letter accounted for three-quarters of referrals while those derived from people calling into the area office accounted for less than one-fifth of referrals.

Once the referral had been made, three-quarters received a follow-up visit during the study period. On average the number of days to a follow-up visit was ten, although this varied considerably from those which were dealt with quickly to those which took over a month to follow up. In practice the key factor was the nature of the referral linked to organizational factors. 'Urgent' referrals would be passed from the duty officer to a social worker for immediate action, otherwise they would await the weekly allocation meeting. Referrals for aids and adaptations would normally take over a month to follow up. This is why a proportion of referrals were left without follow-up at the end of the study period. Some would be awaiting allocation, others would be for aids and adaptations.

Bearing in mind that we are only talking about 16 referrals, we found the formal sector was the principal source of referrals and that delinquency was reported most often as the cause, followed by the need for aids and adaptations, and assessment for a place in a local authority old people's home. On each occasion the follow-up involved a visit to the client's home. Little evidence exists to suggest that much use was being made during this initial contact period of wider community resources. On average 0.75 contacts were made for each referral and these contacts were mainly made back to the referring agency. In only 31 per cent of cases was any contact made outside the source agency. No contacts were made to the voluntary sector and only one to family, friends and neighbours regarding a referral. The reliance on meeting need from within their own service was clear and there is little indication of the area office being used by people as an information and advice centre or as a referral agency in relation to financial difficulties, as suggested by Goldberg and Warburton (1979, p. 63).

The lack of what might be called a 'network dimension' to the department's handling of referrals highlights an area where we would expect to see a marked change. The ability of social work to move from a relatively self-contained framework of services to a broader context of work including client and other networks is a key indicator of what we would describe as community social work practice. This assumes that social workers are taking more account of alternative kinds of help that a potential client may have, of the 'lay referral network'. As Gilbert Smith (1978, p. 217) says:

> to offer an effective service from the client's perspective, social work agencies must be able to see themselves as just one part of a wider system of social and extended family networks of mutual help   (ibid., p. 27).

The data derived from the 1980 Referral Study from Dinnington show that at the stage of initial contact with clients this wider community perspective was not part of the social work team's style and method of work. The description we have given of the pattern of referrals and of the department's initial response to them illustrates the inaccessibility of the department and the restricted role it plays when working 'outside the community'. The combination of distance from Dinnington and the organisational arrangements for referrals resulted in low numbers of clients and members of their networks visiting the area office. The response of the department to referrals was a conventional bureaucratic procedure with little attempt to work outside the boundaries of its own service. There are two points to comment on here. Not only is there the possibility that unmet need existed in the community because people did not perceive the social services department as either relevant or competent, but there was also the problem for those people who did pass through the referral process, that their early experience of social services influenced the relationship between worker and client at other stages of the client career (Gilbert Smith 1978). The routinized procedures followed at reception, intake and allocation may well establish a dependent relationship between professional and client, thus inhibiting any moves by workers towards a more participative form of decision-making with their clients. Both organizational and attitudinal characteristics of social work 'outside the community' possibly have important effects on the overall pattern of service that is given.

So in 1979 and early 1980 social work was practised according to Stage One of our model, that is 'outside the community', and reflected many of the characteristics of conventional practice. We saw that long-term work was primarily directed towards families with problems, who were given counselling and information about benefits, and that quite extensive contacts were made with outside agencies about such cases. In addition, there was some evidence that social workers linked into the wider support systems of their clients, but only in five cases were there any contacts to the voluntary agencies, and none of these involved individual volunteers. Four contacts were to the WRVS and one to a local church.

Short-term cases, and those that spilled over into the four-to-six-months group, were mainly concerned with elderly people receiving practical assistance, for whom social workers were making limited contact with informal networks. Even the restricted range of contacts that took place within the formal sector were contained within the departmental boundaries or made to health agencies.

This over-dependence upon departmental resources was reflected in the response made to referrals. Little evidence existed to suggest that social workers engaged in any systematic integrated practice either with other workers, informal networks or with the community at large.

The home helps
This was much the same for the home help service. Rotherham Metropolitan District Council (MDC) provided an extensive home help service for its population, so that in 1979 its provision of 12.4 whole time equivalent (WTE) home helps per 1000 people aged 65 and over was marginally above DHSS guidelines.

Dexter and Harbert (1983, pp. 83–5) laid out a schema for describing the nature and extent of the home help service, which makes it possible to compare changing patterns of service within an authority, or to compare different authorities. The traditional measure of the service, that enshrined in the DHSS guidelines which we mentioned above, is the number of WTE home helps per 1000 people aged 65 and over. This Dexter and Harbert call the 'extent' of the service, and in 1979 in Dinnington, as in the Rotherham MDC as a whole, this was 12.4.

The number of hours of home help time which are made available to clients, expressed as the average weekly hours available per 1000 of the population aged over 65 years, which they call the 'level' of service, was 497 in Dinnington in 1979. This is approximately two to three times greater than the level of the south-western counties they quote in their book, which emphasizes the commitment of Rotherham MDC to extensive home help provision.

The average number of weekly cases per 1000 of the population over 65 years they call 'cover', which in Dinnington in 1979 was 105, again much higher than the counties they quote and indicating that more than one in ten of the elderly were receiving the service at any one time.

Regardless of the number of clients covered, another important factor to consider is, on average, how many hours are given to each client? In Dinnington in 1979 it was 4.7 hours, and this Dexter and Harbert call the 'intensity' of the service. We are able to compare the village level of 4.7 against national figures of 2.1 in 1979–80 (CIPFA 1981). These measures are linked with the formula 'level = cover x intensity'. Dexter and Harbert argue that the formula allows one to determine crude differences between authorities, not only with respect to the level, but also the emphasis of the service. For example, some authorities may provide a limited (low) cover but give many hours (high intensity) to those whom they do care for. Others may choose to cover many people, but to give only a little time to each (low intensity). For Rotherham MDC in general and for Dinnington in particular we must recognize that in 1979, the extent and level of the home help service was high, and that a high cover (105) and an intensity (4.7) of more than twice the national average reflect a level of service which was among the most generous in the country.

This has important implications for an experiment like the Dinnington Project, or any project which aims to capitalize upon the extent and knowledge of the home help service, particularly the local knowledge of the home helps themselves. The base from which the project begins with respect to the home help service is comprehensive. Theoretically, the use of local knowledge and attempts to integrate the planning of care should be easier than in areas where the level is low and this pool of local knowledge is smaller.

When we examined the service given in 1979 to clients living in the village we found that two distinct groups emerged. The median visit level (from the home helps) of all clients was 1.8 visits each week. Using this figure as a guide we identified those clients who received two visits a week or less, most of whom received a weekly visit, and those who received more than two visits a week, most of whom received five or seven visits a week. In 1979 two-thirds of clients received the weekly service (which is the name we shall use for those receiving two visits a week or less), but they accounted for only 28 per cent of the total visits made by home helps. On the other hand, the remaining one-third of clients received the daily service (which is the name we shall use for those receiving more than two visits a week), and they received 72 per cent of the total visits made. In general those receiving the weekly service would have two to three hours of home help time each week while those receiving the daily service would receive approximately five or six hours each week, but some much more. This division is due largely to the fact that Dinnington is a mining community and consequently there is a need for firelighting. Where this is absent the pattern of care is likely to be different. For example, Hillingdon (1977) reported that 89 per cent of clients received visits on two days a week or less.

In 1979 the average number of visits made to the 'weekly' group was 1.4, which represented less than one-fifth (19 per cent) of the total visits from all statutory services received by clients in this group. However, as most of these other visits would be made by the warden service (whose brief is a daily checking call on around 30 clients), it is likely that the home helps contributed approximately one-half of the total time given to clients by the formal sector. In contrast those receiving the daily service averaged 7.1 visits each week from the home help, which represented two-fifths of all visits from the formal sector. Once again many of those other visits from the formal sector were the five-to-ten minute check by the warden. Thus for most of those 32 clients receiving the daily service, the home helps would be contributing the substantial part of the hours committed to caring by the formal sector.

The principal difference between the weekly and daily service was, as we mentioned above, that the latter included a morning fire call. While nearly all clients (96 per cent) had housework done by their home help, only a little under two-fifths (38 per cent) had services under the category which we have called warmth – cooking meals and making the fire. Warmth is sharply divided between the two groups, for while nearly all (91 per cent) of the 'daily' group received this service, only a few (12 per cent) of the 'weekly' group did.

In addition to this basic difference between the two groups, clients who received the daily service were given a wide range of help, particularly in shopping and collecting pensions (53 per cent) and in nursing care (16 per cent). Here we find ourselves considering a service which, for some clients, was providing a wide range of care generally spread over five or seven days each week. There is, therefore, a considerable difference between the two groups, not just in the frequency of visits and hours given, but also in the nature of the service given.

We found little evidence to suggest that the home help service related to the level of informal care available, other than at weekends where it was policy not to allocate service if local relatives were present. Thus the service was extensive, but appeared to operate in isolation from other formal and informal care. This view was confirmed when we looked at the response to referrals during early 1980. These referrals were received by the assistant home help organizer based in Maltby and this gave an annual rate of seven per 1000 non-elderly people served. For the elderly the annual rate of demand was 215 per 1000 people over 60 years of age. Almost four in five of the referrals were received over the telephone, with 16 per cent being received at the office, mostly from social workers. Over one-third of referrals came from the village home helps; three-fifths of referrals from local authority staff. Only five referrals (16 per cent) came from health services. This is in sharp contrast to the pattern of referrals recorded in other home help services. For example, Hedley and Norman (1982) illustrate demand from an example in Cheshire where 61 per cent of referrals originated in primary and secondary health care. They state that: 'A similar pattern has been shown in many other local authority studies, and was found in the authorities visited' (ibid., p. 18).

This general pattern did not apply in Dinnington, although this may have been affected by home helps bringing forward new demands from existing clients. However, exclusion of these referrals only raises the health-service proportion from 16 per cent to 25 per cent. Almost three-quarters (74 per cent) of all referrals were followed up during the study period, taking on average four days each.

There were many reasons for requesting the service, ranging from the need for general assessment (20 per cent) or post-operative clients (13 per cent) to requests for shopping (seven per cent). The key point is that, generally speaking, requests were dealt with within the service. Contacts made to others as part of the response to demand were very low, at only 0.3 contacts per referral. Only one contact was made to the informal sector. This insularity is further illustrated by looking at the source of referrals to all the participating groups of workers. Out of the 155 referrals received by the various agencies in the 1980 referral study none were from the home help organizer.

So, we have evidence to suggest that the planning and delivery of the home help service was largely carried out in isolation from both other statutory services and informal care – a familiar picture of the services in Dinnington working at Stage One of our model.

The wardens

In many local authorities responsibility for sheltered accommodation falls under the remit of the social services department. The warden service for the elderly in Rotherham was the responsibility of the housing department, and consisted of two types of service. The first was associated with sheltered accommodation where a resident warden lived amongst a group of dwellings specially built for the elderly; the second a peripatetic or visiting warden service in which wardens visited elderly people in their own homes.

In the summer of 1979, there were 73 households in the village living in sheltered accommodation, three-quarters of whom were single elderly people. These households were spread amongst three separate sheltered schemes, two immediately post-war, without any form of communal facility, and one built more recently with a community centre attached. The three resident wardens serving these elderly people each had a relief on one day a week. In addition to those living in sheltered accommodation, a further 112 households were being visited by the visiting wardens and their reliefs. Just over seven out of ten (72 per cent) of these households were single elderly people.

A much higher proportion of those in sheltered accommodation were crippled or disabled, sick or ill, housebound or bedfast. The only problem consistently noted more frequently by visiting wardens was social isolation. By far the largest group served by wardens were those elderly people aged 75 and over who lived alone. They represented over half (54 per cent) of all warden cases, and over half of the cases of each type of warden. For this group the proportion of those housebound and/or sick or ill was marginally greater for those in sheltered accommodation than for clients of the visiting warden. Other problems, such as disability and depression, were much more evident in the clients of the resident warden. By contrast, in the younger elderly group aged 60–74 who lived alone, those in sheltered accommodation had much greater frequencies of *all* problems other than social isolation, than those still living in their own homes.

This would suggest that, in general, for those elderly clients served by the warden service, those in sheltered accommodation had a greater range of problems than those still living in their own homes. That over one-half (54 per cent) of the wardens' clients were cared for by the warden alone emphasizes the key preventive role played in the community by this group of workers. Often the wardens' role is much more than checking to see if the client is well. The wardens in Dinnington were involved in providing a wide range of basic services to their clients. They provided much more simple nursing care than home helps. It was given to nearly one-fifth (19 per cent) of clients, but the bulk of it was from the resident wardens who provided this more intensive style of care in over one-third (36 per cent) of their cases. Those aged 75 and over who lived alone received the greatest range of service but for all clients collecting prescriptions was the most frequent task apart from checking visits. Tasks such as making the fire, cooking or shopping were rarely done for elderly couples. Checking to see if they were well was the principal task.

It is not unknown, however, for wardens, mainly resident wardens, to provide very intensive care, including night-sitting for some of their clients. They often took on responsibilities for caring far beyond their official role. Even though they may be expected to care for clients suffering from temporary illness, they should not have had to face this on their own. Age Concern recognized this: 'Such care pre-supposes that the necessary medical and domiciliary services are available, and that support will also be forthcoming from relatives, other tenants and voluntary workers as required' (Willcocks 1972, p. 14).

It is certainly true that the wardens were potentially in contact with such support for their pre-project cases. Resident wardens, whose clients on average had most problems, were in touch with the general practitioner in nearly half (49 per cent) of their cases, with relatives out of the household in over two-fifths (41 per cent) of cases, and with the home help organizer in one-third of cases. The visiting wardens, whose clients on average had less problems, were in touch with the general practitioner in one-third of their cases and with relatives out of the house in just under a quarter (24 per cent) of their cases. They were much more likely to have been in contact with the home help (over a third (34 per cent) of cases) than the home help organizer. The contact with social workers was noticeable by its absence.

It is clear that the warden service stands at the boundary between statutory and informal care for the elderly in the community, and wardens are ideally suited to act as gatekeepers for resources. It was because of the potential for development of the wardens' role that the appointment of a housing assistant was to be made to work alongside the social workers in the village. Although the latter, as we shall see shortly, were to be devolved to a base in the village and required to adopt a new style of community-orientated work, the appointment of the housing assistant with specific responsibility to develop the role of the wardens was seen as the most experimental aspect of the project. Whether or not the new appointment would be instrumental in bringing about a much more efficient and inte-grated pattern of care for the wardens' clients, as well as reducing the isolation felt by the wardens, a fact identified in the project pilot study and by Age Concern (Willcocks 1972, p. 27), remained to be seen.

The wardens were the only group of workers closely associated with the project whom we would regard as working 'alongside the community' in 1979, which stands in contrast to what we found with the home help service.

The educational welfare officer (EWO)
In the summer of 1979, the EWO held eight cases from the village but his catchment area was considerably larger. Of these eight cases, three were cases where a social worker was already involved. Of the remaining five cases, in only one was contact made with any social worker. In terms of the range of problems faced by his clients, there was no clear pattern which might determine why in one case a social worker was involved, and in another case not. The most frequent problems were school behaviour, truancy and family problems, and the response to these was checking up on the client, financial and material aid and non-attendance casework. The EWO counselled families in half of his cases, and it is noticeable that in three of these four cases the social worker was not involved.

The direction in which the role of the EWO was expected to evolve was not made explicit in the preliminary papers for the project, although clearly with the overlap of cases between the social worker and the EWO there was considerable scope for co-operation between the two. He was, therefore, to be included in the proposed fortnightly meetings between the workers principally concerned with the project. It is interesting that recent examinations of the role of the EWO, (for example Robinson 1978 and MacMillan 1977) when putting forward strategies for the future, have tended to stress the 'community' focus, later developed in the Barclay Report (1982). We shall see how far the project enabled the EWO to adopt a community focus.

Summary
The overall pattern of formal provision in Dinnington before the project was unremarkable. The various workers did make some contact with one another, but it was on a one-off basis. There was some contact with family, friends and neighbours but it was not very extensive and there was very little contact with voluntary bodies. It was generally the social workers with whom there was least contact. This is not surprising as they were based five miles away and nine different social workers had cases in the village. The individual services' response to client need was primarily through the resources of their own department. There was little sharing of cases or pooling of resources. Though we found some instances where services were working 'alongside the community', the lack of any systematic contacts indicates that overall the organization and practice of formal care in the village prior to the project conformed very largely to Stage One of our model – working 'outside the community'.

7 Four Important Influences on the Action

There is an inherent difficulty about describing the changes that took place in the workers' practice as a result of the project. As the work moved from being 'outside the community' to being, at times, for some, 'within the community', so the workers tended to work more with one another and adopt a more corporate and broader approach to clients' or patients' needs. This means that it is inadequate simply to run through the various worker groups showing how the work of each has changed, or not, and what the impact on the users appears to have been. Before we can do that we have to make readers aware of the changed context within which the workers operated. That context was not coincidental, but was both part of the process of change and an integral part of the changed method.

We have just sketched a picture of the structure and pattern of statutory services before the project started, showing little regular contact between workers in different services, few contacts with volunteers or voluntary bodies and a rather narrow, departmentally limited, approach to the needs of clients or patients. In addition the social workers had no local base.

There are four contextual elements that we have to consider. The first three are structural/organizational factors, namely the local base (the project office); the core team's (the two social workers and the housing assistant's) induction course; and the fortnightly meeting of fieldworkers. The fourth arises out of the previous three and is the result of changed practice: nevertheless it must still be mentioned as part of the changed context, that is the creation of additional local resources.

In order to consider these elements, it is worth recalling the model of change which we outlined on pp.51–5 and in Table 5.1. on p. 53. This stipulates that, for change to occur, both organizational and attitudinal changes must take place. It will be noted that both aspects are covered in the list above and the interplay between these two elements is one of the critical features of the story.

Project office
The first change that the people of Dinnington saw was a portable classroom, which was installed next to the district offices in the centre of the village. The office was an unprepossessing building 24 feet long by 15 feet wide. It had no notice up outside saying what it was (nor did it six years later). It came to be called 'the Hut'. The name has stuck and reflects accurately the informal style of operation which the workers developed

and the way clients, relatives, other carers, and other workers used it. It was on a road which led to the main shopping centre. The district offices next door housed the district housing office and the education welfare officer. The assistant registrar was also there three half-days a week.

Originally the office had no internal dividing walls but, once the workers had decided what they wanted, it was divided up. There was a small entrance lobby with room for a chair, a table and generally bags containing washing waiting to be collected by the laundry service. To the right a door led to a small, and usually rather hot, interview room, which was not used very often. To the left a door led into the main office where there were four desks, one for the three workers based in the project office (that is the two social workers and the housing assistant), and one for the assistant home help organizer or whoever else might call in and need somewhere to work.

There was no receptionist. Some secretarial help was available at the district offices and the telephonist took messages if there was no-one in the project office, which was the case occasionally. There was little privacy, nevertheless most interviews tended to take place in the main office. The office was accessible and the informal approach adopted by the core team made it friendly and welcoming. Callers were received by whichever of the workers happened to be in. As a result the project office was used a great deal. It proved to be of major importance as a focus for the project, and also as a place where people met informally without having to make any arrangements.

The organizational change of setting up a local project office had certain consequences for the workers. They were subjected to very different pressures to those to which they would have been subjected in a conventional setting, where they would have been protected by a receptionist. But the effect would not have been the same without a change in attitude on the part of the workers. The importance of this has been illustrated in the Normanton scheme, where one of the patch teams continued to practice what Hadley and McGrath (1984, p. 53) call the 'client model' which 'corresponded closely to the traditional view of relations between social service teams and their clients'. Helping to promote a change in attitude and emphasis was a major aim of the induction course, the second important influence on practice.

Induction course

This took place during the four weeks immediately before the project office became operational and started the process whereby the members of the core team could develop their practice and learn from their experiences. The induction course was run by the University research team with Paul Parker playing the major role. The availability of the research team acting in a consultant role was an important part of the process of changing the attitudes of the workers. The major theoretical influence was the work of Pancoast and Collins (1976) which had been reinforced by Parker's visit to them in Oregon, USA, in 1979.

Three main issues were considered. First, issues concerning organization. It was necessary for the core team to work out a point of view regarding team and project management and to learn how to work together to develop project initiatives. Second, co-operation with other fieldworkers. The induction period enabled the core team to make contact with existing statutory services working in Dinnington. The range of workers extended from those mentioned just below in connection with the fortnightly meeting, to the domiciliary chiropodist, the MSC Dinnington Youth Project director, head teachers and year tutors, the job centre, community psychiatric nurses, and the local DHSS office. Third, and most importantly of all, they began to gain an understanding of how the community functions as a resource to itself. During the induction period consideration was given to the roles of both individual key figures and groups. The core team made a study of the voluntary bodies active in Dinnington, obtaining information about the purpose, membership and activities of the organizations. This was useful for two reasons. First, it provided data about the extent and nature of participation in voluntary activity in the community. Second, and more importantly, it provided an opportunity for the core team to contact some key figures and to begin to discuss the project with them. How to relate to *key* family, friends and neighbours and how to seek out carers was the aspect of the work that the workers found most difficult to grasp and to put into practice. However, by the end of the induction period it had been put firmly on their agenda. At the end of the four weeks, the core team identified the following objectives:

(a) they should aim to increase their accessibility both to other
    workers and to the local community;
(b) they should seek to identify and support informal carers;
(c) they should work towards a team approach that goes beyond
    being a unit for management and administration and includes
    shared planning of workloads, exchange and pooling of information
    and resources (for instance volunteers), and the development of joint
    schemes to respond to identified needs;
(d) they should give greater emphasis to preventive work on a community-wide basis;
(e) they should be alert to needs as defined and expressed by the particular
    community in which they worked.

Fieldworkers' meeting

Only the two social workers and the housing assistant were able to attend the induction course, though other workers were involved occasionally. However, the interdisciplinary, inter-departmental and inter-authority aspect of the project was seen as very important. In order to give expression to this at the fieldworker level, it had been agreed as part of the management structure for the project, that there should be a fortnightly meeting of fieldworkers (see p.78). The workers who were involved were the two social workers and the housing assistant from the project office, one district nurse, one health visitor and the education welfare officer. The meetings were also attended by Paul Parker, who played an active role in developing the meetings in the early stages. After he left in September 1981, another member of the research team attended as an observer until the following summer.

These meetings proved to be of central importance for the development of the project. They gave the workers the opportunity to get to know one another, to learn what the others could do, but also the constraints under which they worked and therefore what they could not do. It enabled them to think together about the way in which the project should be developing. Originally the meetings operated as a sort of standing case conference, but after a year of working together such liaison occurred routinely and the workers turned their attention to broader issues concerning the village as a whole. We look at this below.

The fieldworkers' meeting played a critical role in the development of the project and if we consider our model of change, it is clear why. The provision of the project office was an organizational and managerial matter: the induction course (an organizational matter) was also to change attitudes. The fortnightly meeting brought these two together. The meeting was a very simple organizational device that brought workers from different disciplines together in such a way that they were able to understand one another better and to learn from one another. It should be noted that the assistant home help organizer did not take part in these meetings, although she had been invited. This was largely due to the staffing shortages which we noted earlier.

Creation of additional resources

One of the broader issues to which the fieldworkers' meeting turned its attention in spring 1981 was the needs of housebound elderly people, and they were instrumental in setting up a voluntary group (called VOLT-AGE). By autumn 1981 VOLTAGE had 23 volunteers and was receiving five new referrals a week. Its activities ranged from practical household tasks, to visiting a deaf and dumb couple, cooking lunch, taking people by car to the shops and and social visiting. This was a major new resource for the statutory workers and had a considerable impact on the development of their practice. During 1983 the district nurse, supported by the others, played the key role in setting up a small voluntary body called RALLY to help families where a member was seriously, generally terminally, ill at home. We shall examine these and other initiatives in more detail below.

The interplay of attitudes and organization is apparent again. New attitudes create a new organization which enables practice to develop, which encourages attitudes and practice to develop further. Now that we have looked at these four important influences on the workers' practice, we can look at the ways that the service developed and their impact.

8   The Health Service

The general practice
Returning to the primary health care team and the work of the general practitioners, the first fact we noticed when we examined the pattern of consultations as the project developed throughout 1981 and 1982, was that age-specific rates were highly variable (Table 8.1). This, we think, was caused by two factors. Firstly, the way we collected our data in two one-week blocks which stressed variability. Second, the volatile nature of morbidity. Take for example, measles. Traditionally there was a two-year epidemic of measles, but the use of immunization altered this pattern and reduced cases in the 1970s. Nevertheless a recent *Social Trends* reported that 'while the number of notifications in the United Kingdom in 1981 totalled only 61.7 thousand, they increased by over 70 per cent in 1982 to 105.6 thousand' (OPCS 1984, p. 99). So perhaps the first lesson that we learn about demand placed upon the general practice is its volatility, no doubt affected by simple factors such as the weather, but also by the cycles of our well-known diseases.

One clear change emerges from our observations over two years. Whereas in 1980 the level of consultations from the village was 81 per cent of the national average, by 1982 the level was equal to the national average. This increase was almost entirely connected with a substantial increase in the consultation rate of the elderly. For example, the rate for males aged 65–74 almost doubled from 67 per 1000 in January 1980, to 126 per 1000 in July 1982. Likewise the rate for females aged 65–74 rose from 80 to 148 per 1000 during the same period. These represent major changes in the profile of those consulting, reducing the emphasis given initially to the under-fives (although they are still slightly above the average) and increasing the emphasis on the elderly (although they are still slightly below the average). There was a slight decrease in the proportion of one-off consultations during the period, from 49 per cent in 1980 to 44 per cent in 1982.

There were probably many reasons for these changes, but there is no doubt that a significant factor was the sharp change in the perceptions of the general practice held by those working with the elderly. In 1980 there was much criticism of the practice by wardens and home helps, particularly of the appointment system. By 1982 those workers had gained special access to the doctors and were commenting upon their much improved relationship with the practice. This in turn encouraged them to approach the practice, so for example, the proportion of clients referred by the visiting warden (in the three months prior to our caseload study) rose from 34 per cent in 1979 to 52 per cent in 1982. We are not suggesting that the project was responsible for all this increase. However, it would be correct to say that the integrated approach which the project promoted, and the close working relationships between for example, wardens, home helps and nurses, helped to create a positive relationship between health and welfare services which encouraged such changes.

This positive approach to co-operation did not always promote an increase in referrals to the general practice. Referrals from social workers declined from 18 per cent of their cases over a year in 1979 to seven per cent of cases in 1982. However, referrals from social workers to the district nurse rose from three per cent to 11 per cent of social work cases during the same period. As workers came to know and understand one another, referrals were made more appropriately. This, in a small way, must have played its part in reducing those consultations which doctors felt inappropriate from 19 per cent of consultations in January 1980 to seven per cent in July 1982.

Doctors themselves were also referring more patients to other sources. These were mainly patients who were coming for continuing consultation who were suffering predominantly from chronic illness. Thus we have our first clue that some movement had been made towards the second stage of our model of community practice, working 'alongside the community'.

This increase in the use of additional resources by the doctors was set against the background of almost static morbidity characteristics of those seeking consultation. Throughout our study approximately one-half of clients suffered from acute illness, and one quarter from chronic illness. Not that we would expect any change in morbidity over such a short period in normal circumstances, but there was a substantial rise in the consultation rate of the elderly, and this could have altered the pattern in the short term. However, there was little difference between the increase in one-off consultations (that is, predominantly acute illness) for the elderly and the increase in continuing consultations (that is, predominantly chronic illness) and so this left the general morbidity pattern unchanged.

The increase in resources brought to bear by the doctors was predominantly from the primary health care team, particularly the district nurse. At first sight this seems disappointing, but we found that the doctors used the nursing sister responsible for the village as an entrée to community resources. Thus elderly patients needing the services of the aids and adaptations officer would be first referred by the doctor to the district nurse. Although the route of referral is somewhat circuitous, what matters is that wider resources were mobilized, rather than the precise method as to how. Perhaps given the demand upon the doctor, having a nursing sister

Table 8.1 Persons consulting a general practitioner by sex and age, 1980–2 (rates per thousand)

	1980		1981		1982[1]	
	Dinnington	General Household Survey	Dinnington	General Household Survey	Dinnington	General Household Survey
Males						
0–4	241	190	156	210	196	210
5–14	85	100	51	80	82	90[2]
15–44	78	90	69	70	103	80[2]
45–64	108	120	104	120	96	130
65–74	67	170	115	130	126	150
75 and over	103	210	146	170	129	190
Total	95	110	85	100	106	110
Females						
0–4	236	170	126	170	216	200
5–14	96	100	56	90	104	100
15–44	121	170	134	150	188	160
45–64	121	140	135	130	120	160
65–74	80	170	136	160	148	170
75 and over	98	200	149	200	153	180
Total	118	150	122	140	155	150

Notes: 1   Based on one summer week only. Figures have been weighted to reflect average contribution of summer weeks to two-week period in the previous two years.

      2   5–15, 16–44 in 1982

to hand who had wide access to community resources was the most effective way for the doctor to work.

What we observed therefore throughout 1981 and 1982 was an increase in the demand placed upon the general practice, together with a slight increase in the resources brought to bear upon that demand. Immediate action on the part of the doctors, that is treatment, prescriptions and support, changed little, although 1982 saw much more emphasis upon supportive action by the doctors.

Thus there was movement towards Stage Two of our model but, we would argue, not enough evidence to suggest that the doctors had reached it. In particular, we were disappointed that the doctors never took up the invitation to attend the fortnightly meeting of fieldworkers held in the village. The fact that the district nursing sister was central to the developments that took place within that meeting did not, we feel, excuse the total absence of the doctors. They, too, would have had a considerable contribution to make to the many initiatives put forward by this group. In many respects the fact that they had wider resources to rely upon in 1982 was not due to their own initiatives but to those of the nurse, the social worker, and others. As such the general practice had only moved a little way towards Stage Two of our model. Doctors were, in 1982, still practising according to the characteristics of working 'outside the community'. This was in sharp contrast to the work of the nursing sister in the village.

The district nurse

For the district nurse the single most important innovation in terms of developing integrated health and welfare practice was the fieldworkers' meeting. The presence of the district nurse at this meeting was the source of considerable tension between staff and management. Nursing management considered attendance at such a meeting an inappropriate use of the nursing sister's time, particularly as later in 1980 and early in 1981 they were short staffed. The matter was circumvented, but not resolved, by arranging for the meetings to be held at the end of the nursing sister's day's work. Most of the developmental work towards community practice, which we shall review shortly, was done by the nursing sister in her own time. However, we shall also show that as time progressed the nursing sister brought an entirely new perspective to her routine work.

As we have said, for much of the first year the fieldworkers' meeting was effectively a standing case conference. The value of these routine meetings cannot be underestimated in terms of project development. They enabled workers to come to know one another gradually over a sustained period. They enabled workers to understand the roles of others more clearly and the resources that others had available. They enabled one worker to learn to listen and absorb what another was saying. This took time. It was not uncommon for the district nurse to repeat what she had said several times in earlier meetings. Originally participants were strangers making sure that the point they wanted to make was understood. As time went by workers began to understand the restrictions and limitations under which the others worked. By the end of 1980 the nursing sister was able to say, in response to a question on the most important idea of the project that 'for me it is the liaison that has been created between the health authority and social services'. However, the development of liaison had not yet had any significant impact upon nursing practice.

The nursing sister had a strong belief in the importance of rehabilitation of the patient and the training of family members in day-to-day care. She was critical of those nurses who stripped patients of their independence and insisted on controlling all nursing activity. This, she thought was akin to a 'prison sentence' to the patient. However, she stressed that emphasis on rehabilitation was hard work. 'It is hard work to help people help themselves'. We must be aware, therefore, that considerable variation exists within district nursing practice and that this may predispose nurses towards different stages of our model of community practice.

Most of the traditional work of a district nurse, together with the focus of that work, can be displayed in a simple practice matrix, as in Figure 8.1. (on p.92). All eight of these modes of practice (boxes 1,2,3,4 and 7,8,9 and 10 in the rectangle) were in operation in our two case studies earlier. The question is what does development through the stages of our model of community practice do, if anything, to the practice of the district nurse?

To begin to answer this we shall return first to the fieldworkers' meeting. By early 1981 the crucial shared learning experience which was the essence of that meeting had begun to lead the workers to widen their concern away from the individual patient towards the community at large. This shift in direction was prompted by an increasing awareness that there were simple but important deficiencies in the range of care available to the patients that they had been discussing over the past year. Many of these deficiencies concerned the care of the housebound elderly and so by the spring of 1981 the fieldworkers' meeting was concerning itself not with a particular case, as it had for the previous 16 months, but rather with a scheme to establish a local voluntary group to help care for the housebound elderly. The nursing sister, together with the social workers, had moved to Stage Two of the model of community practice. They were now having regular meetings to plan the care of patients, and they were also involved with developments concerned with preventive care in the community. Such developments were still, however, something extra to normal work. Nowhere was this clearer than with the district nurse. When she asked her management whether she could attend the evening meetings which were to establish the voluntary group, she was told she could do what she wished 'in her own time'!

In fairness to the nursing management the nursing team was critically understaffed at the time (because of illness). In 1981 the caseload for the village was being carried by the nursing sister and an auxiliary. Although there were fewer patients at this time than at any other during the four years we observed (25 in 1981) pressure upon nurses was excessive. No doubt the situation was made possible by the fact that in the summer of 1981, the number of patients receiving 'daily' care had fallen to only eight, 'daily' at that time being somewhat euphemistic as they were only receiving on average 2.92 visits each week. Seventeen patients were receiving 'occasional' care, the bulk of which was other nursing care with some technical procedures. We are unsure how much discharge into the community was restricted at that time because of staff shortages.

By the autumn of 1981 we observed important changes in district nursing practice. The sheer pressure of work meant that much of the nursing sister's time was spent on essential routine tasks. However, in her own time she was rapidly moving towards the point where her perspective on day-to-day nursing practice would be changed.

By this time the fieldworkers' meeting had changed, too. Having established the voluntary group to care for the elderly (VOLTAGE), the workers considered what further initiatives they could turn their minds to next. The district nurse was now working so closely with other workers that there was no longer any need for formal case conferences. Attention was increasingly focused upon the community as the target for intervention, rather than upon the individual patient. Over the next two years the nurse and other workers would be instrumental in establishing a special voluntary group to care for the terminally ill at home, an annual scheme in the summer holidays for some of the village's more needy children, and an attempt to set up a community-provided day care scheme for the elderly.

The critical impact of these developments upon nursing practice was that they liberated the nurse from relying entirely upon health authority resources, and gave her the confidence to be able to tackle the non-technical problems of her clients. Although in theory district nurses have always been trained to consider the wider social problems of their patients, in practice there have very rarely been any resources for them to be able to do anything about them. Consequently nurses have tended to stay clear of raising problems about which they could do little.

The change in the way the nursing sister approached her patients was clearly observed in the study of referrals in early 1982. In 1980 we had observed that while on average the nurse had made 0.8 contacts per referral, three-quarters of those contacts had been directed to the health sector. In 1982, although referrals had fallen from 37 to 28 during the period (an annual average of 42 per 1000 people served) and the level of contacts had remained the same at 0.8 per referral, less than half (46 per cent) of contacts were now made to the health sector. Over three in ten (32 per cent) were made to social services, and 14 per cent were made to the informal and voluntary sectors.

Clearly the nature of referrals had something to do with this change. There was only one referral for a patient being discharged from hospital in 1982 whereas there had been six in 1980. In 1982 there were five referrals for aids and adaptations (from the GP) whereas there had been one in 1980. However, this latter group of referrals in particular was a result of the district nurse's wider role in the health care and welfare of the community. The doctors were aware of this and, as we said earlier, were making use of her wider contacts. She had become a gatekeeper to wider community resources.

This increasingly broad perspective of the nurse's role is further confirmed when we examine the cases held in the summer of 1982 and her response to them. Twenty-seven patients were being cared for at the time, still substantially fewer than the 38 patients in 1979. However, in contrast to both 1980 and 1981, there were once again, as in 1979, more patients receiving 'daily' care than 'occasional' care. The frequency of visits to these patients was still low, almost half (at 2.71 per week) of the level (5.35) which existed in 1979. Clearly 1979 was quite exceptional, but by the summer of 1982 there were signs that demand from existing patients was once more on the increase.

A sharp increase in the level of contacts made on behalf of patients was observed over the period 1980–2. Once again 1979 was exceptional, but it is very interesting to note the differences between then and 1982. While the average number of contacts (3.0) in 1982 was below that of 1979 (3.4) the focus of those contacts was quite different. Generally speaking, there was a substantial fall in contacts with health sector personnel, but a sharp rise in contacts with social services and housing staff. For example, contacts with the health visitor had fallen from 44 per cent of cases in 1979 to four per cent of cases in 1982. Contacts with housing wardens had risen from 14 per cent of cases in 1979 to 39 per cent of cases in 1982. While contacts with relatives of the patient were relatively constant throughout, contacts with friends and neighbours rose from 13 per cent in 1979 to 22 per cent in 1982. Also in 1982, the first contact with the voluntary sector was recorded.

Perhaps of most importance is that there was a rapid shift in the nursing sister's approach to care late in 1981 which was not evident in our evaluative studies until 1982. Contacts in 1981 were much the same as they had been in 1979, although much fewer in number. It was the crucial step of getting the first community initiative under way which encouraged this changed style of practice. Thus by the end of 1982 when we asked the nursing sister how the project had affected her job she was able to reply that it

> gives greater satisfaction for me to know when I see a patient who says I'm lonely, or I would like to go down the street but there's no one to take me ... because of the project I am able to find someone to do these basic things.

The nursing sister had internalized this style of working to the extent that it was now part of her routine practice. This is consistent with Stage Three of the model of community practice. Working in this way was no longer something extra to her ordinary work.

Having said this it was *only* the nursing sister (out of the primary health care team) who had achieved this stage of the model. The other nurses had kept to the same style of practice which was evident in 1979. This was a great disappointment, not least to the nursing sister herself. She identified what was missing: '... should come from managers ... should give more encouragement to fieldworkers to be involved in the project and with the ideas of the project'.

Given the history of the development of nursing involvement in the project and the fact that the nursing sister had to come to terms with the project's ideas largely in her own time, it is not surprising that other nurses were not involved. It was only through the nursing sister's own tenacity and willingness to work out of hours that we were able to see what those ideas meant in practice. What she had done was to expand the role of the nurse, both in terms of the tasks done, and in terms of the levels at which she would intervene. Thus we are able to develop the model of nursing practice from the tasks which appear in the rectangle to the full range shown in Figure 8.1.

In this we introduce the task of entrepreneur, that is someone who goes out into the community and creates resources. The nursing sister and, as we shall see, some other workers, were very successful at doing this. As a result of these extra resources the nursing sister became what Whittaker (1983) has termed a 'network system consultant'. That is, from a wide range of resources she was able to put together packages of care for her patients, not just nursing care, but a wide range of social and medical care.

The nursing sister was also able to increase the levels at which she intervened in the community. Traditionally much of her care went to the patient and, as we have seen above, depending upon her outlook, the patient's family would be taught to help with the care. Now the focus also included identifiable groups in the community, for example the terminally ill, or the whole community itself in the sense of reviewing with other workers what major needs were still unmet by current services. We have filled in some examples in Figure 8.1, but perhaps readers can think of others.

The key point in this development of practice is that it does not seek to replace existing tasks. Rather it seeks to complement them with a wider range of tasks or roles which can harness a whole range of new resources. Acceptance of these new roles entails viewing nursing from a rather different perspective. This views nursing care as part of a wider pattern of care which involves different members of the community and may be very complex. Much of that care will be given by relatives, friends and neighbours. The Cumberledge Report (DHSS 1986a), to which we referred in Chapter 2, develops these ideas in its consideration of the neighbourhood nursing service.

The health visitor
At the beginning of the project we found that the health visitor displayed characteristics of practice which placed her at the boundary of Stages One and Two of our model of community practice. She was locally based and in touch with other workers, particularly social workers from the area office. However, there was no evidence of sustained co-ordination with other workers, a fact which would have clearly placed her within Stage Two – working 'alongside the community'.

Two principal characteristics stand out with regard to health visiting practice as the project developed. First, as a member of the fieldworkers' meeting, the health visitor became part of the regular inter-agency planning forum that, as we have already seen, originally concentrated upon case conferences and subsequently upon community initiatives. Secondly, possibly as a result of the emphasis of the evaluation pro-gramme upon her non-routine cases, but also partly as a result of her own preferences and the inability of her management to grasp new ideas, the health visitor and her colleagues were unable to view the project as anything but 'something extra'. By 1981 and 1982 the health visitors were taking part in the development of community initiatives, but these were seen as an adjunct to their mainstream work. In other words, they became firmly embedded in Stage Two of our model – working 'alongside the community'.

Indeed, we found that the 'non-routine' aspect of the health visitor's caseload diminished substantially as the project progressed. This was partly due to people taking their needs to the newly opened project office, whereas once they would have gone to the clinic, and partly because the health visitor referred patients on to the project office rather than taking the case up herself. As she herself said in an interview at the end of 1980: 'Once the Hut (local name for project office) was here people stopped coming to the clinic. We can send ... there now. They used to drop in to the clinic for help or advice but now they go to the Hut'. This no doubt accounts largely for the fall in 'non-routine' cases held by the health

Levels of intervention	Tasks					
	Technical tests	Technical procedures	Other nursing care	Advice/ counsel	Network system consultant	Entrepreneur
Patient	1. eg. blood samples skin testing	2. eg. injections dressings	3. eg. bathing	4. eg. on self-care	5.	6. eg. one patient to counsel another eg. colostomy
Family	7. eg. teach family how to test urine	8. eg. teach family how to give insulin	9. eg. teach family how to lift patient	10. eg. talk about conse-quences of diseases	11. eg. link to commercial care	12.
Network-Centred	13.	14.	15. eg. use of volunteer to care for terminally ill at home	16.	17. eg. key-worker packages	18.
Group	19. eg. colostomy clubs etc.	20.	21. Young Chronic Sick	22.	23.	24. eg. RALLY
Community	25. eg. Health Education	26.	27.	28.	29.	30. eg. VOLTAGE

Figure 8.1 District nursing practice, 1980 and 1982

visitor from 23 in 1979 to ten in 1980, nine in 1981 and just seven in 1982.

In many respects we can argue that the presence of a locally-based social services office enabled the health visitors to offload their non-routine cases and concentrate on their routine child care work, only occasionally giving time to community initiatives. As we have no quantitative data to indicate how that routine child care work was affected by involvement with the project, we cannot say whether the loss of non-routine cases was good or bad. However, in late 1982, when asked how the project had affected her work, the original health visitor responded that 'community help hasn't changed for 0–5 group that I am mainly involved with'.

Although the health visitors had been instrumental in setting up a series of summer holidays and daytrips for deprived children in the community, by and large it would seem that the project had not affected their day-to-day practice, and gave them the opportunity to offload non-routine cases onto the social workers. This came as a disappointment to many involved with the project. We can contrast the health visitors with the district nursing sister and social workers, whom we will now show to have moved firmly to practising 'within the community'.

9 The Social Workers

For the social workers the early weeks of the project were devoted to creating an office layout and style of work that made social services more accessible to the public. Considerable time was spent discussing issues of record-keeping and administration with the team leader from the area office at Maltby. The other aspect of accessibility was the need to become known in the community. Time was spent in meeting and gathering information about local voluntary groups and in getting to know workers from other agencies. This is part of what Thomas and Shaftoe (1983, p.32) call the process of localization, and it involves being accepted *by* local people as much as learning *about* the community.

Two weeks into the project an interesting example of acceptance by clients occurred. A long-term client, the mother of a large and complicated family, called at the office and was having a cup of coffee with one of the social workers when another client, a neighbour of the first client, arrived. The social worker had not known they were acquainted, though she had worked with both families before being transferred from the area office. Shortly afterwards a third client came into the office and the three women spent the following 45 minutes talking to each other, comparing problems and appreciating each other's difficulties. The social worker's only role in this unplanned and spontaneous self-help exercise was to provide the coffee.

Other declared priorities proved more difficult to achieve. Though they quickly established close informal working relations with other workers, which led to constant information exchange and better appreciation of the ability of other departments to deliver certain services, they found the informal sector harder to come to terms with. This is not surprising. Relating to fellow professionals is only one step away from one's own practice. Relating to local lay people and clients' networks is a more ambitious process and requires patient work over a long time.

After four months the social workers were becoming anxious about what strategies they could use to work with client networks. They could no longer talk in terms of general approaches and needed a clearer focus. A variety of methods were suggested by the university research team, acting in a consultative capacity. These were a street survey to identify needs and resources within a small area; an exercise in goal-setting for particular, mainly elderly, clients; and an initiative to develop collaborative work with the home helps. The suggestions all came to nothing. The workers appeared to resist ideas put to them from outside and the suggestions themselves were alien to the established ways of working with which they were familiar.

Perhaps such strategies for changes in work style and method are acceptable only when they come from within the management structure. However, at this time social services management were putting considerable pressure on their fieldworkers to produce quick results in the form of voluntary help. At no time did management fully understand the implications of the project they had established, constantly seeing it as a vehicle for recruiting and using volunteers and never accepting the need for flexibility in working methods and a good deal of devolution of decision-making to fieldwork staff. The difficulty experienced in beginning to work with clients' networks was compounded by management's inability to accept that time spent on a particular street or estate, getting to know its needs and local key residents, was a legitimate part of social work. During the early months of the project social services management was firmly wedded to the principles and practice of Stage One of our model.

There was a series of misunderstandings and tensions between the social workers and their management during the first year of the project. Some of these issues were argued out in management committee meetings that occurred every two months. An example of this is the clothing issue. The social services area officer forbade the social workers to keep a second-hand clothing store at the project office. However, the Project Management Committee recommended that this should be allowed as it was an imaginative use of office space to meet a legitimate need in the village. The Director of Social Services then overruled this recommendation, causing confusion and tension among the local staff about the lines of accountability and decision-making.

Other issues died because line managers failed to argue the case for changed practice to their own seniors. An example of this is the attempt to enable the housing assistant to make initial assessments for aids and for temporary short-term accommodation for elderly people. Often these requests came from elderly people with whom she was working, yet she had to introduce one of the social workers to complete the relevant forms. Immediate supervisors in the housing and social services agreed to take up these issues with their department, but nothing came of them. As the housing assistant said to us: 'Eventually you give up and move on to other things. You can't wait for ever'.

A third way in which initiatives were stifled during this period was by colonization. The first piece of thinking about the community dimension, matching up groups of people and viewing the elderly as a resource, was a scheme to provide lunches at the Catholic primary school for elderly people living in one of the sheltered housing schemes close to the school. The scheme was jointly planned by one of the social workers and the headteacher. They envisaged mixing elderly people and children at tables and calling upon old people's knowledge of Dinnington history, particularly of the pits, for project work by the children. However the home help service laid down that the meals should be provided according to the normal rules with guaranteed numbers attending each session. The original less formal elements to the scheme were eradicated and after much argument the scheme eventually operated as a conventional lunch club. An attempt to develop a community-orientated service had been colonized by bureaucratic procedures.

During this period there was no encouragement by management to innovate, only a series of blocks. Management constantly applied pressure for results without giving the means to achieve such results! The fact that the social workers progressed through Stage Two in spite of the management constraints owes much to two things, their inter-agency fieldworkers' meeting and their openness to community pressures because of their local base.

However, if social work 'within the community' is to be achieved then organizational and attitudinal changes on the part of both management and fieldworkers must occur. We have suggested that management, particularly senior management, had not responded at that time to the challenge of new responsibilities and styles of worker management. We found no evidence to suggest that social services management had reached a stage in their thinking or actions that we could define as community social work at Stage Three of our model of practice. On the other hand, when we considered the orientation and practice of the fieldworkers, there were a number of indications that they had incorporated some of the major features of community practice into their work. Some of these changes can be shown by comparing Dinnington and the rest of the South area of Rotherham social services. Others can be measured quantitatively from studies of their caseloads and referrals to assess the extent to which the social workers had reached Stage Three of community practice. This is what we shall now look at.

Social work caseloads

There is a technical problem about which caseload study should be used to analyse the social workers' practice. It arose because one of the two social workers left in January 1982 and was not replaced until May. At the same time the housing assistant had a lengthy period of leave and the remaining social worker was under enormous pressure. The depletion of the team and the removal of a number of social work cases back to the area office for a period of months meant that 1982 was atypical. As a result we have had to use data from the 1981 caseload study, even though this was run only 18 months into the project.

The number of social work cases in Dinnington in 1979 was 67. By 1981 this had increased slightly to 74, 63 of which were held by the two workers based in the village. The remaining 11 were held by social workers based in Maltby; seven were long-term family cases, the remainder being one long-term elderly couple and three shorter-term clients. Unless stated otherwise, we shall focus on the 63 cases held by the two project social workers.

The grade of workers involved with these cases changed quite sharply from 1979. The main change was the major increase in the proportion of cases held by qualified social workers. This is due to the large majority of cases being held by the two social workers based at Dinnington, both of whom were qualified. Goldberg *et al.* (1970) have shown the benefits that can flow from qualified staff working with elderly clients and this is likely to have had some effect on the results we report. The unqualified staff still holding cases in Dinnington were all based at the area office at Maltby. That applied to only four cases but it should be noted that the housing assistant, who was working in the project office with the two social workers as a member of the core team, was holding 18 cases in 1981, all except three being elderly clients. Under normal circumstances these cases might well have been part of a 'review' system, which would have involved no visiting unless a request was made. This was the practice for many elderly clients at the area office.

The overall pattern of social work in the village in 1981 showed considerable change from that we described earlier for 1979. Both the characteristics of the clients and the social work response had altered. More elderly clients were remaining on the caseload for over six months, thus blurring the characteristics of long- and short-term clients. The response of social workers had shifted from individualized casework to a focus on client networks and to use of a wider range of extra-departmental resources. For example, whereas contact was made to the voluntary sector for only five cases in 1979, this had increased to 19 by 1981, ten of which involved individual volunteers, most though not all working with elderly clients.

The changed pattern of contacts and negotiations with outside groups and individuals, both statutory and non-statutory, on behalf of clients, was striking. Overall there had been a 45 per cent increase in the average number of contacts made by Dinnington workers over that made by area workers in 1979. Contacts within the statutory sector were directed towards more appropriate agencies than previously. For example, we know from earlier work on the caseloads of a range of agencies that the doctors were a referral point for workers in Dinnington and that the doctors then re-referred information on to the district nurses. We can see that by 1981 social workers were liaising directly with the nurse, with whom they had almost daily encounters. Contacts to the GPs decreased from 11 to six, and to other community health staff from 16 to ten, while those to the nurse increased from two to nine and to the health visitor from ten to 15.

Similarly, contacts to the education welfare officer dropped from 17 to 12, which is more than matched by an increase from 16 to 25 in negotiations directly with school staff. These data confirm other qualitative data on the strong links that the core team had developed with other local professionals, like the heads and other teachers in the primary schools and pastoral care staff in Dinnington Comprehensive School.

The drop by one-fifth in contacts made with DHSS and the Department of Employment is harder to explain since financial problems amongst clients were as prevalent in 1981 as they were in 1979. Moreover, the social workers claimed that for new referrals they were in regular contact with DHSS regarding clients' benefits, though this advocacy role was primarily undertaken with new and 'one-off' referrals that did not become cases. Detailed analysis of social work with long- and short-term cases showed that negotiations with the DHSS increased with short-term cases and decreased with long-term clients.

The other major changes in contact patterns showed increased use of specialist social work help to both elderly and non-elderly clients (from seven to 16), and of services that cater for elderly clients, such as the aids officer, the home help section and housing wardens. Contact with different parts of clients' informal support systems increased, most markedly with friends and neighbours (from ten to 21) and with volunteers (from five to 19).

Long-term cases

When we examined the long-term clients in 1981, there were 41 such cases, 33 of which were held at the project office and the remaining eight at the area office (Table 9.1).

The nature of cases receiving long-term support had altered by 1981. Increasing numbers of elderly clients had been on the case-load for at least a year. The number had more than doubled from 1979, from four to nine, reflecting the social workers' practice of maintaining a continuing involvement with elderly clients. However, the major group of long-term clients were families (18), with or without statutory responsibilities.

By 1981 the visit levels by social workers had fallen by 28 per cent to an average of a monthly visit, but part of this drop was due to the fact that the workers had more elderly clients on their long-term caseload. We found considerable variation in visiting levels for this group. For example, four elderly clients with physical handicaps were visited every two to three months while the two child neglect cases had fortnightly visits and the two cases where financial stress was the problem were visited almost as often. The drop in overall visit levels reflects several characteristics of Dinnington practice, which need to be related to the lower visiting levels, in that they provided alternative ways for the workers to keep in touch with their clients either directly or indirectly.

Clients or members of their networks were far more likely to call in at the office than they did when it was at Maltby. A study of the number of visits made to the project office during two separate weeks early in 1981 showed that 47 visits were made by clients or their carers. This represents a rate of 175 visits per year per 1000 people served. For an area office like Maltby serving 56 000 people this would give a rate of visits of 188 per week (based upon a 52-week year), or 38 each working day.

Also, social workers frequently saw their clients elsewhere, either in the street or in the shops, or at the house of another client, or in the context of one of the community groups initiated by the workers. For example, there were two families who were on the At Risk register whose children walked past the project office every day on their way to school. The social worker found it easy to contrive to talk to them or to members of the family.

Such settings might be thought inappropriate for a counselling role but in practice this does take place on occasion. More commonly though, they are means by which a monitoring role may be sustained and which, from the clients' point of view, may be more acceptable than the normal mode of worker–client transaction, namely the interview. It is difficult to quantify the range of situations in which clients may meet with social workers, let alone make qualitative judgements about their value. But it is likely that the increasing number and variety of social encounters led to a less dependent relationship. It gave social workers the ability to develop a more holistic view of clients, seeing them in a variety of social situations and, for those clients who were involved in the voluntary and self-help initiatives, relations were developed on the basis of shared skills and resources. Of course, the client perspective on this changed practice may not be so positive, as we shall see.

The changing pattern of social work tasks reflects the workers' informal social interaction with their long-term clients or members of their networks. The actual contact might be with the social workers themselves or, very often, with one of the home helps or wardens. The home helps and wardens played a key role in monitoring the elderly. The effectiveness of the social workers in this task was vastly increased by the close contact they maintained with the wardens and a number of home helps.

These contacts with home helps and wardens were not only helpful with regard to the elderly. One warden had reported how a very old lady was looked after by her daughter, who had been a nursing sister. About a year

Table 9.1 Principal characteristics of community social work

Case length (months)	No.	% of clients who were Elderly	Statutory	Weekly visits	Average No. of contacts
1979					
12 or more	33	12	48	0.35	4.1
7 – 11	7	28	0	0.54	3.6
4 – 6	5	40	0	0.44	3.4
3 or less	20	50	0	0.43	1.8
Unknown	2	100	0	0.33	4.5
Total	67	50	24	0.40	3.3
1981					
12 or more	33	24	48	0.25	5.3
7 – 11	10	60	20	0.20	6.0
4 – 6	6	51	0	0.25	4.0
3 or less	14	50	21	0.68	3.1
Total	63	38	33	0.34	4.8

A further 11 Dinnington cases were held at the Maltby team office in 1981 *practice: long, medium and short-term cases, 1979 and 1981*

Major client problems	Major S.W. tasks	Focus of contacts
Family rels, child behaviour	Counsel, info., advice, finance	Other agencies and family networks
Family rels, finance	Counsel info., advice	Education, housing, other agencies, informal networks
None predominate	Check-up	GP other SS staff
Physical disability, finance	Finance	GP, other SS staff, relations
Mental handicap, social isolation	Holidays, clubs, advice, check	Health and SS staff, informal networks
Family rels	Check-up/support, material/financial aid	More accurately focused statutory contacts; more friends and vols.
Physical disability, family rels. financial	Material/financial aid	To wider range of statutory agencies; to wider range of informal carers
None predominate	Counselling/ info./advice	Drop to health services; increase to non-relative informal sector
Physical disability	Material/financial aid; and counselling/ info. advice	More diversified both to formal and informal sectors

previously the daughter had given up her job in order to look after her mother. Before that the warden had only called in when the daughter was not there; and so, once the daughter had given up her job, she ceased calling in. However, on her round one day, she saw the daughter through the window looking distressed. She went inside to have a word with her and discovered that she was totally overwhelmed with the problem of looking after her mother. She felt she had no life of her own left. The warden was so concerned that she called in at the project office and as a result one of the social workers called round quickly and had a talk with the daughter, as a result of which the daughter felt considerably happier with life. If a referral had been made to the area office at Maltby, it would have gone to the bottom of the pile, nothing would have happened for at least two or three weeks, and then, in all likelihood, no visit would have been made because it did not come high enough in departmental priorities. As it was, the social worker was able to do something quick and effective because of the close contact with the wardens and because of greater personal freedom from the constraints of departmental work priorities.

We can see the effect of this. While counselling with the giving of information and advice was the dominant social work task in 1979, offered to nearly four in ten clients, by 1981 this more intensive visiting pattern had almost halved while those given friendly support and checking visits had doubled. The proportion of cases where material or financial aid was given remained stable, at around one-quarter. In part, this reflected the changing characteristics of long-term clients, with higher numbers of elderly, but it also reflected the changed mode of social work practice, for, alongside the drop in visit levels and the changed form of social work support to clients, there was also a change in the other resources brought to bear by social workers. We can see this in the contacts they made on behalf of their clients.

The number of contacts had increased by 29 per cent over 1979, to an average of 5.3 per case (Table 9.1). There were increased contacts with people such as home helps (from one to five), the home help organizer (from two to eight), the aids officer (from one to three), and the district nurse (from two to four), which is largely a function of the increasing numbers of elderly; but also with specialist social workers (from three to ten), friends of clients (from five to 14), and to voluntary bodies (from four to ten). At the same time there was a decrease in contacts with other health workers (from 12 to eight) and with the education welfare officer (from 12 to seven).

We would argue that the decrease in contacts with certain departments illustrate how the social workers' more sophisticated knowledge of other agencies enabled them to make more appropriate contact. Thus, as we mentioned above, the drop in contacts with the education welfare officer was matched by increased contacts with school and special school staff. We know that close links had been built up with the school counsellor at the local comprehensive who was better able to negotiate with year tutors and other pastoral care staff than the EWO, working from outside the institution. Again, however, this obvious advantage of locally-based social work highlights a corresponding problem area within the community model. This is the question of the boundaries between different areas of professional competence.

Another illustration of workers' focusing their agency contacts more appropriately is in the field of health. The drop in contacts with undefined 'other' community health staff in 1981 was matched by the increased liaison reported with both district nurse and health visitor.

Overall, these data suggest an increasing use of specialist statutory help with more extensive links with friendship networks and the voluntary sector. As one of the social workers explained to us, their long-term cases put less strain on them because they had other options open to them and other sources of information available to them. They did not feel the need to visit as often because they were sufficiently involved with the network of the client to be aware of the current situation without recourse to a formal interview.

Understanding client networks and the state of support or antagonism within them at any point in time is a central feature of locally-based work. Unless fieldworkers are able to appreciate the dynamics of such networks and the ways in which a souring of relationships within one part of a network may have repercussions for other parts, they will not be able to practise according to this model. Decentralization alone will not bring about changed practice, unless accompanied by a changed orientation towards clients as people within social situations.

One of the social workers explained to us the way in which he used his detailed knowledge of the state of relationships within a network at any one point in time to guide his own interventions. For example, he had recently been contacted by the local DHSS office about an anonymous letter claiming renewed domestic violence in a family well known to him. A medical examination showed no injury to the children involved. The social worker was familiar with various family members within the network, both through earlier involvement with the family and also because several of them featured in other cases he carried. Because he knew that the extended family was currently supportive to the E family in question he was able to arrange for Mrs E's mother to take the children for the night. For the same reason he was able to work with Mr E's brother-in-law (himself the father of a child who had been on the NAI register) in defusing a potentially hostile situation between Mr E, who had been drinking in the local club, and the police. The volatility of relationships within such a network meant that this particular use of informal resources would not have been possible if this crisis had occurred a few months previously. The use of family members as intermediaries between Mr E and the police would not have been a viable method of intervention, and had it been tried it is likely that the tension within the E family would have increased still further. It was situations such as this which led us to include 'volatility' as one of the three key characteristics of informal care highlighted in Chapter 4.

We showed earlier the extent to which workers brought other formal agencies into discussion about their cases. The data on long-term cases in 1981 show the extent to which they related to the extra-family networks of such clients, too. Social work contacts with friends and neighbours increased from five to 13 and with volunteers or voluntary bodies from four to ten. An example of volunteer help with a long-term family case is shown by the case of Mrs F. Her husband was in a long-stay ward in hospital after a pit accident. He had been home and was now back in hospital. Mrs F, whose two adult children lived at home, was finding it hard to adjust to her changed circumstances and needed help in trying to create a new life for herself. The social worker, therefore, supplemented her own visiting with help from a volunteer who visited weekly giving moral support, companionship and advice. In addition to this the social worker worked with friends and neighbours of Mrs F, also contacting the health visitor and the district nurse and liaising with the hospital social worker and the aids officer about her husband.

Those eight long-term cases which were still held at the area office in 1981 were predominantly statutory cases that were receiving just checking visits with friendly support from their social workers. None of the eight cases were given counselling help and only one had financial or material assistance. The visit levels to these clients matched that given by the local office, but without the opportunities for informal interchange. Moreover the average contacts made regarding the area-held cases was only 1.6 compared to 5.3 for the locally-held cases. Even comparing the statutory cases, we found that the project social workers made nearly twice as many contacts (3.3) as the area social workers (1.8) and to a far wider range of people. The full transfer of cases was never achieved during the period of the project, although only a few were held at the area office. It was another reflection of the lack of commitment of management to the new way of working, although it inadvertently gave the evaluation programme some useful comparisons.

Seven- to eleven-month cases

Those cases that had been ongoing for between seven and 11 months showed similarly changed characteristics. Four out of the ten clients held at the project office in this group had physical disability problems. There was a reduction in the visits made to these clients from an average of once a fortnight in 1979, to once every five weeks in 1981. This was matched by an increase in contacts from an average of 3.6 per case in 1979 to 6.0 per case in 1981. This included an increase in contacts with relatives of clients who lived outside the household from one in 1979 to seven in 1981. The fact that some clients with disability were now carried through to medium- and long-term caseloads influenced both the average number of visits given by social workers to those types of cases, and the pattern of contacts. Such clients received social work visits only about once every three months and the majority of contacts were with people like the specialist social worker, aids officer and home help organiser.

On the other hand, a wider utilization of resources was occurring for other groups, too. Two cases with family relationship problems in 1979 had three contacts made on their behalf, while the one case in this group in 1981 had seven contacts made. Similarly, the response to a client who suffered from social isolation in 1981 was to make three times as many contacts (six) as were made for a similar case in 1979, although we must be extremely cautious of drawing implications from individual cases.

Overall social workers were making a broader response to medium-term clients, moving away from a predominantly counselling with information-giving role to make a more varied personal response and bringing in a wider range of additional resources. As with their long-term cases they were able to monitor current situations, even though visiting less, by working with a wider range of outside agencies, liaising within formal networks and bringing in the voluntary sector.

One example of the broader response to the needs of an elderly client in this group is the case of Mrs H. She was an elderly widow with a son and daughter-in-law living close by who were very supportive, but had other commitments to the daughter-in-law's parents. As the elderly people became more frail the pressures increased on the young couple until they had nearly reached breaking point. The social worker was able to organize voluntary help through the local Toc H group and the Housewives' Register. A volunteer visited on Thursdays and another took a fish lunch on Fridays, relieving the younger couple of cooking a meal at least one day a week and they knew also that the old lady now had additional visitors who would help out with small jobs where necessary. It was also possible to arrange firelighting and meals at weekends by friends and neighbours in order to give the younger couple a complete break. Mrs H had asked for a permanent place in a local authority old people's home, but as this would take time it was necessary to rely upon community resources in the meantime.

Should statutory provision in the form of home help have been provided to ease Mrs H's problems, rather than plug gaps by drafting in voluntary help? Under policy current at that time there was no way in which home helps would be allocated to provide weekend meals, and they provided lunchtime meal calls only to those clients who were most disabled at domestic tasks. So the project was extending the normal intervention by organizing a more comprehensive system of support for the old lady. Not only was Mrs H receiving more visitors, but her primary carers were given help before their ability and willingness to care had collapsed.

The example illustrates extending the scope of care given, supporting carers and also the process whereby responsibility for areas of help can be transferred from informal to formal and voluntary carers. Though the day-to-day responsibility for meals and so on rested with neighbours and volunteers, the responsibility for the package remained with the social worker, and it was she who initiated and organized the arrangement.

Four- to six-month cases
Cases that had been carried for between four and six months in 1979 involved social workers with almost fortnightly visits to carry out a range of activities and an average of 3.4 contacts per case, mainly to health services and other workers within their department. Contacts with carers were limited. By 1981 the average number of visits had dropped by 43 per cent and the average number of contacts increased by 18 per cent (from 3.4 to 4.0 per case), principally with people such as friends, volunteers and voluntary groups, and local service-givers such as shopkeepers and milkmen. At the same time there had been a drop in contacts with health services. In contrast to the other groups, however, the social workers had switched more into a counselling role with these clients. Half received counselling support, which was due to the fact that in 1981, three of the six cases were to do with family relationships.

Short-term cases
Short-term cases in 1979 had a high proportion of clients with disability associated with ageing, and workers responded by making almost fort-nightly visits to give financial or material aid. The range of contacts (1.8 per case) was lower than for any other group of cases.

In 1981 we found a basically unchanged set of problems in that elderly clients with disability still accounted for 50 per cent of the caseload. However, the response was significantly different. First, and in contrast to other groups, there was a 58 per cent increase in average visit levels so that social workers were making a visit every ten days to these short-term cases. Second, though financial and material assistance remained the dominant response, its importance had diminished since other tasks had become more significant. For example, counselling was given to twice as many clients in 1981 compared to 1979.

Third, a much wider range of resources, both formal and informal, was brought to bear in 1981. Contacts per case rose from average 1.8 to 3.1 and while they were heavily department-orientated in 1979, by 1981 there were highly diversified. Thus, liaison with specialist social workers, the home help organizer and housing wardens had all increased. There was one case where volunteer help was utilized. This client was a terminally sick young woman who was cared for through the last months of her life by a combination of statutory and voluntary help. While the home help service put in additional help at lunchtime, a rota of five volunteers covered the latter part of the afternoon, minding the children after school and preparing a family meal for the evening when the client's husband returned from work. This arrangement was initiated and co-ordinated by one of the social workers.

We can see, therefore, that in 1981 more intensive social work was given to this short-term group of clients and a wider range of resources were utilized. Workers were able to make this response in part because their changed management of long-term cases allowed them the flexibility to make an intensive input into new cases when this was needed. This reflects the principles of intake work but in a radically different setting from the normal area team office.

It seems that the organizational arrangements that facilitate a flexible and quick response to sudden demands, combined with a changed pattern of case management for longer-term clients, enabled the project social workers to make a more positive response to relatively new cases. It is true that in 1981 the two short-term cases on the area office books averaged a weekly social work visit. This was due to one of these two having very intensive visiting (nearly two per week). The contacts made regarding them were only slightly higher (2.0 per case) than in 1979. There will always be individual cases that require frequent visits during periods of stress, but frequency of formal visiting is only one part of social work response and there were no signs of any other elements of a changed response from the workers at the area office.

Referrals to the project office

Analysis of referrals to the project office over a five-week period in early 1982 showed marked changes in the number and source of referrals and in the response made by workers when compared with referrals in 1980. (The 1982 referrals to the project office included referrals to the social workers and the housing assistant. They worked as a team with whoever was available dealing with the client who came in, and so it gives a more accurate picture of the work of the project office to consider all referrals to the office together.) The analysis reinforces the picture of work 'within the community'. The pattern of referrals to the area office immediately before the project started reflected the inaccessibility of the area office and the formal procedures for receiving and allocating requests for social work help. We saw that only 16 referrals were made, mostly via other formal agencies, three-quarters of which were followed up during the study period. The major causes of referral were requests for aids and residential care for elderly people and delinquency referrals from other statutory agencies. Social work response was contained within departmental boundaries, with little evidence of wider community or even other agency resources (for example, health) being utilized.

The pattern in 1982 presents a marked contrast to this. First, the number of people referred to social services (area and local office) showed a near sixfold increase over 1980. Ninety referrals were made in the study period, representing an annual referral rate of 133 per 1000 people served (Table 9.2). Referrals in the rest of the area remained more or less constant during the same period, suggesting strongly that the increase was a direct result of the accessibility of the locally-based office. A small proportion of Dinnington referrals (15 out of the total of 90) were still made to the area office. Eleven of these were for the elderly, reflecting the demand for aids and illustrating the way in which workers in other agencies used their more sophisticated knowledge of the social services department to refer directly to the specialist officer for aids and adaptations. A small proportion of these 15 referrals were self-referrals which may be a result of people having had previous contact with the area office.

In 1980 the level of demand from elderly and non-elderly clients was equal, as shown in other studies (Warburton 1982). This ratio had changed in favour of the elderly in 1982. While there had been a fourfold increase in referrals from the non-elderly, by 1982 referrals from the elderly had increased nearly seven times. Consequently in 1982 the elderly accounted for three-fifths of referrals. The rise in referrals meant that the rate per 1000 non-elderly people served had risen from 14 in 1980 to 65 in 1982. The rate for the elderly had risen from 64 in 1980 to 431 per 1000 elderly people served in 1982. Thus, on average, more than two in five elderly people would approach the local office in any given year.

We also found substantial changes in the method of referral in 1982. The major referral methods in 1980 were phone or letter, with less than one in five referrals made by a personal visit to the office. In 1982 nearly four out of five referrals to the project office were made by personal visit, with the phone accounting for only one in five referrals, and letters were not used at all.

Further evidence of the changed use being made of the social services department by the local community was seen in the source of referrals. In 1980, 69 per cent of referrals came from within the formal sector and only

Table 9.2 Referrals made to project office, 1980 and 1982 (excludes referrals to home help service)

Year, client group and location	Manner of referral expressed as % of service				Number of referrals	As a % of referrals	Average days to action	Annual rate per 1000 pop.
	Phone	Letter	Office	Other				
Non-elderly								
1980 Area	0	63	38	0	8	50	7	14
1982 Area	50	50	0	0	4	4	16	7
1982 Patch	25	0	75	0	32	36	1	58
1982 Total	28	4	67	0	36	40	2	65
Elderly								
1980 Area	75	12	0	12	8	50	13	64
1982 Area	64	18	9	9	11	12	11	88
1982 Patch	19	0	81	0	43	48	4	343
1982 Total	28	4	65	2	54	60	7	431
All referrals								
1980 Area	38	38	19	6	16	100	10	24
1982 Area	60	27	7	7	15	17	18	22
1982 Patch	21	0	79	0	75	83	3	111
1982 Total	28	4	67	1	90	100	5	133

Table 9.3 Source of referrals to the social work service, 1980 and
          1982 (percentage of all referrals)

Source of referral	1980	1982
Health services	19	4
Local authority	25	23
Other formal agencies	25	2
Relatives and friends	19	18
Clients themselves	12	44
Volunteers etc.	0	8
Total	100	100
Base	16	90

31 per cent from either clients themselves or their informal networks (Table 9.3). By 1982 this position was reversed, with 70 per cent coming from informal sources and only 30 per cent from statutory sources. Forty-four per cent of all referrals were now self-referrals and a small proportion (eight per cent) came from the voluntary sector and from local service-givers, that is the milkman, postman, and so on.

The major increase was in self-referrals from clients themselves, but there was also a very considerable increase in the number from informal networks which increased from three in 1980 to 16 in 1982, though the proportions remained nearly the same (19 per cent and 18 per cent). This covered referrals from relatives, both those living in the same household and those living elsewhere, and friends and neighbours. The effect of the accessibility of the local office is very clear. However, although the formal referrals declined proportionately, nevertheless the number increased. Referrals from the health services only increased from three in 1980 to five in 1982 but from other formal sources the figures went up from eight in 1980 to 22 in 1982. No less than ten of these referrals came from the wardens. They only made two referrals in 1980.

Three-quarters of referrals in 1980 had been followed up by the end of the study period, with an average of ten days between referral and visit. In 1982 almost all (94 per cent) referrals received a follow-up visit during the study period and the response time was halved to five days (Table 9.2). This figure conceals great variation and in part reflects the different needs brought to the office by elderly and non-elderly clients.

The average time taken to respond to elderly clients was one week, reflecting the influence of the demand for aids. Even so this had fallen from an average of almost a fortnight in 1980. Some referrals, mostly for aids, were made appropriately to the area office in 1982, where they took an average of 11 days to follow up, compared with only four days for elderly clients referred to the local office. The difference in follow-up times for non-elderly referrals was even greater. In 1982 four referrals received at the area office took an average of 16 days to follow up, compared with one day for the 32 referrals received at the project office. In general, workers at the project office dealt with referrals on the spot, by contacting the relevant agencies and giving any information and advice that might be needed. An early and declared priority of the project workers was a quick response to requests for help. The fact that response time had been halved with a near six-fold increase in referrals shows the extent to which that particular objective was met.

Analysis of referrals from the elderly showed that the greatest single demand in 1982 was for aids, requested in 17 out of 54 referrals. However, there was a wide range of demand for other help. These covered such things as housing matters, failure of other agencies, and health. The average number of contacts per referral from the elderly fell slightly from 1.3 in 1980 to 1.1 in 1982, although due to the considerable increase in the number of referrals. The actual number of contacts rose from ten to 62. More use was made of volunteers, although still only one in nine referrals were linked into this resource.

Other categories of referral indicated ways in which characteristics of locally-based community-orientated work were being put into practice. For example, the number of old people being assessed for residential care dropped from three to two between 1980 and 1982, in percentage terms from 38 per cent to four per cent of all elderly referrals. Obviously the figures are far too small for much weight to be attached to them but the direction in which they point is consistent with other findings. On the other hand, requests for advice and help regarding relief for members of informal networks increased from one to five. One could argue that such referrals represent social work intervention at an earlier stage of dependency in old people, that is, people were seeking help in supporting elderly relatives before crises occurred and networks collapsed. Or again, the appearance in 1982 of four referrals regarding financial problems may be an indication of preventive work; at least it points to needs amongst elderly people that were not brought to the area office in 1980.

Delinquency featured in the referrals from the non-elderly in 1980, but by 1982 financial problems and family relationship problems were the most frequent cause of referrals, accounting for 53 per cent of non-elderly referrals. In each of the six cases involving family relationship problems (compared with only one such referral in 1980) the social worker considered the family to be breaking up, and in one case was considering admitting a child into care. Not all the increase in non-elderly referrals is therefore at what some would call the 'soft end' of the market. In no case, however, was there any indication of child abuse.

Given the project's emphasis upon preventive care, the sharp increase in those with financial problems (from one to 13) could indicate an earlier stage of intervention for social work. As is normal in these cases, contacts with other agencies were greater in number than for any other, not just with agencies like the DHSS, but also with others in the local authority and with health service personnel. Most of these financial problems (69 per cent) were brought to the local office by clients themselves.

Use of volunteers for non-elderly referrals was very restricted. Other than one referral received from a voluntary body which was subsequently recontacted, only one referral was made where a volunteer was contacted to help out the members of an informal network. The use of volunteers with the non-elderly, particularly with intractable family cases, was found to be more problematic than with the elderly. It certainly requires more time (see, for example, Munday and Turner 1981).

Other demands increased by 1982, indicating the way in which the project office had become a general information and advice centre and a first point of referral for people with problems. Callers have gone into the office with the initial query 'Are you the CAB?' This comment raises a pertinent issue. Should trained social workers be fulfilling a Citizens' Advice Bureau type of function? One could argue that it is quite inappropriate and a waste of the time of skilled workers. On the other hand, one could argue that it offered an invaluable opportunity to pick up problems at an early stage and thus makes preventive work far more possible. This important question is considered in the last chapter.

A clear pattern of demand and response had emerged in 1982. Most demand was received at the local (project) office, mainly through personal visit. Generally speaking, this demand was dealt with at once using a wide range of community resources. Thus the average level of contacts per referral rose from 0.8 in 1980 to 1.1 in 1982, even with the sixfold increase in the number of referrals taken. The actual number of contacts rose from 12 in 1980 to 95 in 1982, suggesting an extensive use of both statutory and other resources even at this initial stage of demand. Twelve per cent of contacts were now directed towards the community, either to the voluntary sector or to informal carers. Contacts in 1982 showed a sharp increase in those made outside the referral source: on average, in around 80 per cent of cases contact was made with an agency other than the referral source.

Their greater knowledge and understanding about other formal agencies enabled the core team to direct contacts to the most relevant personnel within these institutions. By means of their detailed knowledge of both formal and informal care the core team were able to function as gatekeepers to community resources, making a broader response to initial assessments and linking newly-referred clients into a wider range of resources.

It may be argued that the increased rate of referral and the changed nature of problems brought to the office in Dinnington were not a consequence of the project, but reflect more general demographic and social factors common to other social services offices. We were able to set the Dinnington referral data within the context of the rest of Rotherham South area, which shows that the trends we have observed in Dinnington were not common throughout the area. We compared two sets of information. The first covers the number of referrals to Dinnington and the rest of the team of which it was part in the South area over the period 1980–2. The second compares the reasons for referral to the whole South area (that is, both of the social work teams) with those to Dinnington itself. We shall consider the first in this section and the second in the next.

Before we do this we must first clarify some different usage of the term 'referral'. We have noted already that the project office was receiving a markedly higher level of referrals in 1982 than were made to the area office in our first referral study. A significant proportion of the increased number of referrals were what the workers described as 'one-off' referrals, needing no further action and for which they did not open a case file. Examples would be enquiries about social security payments, employment queries, and CAB-type enquiries. The referral was dealt with on the spot by giving information and advice and by making contact with the relevant agency to negotiate on the client's behalf. Departmental referral forms were not completed in these situations (although they were for the Referral Study) because the workers felt it was unnecessarily bureaucratic, formalized their relationship to people calling in when they were striving to create a more informal style of work, and required them to ask a range of personal questions of the client that they did not wish to ask. In March 1982 social services management instructed the project office to complete referral forms for *all* requests received at the local office, and this procedure has been followed since then. However, the area figures we shall refer to below do *not* include the 'one-off' referrals to the project office.

Dinnington was one of nine constituent parts of the social work team and in the calendar year 1980 accounted for 18 per cent of all referrals to the team. The 150 referrals over the year from Dinnington represent a rate of 21 per 1000, slightly below that derived from our 1980 referral study, but higher numbers of people are referred in the winter months than at other times of the year.

By 1981 the Dinnington rate had increased to 31 per 1000 people served and the village accounted for 25 per cent of all the area team's referrals. In 1982 the rate had reached 40 per 1000 people and represented nearly one-third of the area team's referrals. During this time, when Dinnington's referrals increased by 88 per cent (excluding the one-off referrals), referrals from the rest of the area declined by 11 per cent. This shows the increasing importance of Dinnington in the total demand placed on the social services department, though since the workers there utilized so many different and varied responses to that demand, the pressure on the department was less than might be expected from these figures.

Two points of interest arise. One is that, even when considering just conventionally defined referrals, the local office with its informal style of work received much higher levels of demand from the community, suggesting that there had been levels of unmet need before, due to the inaccessibility of the area office. Similar comments have been made about other decentralized schemes. Thus, Anne Whitehouse (1982), writing in *Community Care* of the East Sussex scheme, says: 'Referrals are significantly up, especially self-referrals, since going patch. Combined with referrals from relatives, they form half the total figure'. In similar vein, Currie and Parrott (1981) showed a 50 per cent increase in referrals after decentralizing part of Nottinghamshire's social work services.

Secondly, the additional referrals, not recorded by the area office, that were dealt with there and then in the project office, are an indication of new areas of need coming to the attention of social workers. This would appear to be the extension of social work into areas of preventive action, where referrals are made at an earlier stage in the development of a problem. These more 'trivial' problems could eventually have presented themselves as crises to the social services department if there had been no ready means of tackling them early on. Examples of such problems presented themselves to the project office daily, primarily issues of finance, welfare rights and housing. In mid-1984 negotiations were in progress with the housing department in Dinnington, on the latter's initiative, to consider and act upon the question of rent arrears. The housing department maintained that 'housing issues of today may be social service issues of tomorrow' and were working out ways of preventive action by giving support to new tenants. This illustrates also the way in which the housing department was beginning to think in terms of integrated services in the community.

This point is also made in other writing on decentralized schemes. Currie and Parrott (1981) note:

When the team was based outside the town very few people came to the office to ask for help and usually requests were made by telephone. The problems were frequently of a kind that needed to be dealt with by interview and so a home visit had to be arranged and a 'case' opened. Since moving to Hucknall a very much greater proportion of referrals are made by office visit, and the necessary interview and discussion has taken place at the time of referral, often with the person in need, obviating in many cases the need for the social work involvement.

Thus the figures derived from our five-week referral study in early 1982, which gave an annual rate of 133 per 1000 people coming into the project office to be seen by either the social workers or the housing assistant, indicate the extent to which the project had moved into this area of preventive work.

The viability of community social work

There has been considerable doubt expressed, however, about providing such a service. It has been suggested that it is a waste of social work resources to respond to demands which do not reflect the priorities of the department, that such demands are often trivial and can only be met at the expense of 'real' casework. This broad objection is encapsulated by Professor Pinker in his minority report to the Barclay Committee (Barclay 1982, p. 237):

Social work should be explicitly selective rather than universalist in focus, reactive rather than preventive in approach and modest in its objectives. Social work ought to be preventive with respect to the needs which come to its attention; it has neither the capacity, the resources nor the mandate to go looking for needs in the community at large.

A great deal turns on what Pinker meant by 'go looking for needs in the community'. All the evidence suggests that decentralization of social work increases demand, often considerably, and this holds despite the considerable differences there are likely to be between Dinnington and an inner-city area, such as Lewisham (Whitehouse, 1982). Decentralization is, therefore, in one respect a simple but very effective method of looking for needs in the community. Implicit in Pinker's statement is the assumption that social workers ought to be situated far enough away from their prospective clients to avoid the type of demand experienced in Dinnington. His statement is in effect one for maintenance of the area model.

Much more serious is the comment that social work does not have the resources to be able to offer such a service, and that it can only do so at the expense of casework. Two points arise from the Dinnington Project which suggest that this is not so. The first is that locating the social worker in the village not only saved the local authority a certain amount of travelling expenses, but effectively increased the amount of social work time available to the community. Social workers no longer spent that time on travelling. For Dinnington we have estimated that decentralizing social work to the local office effectively gave the community the equivalent of one-third of an additional worker. This helped the social workers to cope with the increase in demand from referrals while at the same time holding the same number of cases as were held from the village prior to the project.

The second point is that such an accusation shows no faith whatsoever in preventive social work – that working today with 'trivial' demands saves meeting with expensive demands tomorrow. While the model of social work developed in Dinnington was that of social work within a wider context of integrated health and welfare provision, not just locally-based social work, evidence has emerged from elsewhere and from the Dinnington Project that locally-based provision, in the medium term, reduced those demands which can be very expensive in social work time and resources. Sharron (1982) argued that social workers in Normanton were able to keep watch sufficiently closely on the community to reduce substantially the number of children placed on the NAI register. No direct link has been established yet between 'trivial' demand and the prevention of something more serious. The general evidence suggests, however, that working in the community, being able to respond to need, at whatever level, and being able to respond quickly does result in such a reduction. The fact is that in preventive social work no demand is trivial.

There are two main ways in which preventive care may be understood. First, it can mean the prevention of the deterioration in the quality of a person's life. We have given a number of examples of this above, mostly in relation to the lives of old people. Second, it can refer to the prevention of problematic anti-social behaviour. This is a much more difficult and debatable area, but in the following section there are indications (we would claim no more than that) that the project has had some effect, especially in the area of delinquency.

The second piece of comparative information used to set Dinnington within the context of the rest of the area concerns the reasons for referral. In this case we have compared the figures for Dinnington with those for the rest of the area in the financial years 1981–2 and 1982–3. The results show sharp differences between the two areas.

For those problems primarily associated with the elderly, like referrals for aids or for residential or day care there was an increase during the period from Dinnington, but a decrease in the rest of the area. Thus, demand for aids in Dinnington increased by 10 per cent, while decreasing by 23 per cent in the rest of the area. Referrals for day or residential care rose by 34 per cent in Dinnington, but dropped by nine per cent in the rest of the area. This, of course, reflects the increased referral rate from the elderly which we noted earlier, and the higher priority accorded in the project to elderly people and their needs. Referrals for adaptations, however, dropped marginally from Dinnington while increasing by 16 per cent in the rest of the area.

Marital and family problems increased proportionately much more in Dinnington than at the area level and there were substantial increases in Dinnington referrals regarding energy problems (208 per cent) and housing (267 per cent), although we think the latter will have been affected by the housing assistant being part of the core team. In 1982–3 Dinnington provided around one-sixth of housing and energy referrals within the area, whereas it had provided only six per cent of them in 1981–2.

Analysis of child care referrals, including child abuse, showed that they increased by 17 per cent for the area, but reduced by 50 per cent for Dinnington. Referrals for the juvenile court (including social enquiry reports) showed a 42 per cent drop in Dinnington, compared with an increase of more than one-fifth in the rest of the area. Thus, while Dinnington accounted for 20 per cent of all such referrals in 1981–2, this had halved by 1982–3. How are we to account for these decreases? We are not in a position to make definite statements. It could be that the increase in referrals for marital and family problems and for energy problems and housing, mentioned above, are a further indication that workers were being contacted or were themselves becoming aware of problems at an earlier stage, before the more serious stages of abuse or court appearances.

It seems fairly clear that the trends observed in Dinnington are not part of a common pattern within the area, but rather form a distinctive pattern characteristic of a decentralized, community-orientated social work service. One aspect of working with informal support networks is the opening up of formal services to the community by easy access and making them acceptable, that is, presenting the services so that it is not considered stigmatizing to use them. Knowledge on the part of people in a network that they can approach the social services for help and support is as important as knowledge about strengths and vulnerability of networks on the part of workers.

This quantitative information, together with the case examples, indicates that social work as it was practised by mid-1981 and early 1982, only 18–24 months after the start of the project, showed subtle but important changes from conventional practice. We have seen that the shape of the caseload was different, with higher numbers of elderly people featuring on long-term caseloads. The proportion of clients who had been on a social worker's caseload for at least a year and who were elderly doubled, from 12 to 24 per cent. Consequently problems of physical disability and ageing were prevalent amongst medium-term clients, along with the more typical family relationship problems of longer-term non-elderly cases.

We have seen, too, that the response of social workers to the demands made on their time had altered from 1979. Visits to medium- and long-term clients occurred with less frequency, while visits to short-term cases had increased markedly. Whether the workers were doing so wittingly or not, this concentration of effort at an early stage when the possibilities of rapid change are at their height accords with crisis intervention theory and the research by Fahsbeck and Jones (1973). At the same time a wider range of other resources was utilized. Contacts with other formal agencies were focused more accurately on the relevant personnel, thus avoiding inefficient re-referrals within agencies. Detailed knowledge, not only of the extent of client networks, but also of the quality of relationships within the network at any particular time, enabled workers to work *with* networks in a more constructive manner. Their appreciation of this volatility enabled them to bring in friends, neighbours and volunteers to a much greater extent than was shown in 1979.

We have also shown that referrals coming to the core team had increased nearly sixfold by 1982 with an even greater rise in referrals regarding the elderly. Most demand was dealt with at once in the office by calling upon a wide range of local resources and thereby cutting down on the number of follow-up visits required of the social workers. In spite of the increased rate of referral, workers were able to liaise with more people, directing such contacts to a wider range of other agencies and groups than previously, when contacts tended to be made back to the referring agency.

There is some evidence that the project had been able to tackle the question of preventive work since the comparative figures for child care referrals, including abuse, between Dinnington and the rest of the South area showed a trend upwards over the whole area, and a halving of such referrals in Dinnington. A similar pattern emerged for juvenile court and social enquiry reports. The drop in care proceedings regarding Dinnington children is something that had been commented on informally by the court liaison officer to one of the project social workers.

Claims about the impact of experiments such as Dinnington on rates of child abuse are hard to verify. Certainly advocates of the Normanton scheme have made the claim that children at risk can be maintained in the community because of the patch system (Sharron 1982). The social workers in Dinnington were aware of the levels of risk they carried by trying to contain difficult family situations in the community rather than resorting to care placements. They were equally aware of the vulnerability of front-line workers if such a situation should escalate into a crisis and they worked hard at maintaining contact so that they were aware of current developments in the families.

The greatly increased flow of demand kept them office-bound for much of the time, taking them away from the streets and traditional centres of the life of the community. However, the evidence we have presented on the use of the 'Hut' suggests that they themselves had become a centre of community life – certainly a centre of community care.

A theoretical model for locally-based work

The fact that many readers will have recognized in our case examples familiar modes of social work practice provides our first principal understanding of locally-based work. It is firmly built upon the base of existing social work experience and practice. There is no revolution here, no epoch-making change in methods of intervention, but rather a widening of the social worker's perspective together with the acquisition of some new skills. This simple, and often incremental, development of the social worker's role could, however, lead to a substantial shift in the nature and effectiveness of social work practice if some of the outcomes of Dinnington are anything to go by.

What, then, are the characteristics of practising social work 'within the community'? The work of Whittaker (1983) is particularly helpful for tackling this question. We have met his work already when considering the work of the district nurse. The significant contribution of Whittaker's work is that it brings into the practice of social work the concept of working with informal networks. So we have the development of a theoretical model of social work practice which explicitly includes the style of working with informal networks that has been at the heart of the theory(if not always the practice) of the Dinnington Project.

Thus, one can construct a theoretical matrix of social work practice from his work. As it stands there are four levels of intervention (person-centred, family-centred, group-centred and neighbourhood-centred) and five different roles (treatment agent, teacher/counsellor, broker, advocate, network system consultant). The key aspect of this matrix is the addition of the 'network system consultant'. We have seen that Whittaker (1983, p. 52) defines this as where 'the professional person works through a pre-exisiting or continued support system to aid an individual client or groups of clients'.

Looking at this matrix from the perspective of social work 'within the community', our experiences in Dinnington suggest to us that one further level of intervention should be added, as well as one further role (see Figure 9.1). We find it hard to envisage working as a network consultant without working to an intervention level which is 'network-centred'. Indeed we have many examples of this type of role at this level of intervention. Due to the special relationship in the Dinnington Project between the social workers and the housing assistant, particularly the development of the latter's role in constructing packages of care for elderly clients, most of those examples came from the housing assistant's work in the project office. We shall examine this shortly. Elsewhere this type of work may be done by a social worker, a health visitor, a district nurse, and so on. A further role, which has emerged clearly from the project, is that of entrepreneur, a creator of resources. As we have shown, from 1981 onwards, the core team together with other local workers, initiated and developed a range of community projects.

The interesting thing about these developments is that they were only possible because local workers had been able to see themselves as a group working with the needs and problems of a particular area. It was the process of shared thinking and information about groups or streets within the village that enabled them to define special needs and to identify shortfalls in provision. Thus, for example, the children eventually selected for the first holiday project were put forward by local teachers, by the health visitor from amongst her caseload, and by the EWO. The funds were raised jointly by all the workers from a variety of local sources. The youth worker was involved in planning the venue and voluntary helpers ranged from one of the wardens to parents. All this reflected the gradual development of a neighbourhood or locality team identity. Given the prerequisite, therefore, of working 'within the community', social workers, as part of the wider community health and welfare team, were able to generate new caring resources for the community. They also had, throughout the project, help from individual volunteers whom they themselves had recruited, sometimes from among their former clients.

This additional role, together with the extra level of intervention, develops the matrix implied by Whittaker's work to that given in Figure 9.1. Here we identify thirty modes of social work practice. In reality any social work situation could use several of these modes at the same time. Whether this is so, or whether one mode is utilized, this matrix stresses what we said earlier, that traditional social work practice forms the basis of locally-based work. However, we believe that the 14 modes of practice marked in bold type can function effectively only from a 'within the community' perspective. They require an extensive knowledge of networks and community resources and deficiencies.

One could argue that, to be really effective, many of the other modes require this perspective; that, for example, counselling a family ought to be set within this wider perspective. It is, we would argue, a question of the perception of the social worker. The individual task and the level of intervention may be the same, but those working from 'within the community' will have assessed a whole range or alternative modes of practice as well (up to 14 above the traditional range on our matrix). It is this community perspective brought to traditional social work practice

Role Cluster

Intervention level	Treatment Agent	Teacher/Counsellor	Broker	Advocate	Network system consultant	Entrepreneur
Person-centred	1. Mrs F. (p. 104)	2. Daughter of old lady (p. 99)	3. Mrs F. (p.104)	4. Negotiating with DHSS	5. Mrs F. (p. 104) Mrs H. (p. 105)	6. Arranging for a severely disabled man to come out of hospital into a specially adapted bungalow with external support services, both voluntary and statutory
Family-centred	7.	8.	9.	10.	11.	12.
Network-centred	13.	14.	15.	16.	17.	18.
Group-centred	19. Single parent group	20. (only at planning stage)	21. Helping RALLY to obtain funds for a radio telephone	22.	23.	24. VOLTAGE
Neighbourhood-centred	25.	26. Improving understanding of what social workers & SSDs do via contacts with voluntary bodies, police etc.	27. Making information available about how accounting systems of electricity and gas boards work, i.e. helping people avoid disconnection. (Also covers 26)	28.	29.	30. RALLY; summer holiday projects

Figure 9.1 Community social work/locally-based work matrix

which identifies Stage Three of our model.

We therefore describe community social work/locally-based work as the traditional practice of social work (blocks 1–4, 7–10, 19–22, 25–28 in Figure 9.1) augmented by two additional roles and one extra level of intervention brought about by the desire to work from a community-wide perspective. Opinions may vary about whether the neighbourhood-centred level of intervention has ever been part of traditional social work practice, or whether this has been the remit of the community work. To the outside observer, therefore, the nature of the social work task and the level of intervention may often be the same for a social work situation whether it is being approached from the perspective of working 'outside' or 'within the community'. The latter will, however, have involved consideration of a much wider range of modes of social work practice. Thus concern at the 'ordinariness' of some social work practice at Stage Three of our model would be ill founded. What matters is not whether the approach adopted eventually is a conventional social work one, but whether, after considering the wider range of possibilities suggested by the community social work perspective we have outlined, it was the most appropriate.

10   Other Local Authority Services

The home help service

A sharp contrast to these developments in social work practice may be seen in the home help service, also part of Rotherham social services department. An extensive home help service with some knowledge about informal networks (on the part of individual home helps) existed prior to the project, as we have seen earlier. This clearly provided a sound springboard for achieving many of the project objectives. That few if any of these objectives were met after four years of action was largely due to a catalogue of missed opportunities. Some of these were outside the control of the project (though not the local authority) while others were related to the failure of the project to address itself specifically to the implications of the project for the home help service. There was a brief period of courtship between the project and home helps which, during early 1983, looked as though it might produce a more permanent relationship. Like many such relationships it was short-lived, but its brief success taught us a lot, as did the reason for its demise.

Without doubt the major element in the failure to integrate the home help service into the project was the delay of 18 months in the appointment of a locally-based assistant home help organizer due to an acute shortage of staff. We can appreciate the impact of this delay by remembering how the team in the project office developed throughout that first 18 months, and consequently the learning process missed by the assistant organizer. It was only after 18 months of hard work, when the project office workers were beginning to develop some community initiatives, that the assistant home help organizer came to work with them. In many respects it must have seemed like landing on a different planet. Not only is it unusual for an organizer to work in the same office as social workers, let alone staff from different departments, but also the emphasis on open access must have been unnerving for someone used to a structured and relatively closed organizational environment.

These problems had not been foreseen, partly as a result of yet more missed opportunities. These were the failure to involve the home help management in certain crucial project meetings, notably the Project Management Team meeting (where the home help service was represented by the social services department area officer, a social worker) though this was remedied later. As a result, when the assistant organizer arrived in the project office, little if any discussion had taken place about how far the home help service in its existing form was compatible with the project or how it could work with it.

Thus the organization of the home help service in Dinnington was still focused on the area office five miles away. The assistant organizer, who worked half-time, spent each Thursday at the area office for the weekly planning meeting, and had to do her share of 'cover' at the area office at other times. This, together with her commitment to visiting, meant she spent very little time in the project office. Given the isolation that the assistant organizer must have felt at that time, together with a total lack of direction with respect to project objectives, it is not surprising that she chose to spend very little time in the project office. As the project moved towards the end of its second year very little change was observed in home help practice. Such change as there was, namely an increasing concentration on those receiving the daily service, would be due entirely to factors of demand and supply, and not related to any project intervention or way of practice.

It will come as no surprise that, as the project moved into 1982, its third year, little impact was recorded upon the organization and practice of the home help service. In early 1982 our referral study recorded a 45 per cent decrease since 1980 in the number of referrals from the village to the home help service. The South area of the social services department reported an 11 per cent fall in all types of referral to the home help service from 1981–2 to 1982–3. We found that, if anything, the home help service at this initial stage of demand was focusing even more on the area office in 1982 than previously. It took longer to follow up referrals, and response was still made entirely within the resources of the department. This was not surprising when we examine the weekly pattern of work of the assistant organizer in March 1982. Every Monday she reported to the area office because Mondays were considered a crisis time for organizers, with home helps off sick, for example. Each Tuesday and Wednesday she called at the project office to collect messages and then went out to visit. Some days she would have to return to the area office to take her share of the duty system to ensure that the office was covered all day. Thursdays were planning days at the area office. Fridays were mainly spent in the village when she would stay in the project office for two to three hours over lunch. Even so, she reported that only those home helps working in the area immediately around the project office would call in at this time. During the summer of 1982, when we once again looked at the care received by home help clients, we found little movement towards project objectives. There had been a 23 per cent increase in the number of clients which with fixed resources meant an increase in cover – but a reduction in intensity – of the service (Table 10.1).

In 1982 nearly 13 per cent of the elderly population was covered by the

Table 10.1 Home help service provision, 1979 and 1982

			Nature	
	Extent	Level	Cover	Intensity
1979	12.4	497	105	4.7
1982	12.4	497	129	3.9

service (excluding meals-on-wheels) which was a considerable achievement for Rotherham MDC. What is more, there was evidence to suggest that the service was sharply focused upon those who needed it most. An examination of all households in the village (222) with persons aged between 70 and 79 years old inclusive showed that while the majority of such households (63 per cent) received no formal project related services, neither did they display serious levels of need. Only five per cent of those not using formal services were considered very disabled and only two per cent in very poor health. In comparison, 45 per cent of home help clients of the same age were rated as very disabled, and 18 per cent in poorest health. Those who were not receiving the home help service, but were receiving other project services, principally from wardens, were in between the two.

For those clients receiving a home help, the service was still pretty much the same as it had been in 1979, although there had been a marginal reduction in their visits and hours. The average number of problems of and tasks done for clients had remained the same. The only significant change in response was a reduction in those receiving simple nursing care – from seven per cent in 1979 to four per cent in 1982, and a 21 per cent increase in those receiving 'warmth' related tasks. This reflected an increase in those receiving the daily service, who accounted for 33 per cent of clients and 72 per cent of visits in 1979, but 39 per cent of clients and 77 per cent of visits in 1982.

The principal carer study gave us further insight into the relationship between home help allocation and informal care. Between 1980 and 1982 these carers (35 in each year) had increased their commitment in terms of hours given to home help clients by 12 per cent over the period, with all the increase coming from friends and neighbours. As the intensity of the home help service had fallen by 17 per cent over the same period, so this was compensated for by a similar increase in care by friends and neighbours. Given our earlier observations about the relationships between visits made by home helps and carers, it is more than likely that caring by friends and neighbours was increased in response to a reduction in service by the home helps, rather than a rational response on the part of the latter to an increase in informal care. Arbitrary reductions in formal service provision run a grave risk of exploiting informal care in the short term, and destroying it completely by overburdening carers in the long term. Fortunately, in Dinnington informal caring resources were considerable, and the reduction in the home help service (from a high level) was marginal. Once again we are left with the impression of an extensive and efficiently allocated system of home help care working in parallel but not necessarily in contact with an extensive informal caring system.

When we summarize our knowledge about the home help service at the end of 1982, we can see the similarity to the 1979 position outlined at the end of Chapter 6 which indicates how little change there has been.

1. It was extensive. The level of provision was one of the most generous in the country.
2. It was efficiently allocated in that those most in need received the service. There was very little unmet need in the community. Also, looking primarily at the level of disability of those receiving the service, particularly disabilities affecting those activities (warmth) which the daily service provides, it was efficiently allocated between those receiving different levels of service.
3. Demand upon the service was met almost entirely within the service's own resources. Little use was made of other resources at the initial stage of demand (referral), nor was there evidence to suggest any wider use of resources (via contacts) for existing clients.
4. The overwhelming impression is of an extensive, efficient service which runs in parallel to, but not necessarily in contact with, other formal and informal carers.
5. Little if any progress had been made in thinking about and developing a home help system which was part of a much wider integrated health and welfare service, which itself worked very closely with, and sustained, voluntary and informal care.
6. The planning and organization of the service fitted that aspect of community practice which we have labelled 'outside the community'. This is typified by large-scale organization, sometimes physically remote from the community it serves, delivering care on a one-to-one basis, with resources being found almost entirely within the same department.
7. Some individual home helps did appear to work more closely with the community. They were in frequent contact with a range of workers and family, friends and neighbours, often giving levels of care well beyond that stipulated in their contracts. Even so, the principal focus remained the home help service itself. Only two home helps re-

sponded to a question about the main ideas of the project in terms of working with or involving the community. Nine of them did not know what the project was about!

None of the principal objectives of the project had been met by the end of 1982. There was no increase in contacts and co-operation between the home help service and other formal and informal carers, nor was there any evidence that people were presenting problems sooner (generally meaning at a less severe stage). The home helps had not been drawn in to the complex web of care that was being woven by the social workers, district nurses, the housing assistant and some wardens. Consequently they did not produce more referrals for these agencies, as had been expected. Nor was there any specific change in the perceptions of users or carers *vis- à-vis* the home help service.

One really must question whether the project approach – that is, the emphasis upon integrated formal and informal care making full use of community-wide resources – had anything to contribute to the home help service, particularly when the level of service was so high in the first place. This was neatly summed up by the assistant organizer when, early in 1983, she expressed her feelings about the project by saying that 'apart from being able to talk over cases with [the social worker] there did not seem to be any great savings'. Yet it was only a month later that the nursing sister in the village said in connection with a patient and another of the nurses:

> This home help had previously been thought to be just a cleaner rather than a carer, but has really taken over the patient and is, for instance, taking her to the toilet straightaway which is helping to keep her continent.

Furthermore, the home help noticed that the patient tended to be incontinent on Tuesdays and Fridays which were the days on which she went to day care. She mentioned this to the district nurse who was going to ask day care what they were doing. The district nurse reported that her continuing contact with the home help helped the latter to feel 'that she had the right to see to the toileting'.

Contacts between the home helps and the district nurse had been helped enormously by the increasing number of home helps who were going into the project office on Fridays, which was increasingly the case during the early part of 1983. Whereas in the first six months of 1982, a log book of visitors to the project office had recorded 55 separate visits by home helps, just over two a week, during the same period of 1983, visits doubled to 110, an average of 4.2 each week.

As there was variation from one week to the next in the number of home helps calling into the project office it was possible for several home helps, the district nurse, the social workers, housing assistant, assistant organizer and some wardens to be crowded into the project office over Friday lunchtime, discussing this or that client.

So three-and-a-half years after the beginning of the project, part of the original concept of drawing in the home helps to participate in an integrated package of care for the elderly was beginning to emerge. Unfortunately, later that year the assistant organizer moved to another area and was replaced by a full-time assistant organizer who had responsibility not only for Dinnington, but for neighbouring villages as well. The day on which home helps were asked to call in to the project office was switched to Wednesday rather than Friday (when they could also hand in their time sheets), and the whole momentum that had been built up dissipated, as it were, overnight. It took a year before home helps were coming in on the Wednesday in similar numbers.

The only difference with respect to the home help service, as the project entered 1984 (its fifth year), was that the home help organizer and the assistant responsible for Dinnington were attending the six-weekly meetings with other workers and the university team. At least channels were open to learn from the missed opportunities and mistakes of the previous four years.

The housing assistant

There were three innovatory elements in the Dinnington Project for Rotherham MDC. The first was the decentralization of social work to the village – locally-based social work. The second was the introduction of mechanisms to facilitate inter-authority and inter-departmental co-operation at fieldwork level in the day-to-day care of people in the village. The third was the appointment of a housing assistant with a brief to bring the work of the wardens closer to the mainstream of care for the elderly, with particular emphasis on reducing the isolation of wardens, a factor which had shown up in the 1978 pilot study.

The housing assistant took up her post alongside the two social workers in January 1980. She had been employed previously with housing in a welfare capacity. The pre-project specification of the post concerned itself with general comments about working with the wardens and developing the care of the elderly in the village. For example: 'The housing assistant would establish and develop co-operation between wardens and other fieldworkers in such a way that the wardens' extensive knowledge of community needs and resources could be utilised' (Bayley *et al.* 1981, p. 24). This was easier said than done. During much of the first year there was uncertainty about the way the post should develop. In practice the housing assistant was doing numerous small housing-related tasks. At a meeting in March 1980 she said that 'my position is odd; neither one thing nor the other'. In May 1980 the vagueness about her role led to an attempt by the district housing manager to define the responsibilities of the housing assistant more precisely. Four aspects of the job were identified:

(a) visit all new tenants in bungalows for the elderly, together with those who have refused offers;
(b) work with the 'possible homeless';
(c) work on rent arrears – but attempting to involve the 'social aspect';
(d) work with wardens.

As the year passed, the first and the last were effectively the major elements in her work. In the summer of 1980 her three cases were primarily housing-related cases and by September 1980 she was still arguing that '60 per cent of my time is housing; not really doing much within the project at all'. She was still practising at Stage One of the model of practice, that is 'outside the community'. She saw the project as something separate and different. As we have seen, some workers did not go beyond this stage. Others passed to the transitional stage, 'alongside the community', which is characterized by learning about others involved with the project and by a gradual understanding of the project approach, although still treating it as something 'extra'. By the end of the first year the housing assistant had reached this stage of development. When asked how the project had affected her own job, she replied that it gave her 'a different slant on things. Now I liaise with other authorities to solve more problems at the beginning. I have a more broadened outlook on clients' needs – not just a pure housing approach now.'

In part this was a result of the initial transfer of some social work cases with the elderly. It had been agreed earlier in 1980 that the housing assistant would take over some of the social workers' elderly clients whose need was primarily a watching brief. Otherwise such cases would have been passed back to the area office and placed on the Central Index on Request. In theory this was concerned with elderly people who needed regular visiting once every six to 12 months. In practice, because of demand, routine visiting was rarely carried out. We must stress, therefore, that transfer of these cases did not in any way affect social work practice by, for example, reducing the number of elderly clients on the social workers' caseloads.

By the summer of 1981 the housing assistant was monitoring 18 elderly cases, visiting on average every two to three weeks, although this varied from visiting some clients weekly to others every five or six weeks. At that stage, problems with bureaucratic procedures inhibited the development of more effective monitoring of the elderly. Quite frequently the clients whom the housing assistant monitored needed aids, adaptations and short-term residential care. Social services, however, insisted that dealing with these matters was the responsibility of a social worker (or social work assistant). It was necessary, therefore, for the housing assistant to take one of the social workers around to meet her clients so that they could then process the necesssary application. Yet it was also at this time that the housing assistant became concerned that she was effectively being transformed into a pseudo social work assistant, carrying a similar caseload but without the same salary. This led to a tense working relationship in the project office during the latter part of 1981.

By early 1982 the housing assistant was involved with a widening range of services. One important part of this service was dealing with the broad range of demand which was being placed upon the local project office at that time. We have already discussed the nature and response to this demand, but briefly the housing assistant was responsible for dealing with an average of eight of the referrals which came to the project office each week. Most of these referrals were from people calling into the office, and were concerned with aids and adaptations for the elderly, and with general financial problems.

Another demand placed upon the housing assistant's time was the increasing use of the local project office by other statutory workers and volunteers. This use was entirely consistent with the overall intention of the project of developing an integrated health and welfare service for the community. During 1982, wardens and home helps were to make 464 visits into the project office. Other statutory workers were to make a further 569 visits during the year; thus on average there were 20 visits to the office from statutory workers each week. To put this figure into the context of the social work area office which served 56 000 people, the level of visits to that office from other statutory workers would average around 32 visits each day. Counting all visits to the local office, from clients, volunteers, workers and carers, the project office staff had to deal with an average of 43 visits each week – the area office equivalent would be 69 visits each day. In reality this would not happen to the area office; it was too remote from the communities it served. However, it did happen in Dinnington and the housing assistant was committing a considerable part of her time to these liaison activities.

Another aspect of her work was an increasing role in the letting of bungalows. This had immediate benefits for the project as a whole when a new set of aged person's dwellings were opened in the centre of the village. The housing assistant dealt with all lettings for these dwellings and so the new tenants were therefore known to and knew about the project office.

By the summer of 1982 the housing assistant was monitoring 19 cases, of whom eight (42 per cent) had some physical disability, seven were socially isolated (37 per cent), and seven had problems with finance (37 per cent). She made checking visits and provided information and advice to these clients, but she was also making an average of four contacts to other people or agencies about each of her cases. These contacts were primarily with the wardens, with whom she shared most clients, the home help service and with relatives living outside the household. This reflects the central development of the role of the housing assistant – the co-ordination of packages of care for the elderly. The development of this aspect of her role is best illustrated by reference to case studies, two of which are detailed below:

Case 1
In the summer of 1979 Mrs J, an 81-year-old widow, had been living in sheltered accommodation for two years. She was crippled by arthritis. The warden visited twice daily, not only to check on Mrs J but also to fetch her shopping and collect her pension and prescriptions. The warden had not made contact with anyone on Mrs J's behalf in the three months prior to our study. By the summer of 1980 the warden had increased her visits to three times a day and had also made contact with the general practitioner, the home help organizer and a sister living outside the household. The sister was caring for Mrs J at that time but the pressures were also increasing upon the resident warden.

This was confirmed the following summer by the fact that Mrs J was receiving 14 visits each week from the home help service, as well as more than two daily visits from the warden. Besides housework, the home helps had taken over the task of shopping which the warden had done previously, and also were cooking lunch five days each week.

There was now little informal care for Mrs J, as the sister had withdrawn. The warden was, therefore, still under considerable strain. She was making supper every night and putting Mrs J to bed. She was also making dinner and tea for Mrs J at weekends. The warden was particularly concerned because Mrs J expected this service as of right, and grumbled if the warden was late. Because the warden had several poorly people on her scheme at that time, it was clear that the situation could not continue for much longer.

The housing assistant visited Mrs J to explain that it was not the warden's job to provide 24-hour care for any one resident. She then tried to contact Mrs J's sister who had earlier given up responsibility for her care. The sister subsequently called into the project office where she explained that she had felt unable to cope with the situation, but that, given the support of the statutory and voluntary services, would be prepared to play her part in looking after Mrs J. The housing assistant then called a meeting at Mrs J's home (with her permission), attended by the sister and her daughter, the warden and her relief, the home help, the district nurse, a volunteer and the housing assistant herself. After a lengthy discussion a package of care was made for Mrs J which relieved the warden of her main burden while allowing Mrs J to stay in her own home in the community. On weekdays the home help would make two calls and see to Mrs J's three meals. At weekends the home help would make a morning fire call and see to breakfast, while a volunteer prepared lunch and tea. The warden would make sure she was safely locked in at night. Her laundry was to be done by her sister. Her niece agreed to bath her once a fortnight. The sister would call when she could for social visits.

This case study illustrates two crucial aspects of the relationship between formal and informal care. It is a classic example of informal care 'burn out' and as such represents a failure of the workers involved to support the sister sooner (although this occurred early in the project). Failure to provide this support necessitated a dramatic increase in formal support when Mrs J's sister withdrew. Nevertheless it also shows what can be done by joint planning at the local level, and how a little extra care (the volunteer at the weekend) can mean the difference between a person staying in the community, or being transferred to an institution.

Case 2

Mrs L, a 90-year-old widow living alone in a National Coal Board property, was already receiving daily visits from both the visiting warden and home help in the summer of 1979. In 1980 when we first interviewed her we found out that she had a friend who visited her five times each week to do her shopping and laundry, as well as taking her out to the 'club'. When we interviewed the friend as a principal carer we found that she spent two to three hours each day with Mrs L; however, there was considerable conflict between the friend and her husband over her caring role.

Other than an increase from seven to nine visits each week from the home help, Mrs L's situation and help remained the same throughout 1981. By mid-1982 Mrs L's condition was deteriorating with suspected cancer of the liver. The district nurse was visiting weekly to assist Mrs L with bathing, and to carry out various tests. Shortly afterwards, Mrs L went into hospital for a seven-month stay.

It was late in 1983 when the visiting warden approached the housing assistant over Mrs L's condition. When she had been discharged from hospital a VOLTAGE member had arranged to be at Mrs L's home to make the fire, air the house and generally help Mrs L to settle in. However, although Mrs L was mobile, continent and relatively independent, she had periods of disorientation worsened by deafness and partial sight.

A meeting was called to discuss the situation of Mrs L and to establish responsibility for the provision of care and support and to highlight any gaps in that support. It was generally agreed at the meeting that the circumstances of Mrs L's discharge from hospital were less than satisfactory but, as she was medically fit, she could not be detained in hospital. She was currently receiving a fire call with breakfast every day from the home help service, as well as home helps providing a lunch call on Monday, cleaning and lunch on Tuesday, lunch on Wednesday: meals-on-wheels came on Thursday and Friday, and the home helps called again on Friday for a shopping and tea call, and a late-morning lunch call on Saturday and Sunday.

In addition to the warden's daily call, after discharge from hospital the warden had been travelling one-and-a-half miles (when she was not on duty) to make an evening check on Mrs L. The district nurse also visited daily.

It was agreed by all those present at the meeting that care for Mrs L during the day was adequate. The problem was the provision from teatime to the following morning. A friend agreed to call in each evening to check that Mrs L was all right and this comparatively simple arrangement made the package for Mrs L viable.

The development by the housing assistant of this care management role had clearly been of benefit to many people in the community, elderly clients or their informal networks. By mid-1983 a triple role had been identified for the housing assistant.

(a) monitoring elderly cases and providing a range of services, from benefits advice to co-ordinating packages of care;
(b) letting of aged-persons' dwellings;
(c) work in the project office which included response to demand through the door, and liaison with workers, clients, volunteers and informal carers.

By the end of 1983 the district housing manager and the housing assistant were discussing the possibility of extending her work into the area of rent arrears, particularly those tenants who had just fallen into arrears, that is with four weeks' arrears or less. Thus three out of the original four points put forward in May 1980 (excluding homelessness) were either operational or at an advanced planning stage. In many respects the housing assistant was coming full circle with her work in relation to the project and she was once again putting more emphasis upon traditional housing matters. The crucial difference was that she had passed to Stage Three of the development of community practice, working 'within the community'. As part of an integrated health and welfare team she was in a position to approach traditional housing matters with a community-wide perspective. The resources that she would bring to any problem were not just those of the housing department, but of other services, of volunteers, and of informal care. This was possible because of the development of an integrated approach and the build-up of a considerable body of knowledge about the community and about informal networks within the community.

The warden service

Residential wardens

One thing we learned in our examination of informal care in Chapter 4 was the variation in both clients and the patterns of care which they received. For example, we argued that it was quite wrong to talk of the elderly as though they were a homogeneous group. Not only can the 'elderly' span 40 years of life, but also they range from those who are fit and healthy and taking a leading role in the community or their work, to those who are seriously ill and bedfast. Even when we focus down to a very small group of people, all of whom lived in sheltered accommodation, we must be wary of falling into the same trap. Within this small group of people we found those who were (relatively) well and those who were very ill. We found those who received considerable informal support and those who received very little. Two case studies reflect the broad spectrum of clients to be found in sheltered accommodation.

Case 1. When we first visited Mrs M, a 77-year-old widow, she had been living in sheltered accommodation for six years. She was housebound and crippled with arthritis. Her mobility within the house was facilitated by both wheelchair and walking sticks. She found it virtually impossible to do many personal and household tasks. The resident warden visited daily and fetched Mrs M's pension, and occasionally her shopping. A home help called five times each week to do housework, make the fire and to cook meals. Little contact was made with other services, although a year previously a social work assistant had assessed Mrs M. As a result of this a new shower unit was being considered at the time of our first interview in 1980, as Mrs M could no longer use the bath.

In addition to the care being given by the statutory services, Mrs M's daughter called in daily. She helped her mother and cooked her breakfast, cleaned the house and did her shopping. Another daughter, living in the Rotherham area, called two or three times a month for a chat. Mrs M was quite satisfied with her care, but at the time of the interview was anxious to get her shower fitted. There was clearly good liaison between her daughter and the statutory workers. We left Mrs M in 1980 with the warden involved in just routine visits and occasional shopping.

When we visited Mrs M in 1981 there were only marginal changers to her condition and to her care. The pattern of care had remained the same, although her other daughter was now calling in weekly to do the laundry.

Mrs M was beginning to have trouble with her digestion and was consequently on a liquid diet. However, the daughter who visited daily was taking her mother three days a week to the centre attached to the sheltered accommodation scheme.

By 1982 the wardens were visiting twice daily, collecting prescriptions, and now making the fire. The home help visited as before – five times a week for housework and to make the fire. The aids and adaptations officer from the social services department was once again involved, although we had heard nothing of the shower since that first interview. Her daughter was now visiting 17 times each week, giving essentially the same range of care as before. The warden had, however, arranged for the voluntary group VOLTAGE to take Mrs M out.

When we examined the extent of Mrs M's care in the pilot to the Diary Study earlier in 1982, we found that she was receiving an average of eight visits each day. The warden was at that time visiting daily, the home help each weekday except Wednesday, which was the daughter's day off from work. The main care was being shared by the daughter and the home help. We can perhaps best illustrate the package of care given to Mrs M by looking at one typical day, Tuesday 16 March 1982:

8.25 –8.45	Daughter: breakfast, make bed, help dress
8.30 –9.00	Home help: make fire
10.00 –10.10	Warden: check
11.25 –12.55	Home help: cleaning, lunch, fire
15.00 –15.05	Warden: check
17.45 –18.30	Daughter: main meal, pay bills, wash up dishes
18.55 –19.05	Daughter: take mother to centre
21.45 –22.00	Daughter: return mother from centre, make drink, make fire, help undress

Approximately three-and-a-half hours care was given to Mrs M in the course of the day. During the week of the Diary Study, 25 hours of care were recorded.

In contrast to some of the wardens' fitter clients, Mrs M needed care continually. This case showed a wide response to Mrs M's need with the result that the warden's role was limited to checking Mrs M, with occasional shopping, in support of the general care package.

Case 2 In 1980, 85-year-old Mrs N had been living in sheltered accommodation for twelve years. Like Mrs M she was receiving a daily visit from the warden, and she also received daily visits from the home help. She had a heart condition, was housebound, bored, lonely and depressed. Her feelings about her situation might be summed up by her comment 'I wish the Lord would take me'.

In sharp contrast to Mrs M, Mrs N had no informal care. At this time the home help was involved with general housework, making the fire, cooking and shopping. The warden, other than the routine checking visit, fetched Mrs N's pension and prescriptions.

In early 1982 Mrs N was referred to the district nurse by the general practitioner. She had pressure sores on her buttocks and was having trouble with bedwetting. The nursing sister visited to deal with these matters and to carry out various tests. She also referred Mrs N to the aids and adaptations officer at the social services department and to VOLT-AGE, as well as contacting Mrs N's home help. In the meantime the general practitioner had contacted the warden, asking her if she would apply cream to Mrs N, a task which the warden agreed to do.

By the summer of 1982 the warden and the home help were still visiting daily, and Mrs N had received two visits during the previous month from one of the social workers at the project office. The home help service was as before, but the warden was also cooking Mrs N's weekend meals. The social worker was assessing Mrs N for short-term admission to a local authority old people's home, but had also contacted VOLTAGE. On the surface nothing appeared to have happened as a result of the district nurse's earlier contact to the voluntary group, but the reality of the situation was that Mrs N simply did not want 'strangers' around her.

During the two-week period of our diary study Mrs N was receiving approximately two hours' care each weekday from the home help, but only a fire and breakfast call at the weekend. The task of caring for Mrs N was shared between the home help and the warden, who, as we have seen, prepared meals at the weekend. Relatives from the area visited once during the two-week period, for three-quarters of an hour, to chat and chop wood for the fire.

In this case we found that the warden's role was more extensive. She was involved for a period in simple nursing care, and later with providing meals at the weekend. Although contact had been made to a voluntary group, alternative community resources had not been mobilized to share in Mrs N's care as she continually refused the help. All the responsibilities fell upon the formal services. Later in that year Mrs N was to become severely ill and, for a short time before she was admitted to hospital, the specialist voluntary group RALLY cared for her in her own home. Mrs N died in hospital.

These two cases illustrate some of the clients cared for by the wardens of sheltered accommodation. Their responsibilities covered:

(a) those clients who were relatively well and who, apart from brief periods of temporary incapacity, placed little demand upon the warden;

(b) those clients who were ill and in need of considerable care, but due to an extensive package of care from both formal and informal sources, still required little input from the warden;

(c) other clients, who were equally ill but lacking in informal care, and required considerable care from the formal services. Here the warden could be involved heavily in day-to-day care, not only domestic, but also simple nursing care.

The three full-time wardens (not their reliefs) covering the sheltered housing schemes in the village had always had an affinity with old people, even before their present work. Two of the wardens had been reliefs for many years, one of whom used to fill in voluntarily for a warden friend before that. When asked in our worker study how they would describe their job to someone who knew nothing about the warden services, one warden replied: 'Rather demanding, rather trying, rather amusing, rather frustrating'.

The two wardens of the older units (without a centre) stressed the satisfaction gained from helping old people. The warden of the newer unit with a community centre attached related to us what she had done the previous day:

9.30	–	Begin visiting 28 people
	–	put eye drops in for two people
	–	put papers down for fireplace to be taken out
	–	picked up bin lid with ashes for another that couldn't bend
	–	two people told me of prescriptions needed so later phoned in and will collect today
11.50	–	Back to luncheon club
	–	Dish out meals for about 20 (brought by meals-on-wheels)
	–	took two meals out to people
14.00 p.m.	–	Cleaned up centre
16.00 p.m.	–	Break
18.00 p.m.	–	Do more eye drops. Look in on one client who is ill.

All three wardens listed a range of tasks that they did which they considered extra to their duties. These would include major shopping and housework. They also involved their husbands, particularly in activities such as mending electrical appliances and putting up curtain rails. The importance of the support of the warden's husband was also mentioned by Duncan Boldy (1976) in his study of the wardens of grouped dwellings. At the extreme of additional care, one of the Dinnington wardens night-sat for a dying client for almost five weeks.

During the four weeks that we examined the caseload of the resident wardens, numbers in the three units remained fairly constant at round 80 households. This would be expected with only slight variation due to the normal lettings process. The largest group of tenants throughout the four years were those aged 75 years and over who lived alone. They consistently averaged about half the total households living in sheltered accommodation. Elderly couples accounted for approximately a quarter of tenants, and those aged 60–74 who lived alone for about a further 15 per cent.

We saw in our case studies how different a visit from the warden may be. It could be a simple check, bringing the shopping, cooking a meal, or nursing. Over the four years the average level of visits made by the wardens fluctuated, rising from 10.6 each week in 1979 (before the project started) to 12.9 in 1980, and falling through 10.4 in 1981 to 9.1 visits each week in 1982. This reflected the pattern of visits from all project services, but as the wardens' visits dominated this pattern then most of the overall change was due to the fluctuation in visiting by the wardens. Visits made by the wardens, as a proportion of the visits made by all the services, fell from 86 per cent in 1979 to 81 per cent in 1982.

An assessment of their clients' needs and problems showed that in 1979 the wardens considered one-third to be housebound, and that this remained constant throughout the four years. Other key indicators of need, such as illness and disability, fluctuated throughout the period, as did the number of those who were considered to be depressed and lonely. The only trend to appear throughout the four-year period was a fall (from 29 per cent to 20 per cent) in those who had difficulties with filling in forms.

This lack of clear trends, particularly lack of evidence of increasing levels of disability and ill health, runs contrary to much of the recent comment about clients in sheltered accommodation (for example Plank 1977), although not to its original purpose. Not only did we fail to find any signs that clients were becoming more dependent, but over the four years there was a reduction in the response made by the warden. While there was some fluctuation during the period, the number of extra tasks done by the warden, shopping, collecting, housework and nursing had fallen. This happened across all groups. Simple nursing duties fell, for example, from 35 per cent of clients in 1979 to four per cent in 1982. However, the level in 1979 was high and in part reflected the fact that the resident wardens had some very ill people under their care at that time. Whether or not other factors have intervened to help reduce the wardens' response (project-initiated or otherwise) remains to be seen. Whatever the reason, by 1982 the wardens were providing a basic checking and supervision service with only the collection of prescriptions as a noticeable additional task. Thus the type of care being given to Mrs N in 1982 was an exception to the warden's normal pattern of work.

Contacts made on behalf of the clients with other agencies also fluctuated over the four years. Wardens were asked whom they had contacted during the previous three months. The general practitioner was contacted most frequently (approximately 50 per cent of cases). with relatives out of the house (approximately 40 per cent of cases) a close second. No trends can be observed over the whole period, but contrasting 1979 with 1982 shows increases in contacts to social workers (up 75 per cent), home helps (63 per cent) and friends and neighbours (45 per cent).

There were equally dramatic falls in contacts to the chiropodist (down 75 per cent), the aids and adaptations officer (50 per cent), and to agencies like the DHSS (57 per cent). However the numbers involved were relatively low, and we think substitution occurred. For example, contacts made previously to the aids and adaptations officer and the DHSS were made instead to the social workers in the local project office. The average number of contacts made for each client changed little (two in 1979 to 2.1 in 1982), which suggests that substitution did take place.

It is clear that one important factor was the maintenance of the balance between the fitter and frailer tenants. In the Metropolitan District of Rotherham this was largely due to their lettings policy. Sheltered accommodation in Dinnington was part of the district's housing stock. It was not reserved for local people. The housing department operated a threefold waiting list system for its aged persons' dwellings, a part of which is sheltered accommodation. Thus in the first instance sheltered accommodation was treated no differently to other aged persons' dwellings which did not have a resident warden. The threefold waiting list consisted of those who were over 80 years old, those with medical reasons for rehousing, and a list which was ordered by date of application. When any aged persons's dwelling became vacant, applicants were taken off the top of one of these lists in rotation. While the medical list was the shortest, it meant that a mix of dependency levels was likely to be maintained in the medium term. It was possible, due to the vagaries of supply and demand, for consecutive lettings to sheltered accommodation to come from the medical list, but this was unlikely to be sustained. So the balance of fit and frail elderly was maintained. What happened to those who were ill who were given other accommodation? They were likely to be covered by the visiting warden service, which facilitated this type of lettings policy.

Peripatetic wardens
The power to employ peripatetic or visiting wardens was granted under the 1968 Health Services and Public Health Act. The village was served by four visiting wardens who worked three hours, six days a week, with, in theory, a full weekend off every six weeks, although some choose to have other days off. The seventh day was covered by a relief visiting warden. In addition a mobile warden, who visited outlying villages by car, visited one or two households at the edge of the village. The four current

visiting wardens had 28 years' service between them. Three of them were relief wardens before that and the fourth came from the meals-on-meals service.

Each warden had her own area, their job being primarily to check old people, not necessarily council tenants, living in their own homes. The wardens cared for about 25 clients on their caseload, but this varied over time. It is obvious that, as with the resident wardens, so the visiting wardens must have their mix of fit and frail clients, otherwise their work would become too great a burden. Here are two further case studies to illustrate the visiting warden's work.

Case 1. When we first interviewed Miss O in 1980 she had been living at the same address for 60 years. She was 74 years old and lived alone in a private rented unfurnished property. She was healthy and active, rising at 6.30 a.m. each morning to make the fire and her breakfast. She had several brothers and sisters living in the village with whom she had frequent contact, both in her own home and in their homes. During the week she would also visit a friend first thing in the morning to help send her boy off to school. The warden visited Miss O each morning purely to check if she was well. The warden was the only formal service with whom Miss O had contact, and thought of her as having no needs/problems and requiring no more than checking each day. It was a purely preventive service. Miss O was active and caring for others in the village.

In 1981 Miss O's condition remained unchanged; she was, however, visiting a neighbour frequently enough to be interviewed by us both as a user (of the warden service) and as a principal carer. She was committing approximately 45 minutes every day to caring for a neighbour and a brother who lived about ten minutes' walk away. Once, when her neighbour had gone out without telling anyone, the warden had immediately come back to Miss O to find out whether or not she (the neighbour) was ill, or had gone out for the day. The relationship between Miss O and the warden was obviously very good – 'I can discuss anything with her'.

By 1982 Miss O was still shopping for her brother, and also cooking for a sister, visiting one or another of her brothers or sisters on average daily, and receiving on average twice-daily visits from them. She had, however, reduced her commitment to her neighbour whom she now only visited occasionally. The neighbour had apparently suffered from a nervous breakdown and was receiving a fortnightly visit from the home help.

When we examined the range of visits Miss O received during a week in July 1982, other than the warden briefly calling in every morning, the pattern of visits was that one or more of her brothers and sisters called to spend several hours with her during the late afternoon and evening. Tasks such as cooking dinner would be shared, and the evening would often end with a game of scrabble. The visits from the warden, first thing in the morning, were isolated from informal care which came later in the day.

It is clear that this case study not only represents that element of a visiting warden's caseload which is purely preventive, but also an illustration of how relationships with clients can also help to monitor and care for others. The fact that Miss O had a good relationship with the warden enabled the warden to use Miss O (a principal carer) as a vital contact when something was amiss on her rounds. It was this knowledge of people and their informal networks that was seen as so important in the project's pilot study. If, it was argued, links could be established with this knowledge of and these relationships with people, then clients would be able to receive a quicker response from a wider range of services should anything go amiss.

Case 2 In 1979 Mrs P, an 82-year-old widow, was receiving daily visits from both the visiting warden and the home help. She was housebound but none of her statutory workers considered her to be disabled or ill. The wardens were visiting and collecting prescriptions, the home helps (one during the week, another at weekends) were cleaning the house, making the fire and doing the shopping.

When we interviewed Mrs P in 1980 the level of formal care was the same as the year before. Informal care was largely absent. A son lived in Sheffield, 15 miles away, and visited once a month to do the garden and occasional decorating. A daughter, who lived locally, did not call at all as she had fallen out with her brother some years previously. Mrs P listed only one friend in a neighbouring village whom she saw twice-monthly for a chat. She put her condition down to 'just old age' and was largely satisfied with her care, although she said that she could do with 'a bit more company'. This situation remained the same throughout 1981.

In early 1982 Mrs P fell ill. The home help had called early one Sunday morning and Mrs P had asked her to call on the warden and asked her to visit immediately. The warden responded, contacting the general practitioner and Mrs P's son in Sheffield. The general practitioner subsequently contacted the district nurse who visited in the week. In the meantime the home help had contacted the home help organizer as Mrs P had asked for extra help in the morning to get breakfast, and a Thursday lunch call. A neighbour was temporarily providing Mrs P with lunch on the other days.

By the summer of 1982 the situation had reverted to the normal pattern of service delivery. The care was given predominantly by the home help service with a daily checking visit by the warden. Significantly Mrs P's concern was for more company, yet apparently she was not known to the project office who could easily have arranged for a volunteer to make social visits.

During the four years that we evaluated the caseload of the visiting wardens the number of clients varied very little, from 110 in 1979 to 112 in 1982. Unlike the resident wardens, visits from peripatetic wardens remained fairly constant throughout the period, averaging 6.3 visits each week in 1979, 6.8 in 1980, 6.4 in 1981 and 6.8 in 1982. This variation was easily accounted for by the natural change in demand in any fortnight period during the summer holidays. Total visits to the warden's clients from statutory services also remained constant, averaging 8.3 visits each week in both 1979 and 1982.

While the level of visits remained constant the needs and problems of clients, as assessed by the wardens, fluctuated considerably. There were no true trends (unidirectional movement over four years) but, despite fluctuations, certain changing characteristics were observed. The number of clients who were housebound rose from one-quarter to nearly two-fifths (38 per cent). There were similar increases in those who were disabled. Those whom the warden considered to be depressed more than doubled over the period (15 per cent to 38 per cent), but there was a fall from one-third to under one-quarter in those considered to be socially isolated.

There was a fluctuating response by the wardens matching the fluctuating needs of clients. There was a general increase in the emphasis upon checking and support. One clear trend that emerged, was that the proportion of clients receiving simple nursing care from the visiting wardens almost doubled over the period, from seven per cent to 13 per cent of clients. This contrasts sharply with the decline in that type of service given by the resident wardens.

As with the resident wardens, three-quarters of clients lived alone. It is quite noticeable that while the eldest group (alone, over 75) were more housebound and more disabled, it was the younger elderly group (alone, 60–74) who experienced the greatest increases in the levels of illness, of disability, and those considered to be housebound. The housebound within this younger elderly group increased more than fourfold over the period (five per cent to 22 per cent), those ill more than doubled (18 per cent to 41 per cent).

Checking and support received greater attention by the wardens in response to these increased needs of the alone 60–74 group, but otherwise there was no clear pattern of a change in response for that group or for any other. There was, however, some indication that the wardens were making more use of certain community resources over the period. Probably as a function of the increased levels of illness of their clients, visiting wardens increased their contacts to the general practitioner from just over one-third of cases in 1979 to over one-half of cases in 1982. Contacts to social workers, although at a low level in 1979 (one per cent of cases) rose sixfold over the period. There was a small drop in these contacts in 1982, but, as we have seen, a change-over of staff at the local project office early in 1982 and the subsequent temporary re-allocation of cases affected 1982 patterns of social work, including contacts to the project office. There was also a substantial increase in the number of contacts made to the home help organizer. This increase, from seven per cent to 19 per cent of cases, occurred in the final year, 1981-2. As the appointment of the assistant home help organizer to the local project office was delayed until summer 1981, it would seem that this change can be attributed to the presence of a locally-based organizer. The increase in contacts to the organizer was matched with a decrease in contacts to home helps.

A key section of the pre-project specfication of the housing assistant post read: 'The housing assistant would establish and develop co-operation between wardens and other field workers in such a way that the wardens' extensive knowledge of community needs and resources could be utilised.' How far was this achieved? On the face of it there was not much change. The resident wardens increased their contacts with social workers, home helps and friends and neighbours, but, on the other hand, contacts with the chiropodist, aids and adaptations and DHSS fell. Likewise, the visiting wardens increased their contacts with social workers but from a very low level indeed to a level which still seems low. There was also a substantial increase in contacts to the home help organizer. This seems a long way from meeting the original expectations about the relationship that would develop between the wardens and other workers.

In practice this only gives a small part of the total picture. Contacts between other workers and the wardens were far more extensive than this. As we have seen, the project office proved to be an invaluable meeting place for all kinds of workers including the wardens. During the six-month period beginning in January 1983, wardens were recorded as visiting the office on 196 occasions, an average of 1.5 visits each working day. This is probably an under-statement as the workers often forgot to make entries in the office day book, from which this information is drawn, when the office was very busy. It seems that these opportunities for contact did enable the other workers to benefit from the wardens' contacts and knowledge in just the way that had been hoped. The research team were only able to record occasional examples, but one such example was when a man rang the project office because he was having problems with his daughter. The mother had sent for 'Auntie Ethel', who turned out to be one of the wardens. The next day the warden concerned came into the project office to discuss it further with one of the social workers. As a result of this discussion the social worker decided that no further action was needed as she could be confident that if further problems arose, and her help was needed, the warden would contact her.

So although the caseload study data suggested only moderate progress, in practice this aim was substantially achieved. The discrepancy is probably due to the fact that the wardens may not have contacted the other workers so very often about particular clients, at least not in a way that they reckoned merited recording, but they had come to the project office and talked about all sorts of people. Maybe much of this could be dismissed as mere gossip, but one of the lessons to come out of the project was that, for the workers to be able to function effectively, they have to be in on the gossip networks. In this process the wardens played a most effective part.

A brief mention should be made at this point about the problems of co-ordinating the visits of home helps and wardens. Despite considerable efforts on the part of all concerned it proved impossible to make any really significant changes to the visiting patterns of home helps and wardens to ensure that they were spaced to give greater cover. Frequently both called in the morning and they often overlapped. The problem was a management one which will be referred to again.

Did the wardens show any greater sensitivity to the needs of their clients, for example their health, and were they more responsive to differing levels of informal support? The evidence here is confusing. The resident wardens' visits in 1982 did relate to the disability of their clients in a way they had not previously, but the tasks they did moved away from household-type chores to simply visiting and support. On the other hand, the clients of the peripatetic wardens, according to the wardens' perceptions, became more ill and more disabled over the period and the wardens appeared to have responded appropriately, for example the amount of simple nursing care increased. However, those aged 60–74 who lived alone became more dependent over the period and the visiting wardens did not change their visiting patterns to match this. This appears to reflect a certain rigidity in the peripatetic warden services which contracts sharply with the sensitive response of informal care to changed levels of need.

The most striking impact of the project on the wardens' work was the three VOLTAGE volunteers who helped in one of the sheltered housing schemes. In 1980 the resident warden here had been under considerable pressure and the assistance from volunteers made possible a reduction in the number of client visits she made. We should question whether the reduction in the visiting levels of the resident warden was entirely desirable. Did this really serve the best interests of the residents? On the other hand, the pressure on one warden in 1980 was excessive, resulting in work outside the normally expected terms of service. This raises the question of the support which the wardens receive themselves. The pilot study (Bayley and Parker 1978) had shown that both they and the home helps were isolated from other statutory workers. If the project was to achieve any positive outcome in relation to the warden service we would have expected the wardens to comment on increased support from other workers. When we interviewed the seven full-time wardens at the end of 1982, only one warden considered that the project had little effect on her work. Even she said that she could 'go round the corner and talk things over'. The other six wardens were very positive about the support the project gave them. There was no doubt that their sense of isolation had been removed. Most wardens expressed this in clear terms, for example: 'Before the Hut (project office) was there you were out on a limb. There was no one you could turn to if you needed moral support ... I think it's great,' or 'lots more co-operation and co-ordination ... old people benefiting ... take smaller problems than we used to ... you are more aware of different services and what can be done'.

However, two of the wardens tended to go to the social workers rather than the housing assistant. As the local office operated a policy of open access this was acceptable. It was in part due to the confusion in some wardens' minds as to the exact role and position of the housing assistant, which itself reflected the actual confusion surrounding her role in the early phase. Nevertheless, it was clear that the project had achieved its main objective as far as the wardens themselves were concerned, well illustrated by one of their comments: 'It's the best thing since sliced bread.'

Finally we should notice the vulnerability and exposed nature of the wardens' position with regard to informal care. The wardens often said that if you let them, the relatives would let you get on with the caring. It is often the wardens who have to hit the balance between what the family should be doing and what they should be doing themselves. If we are concerned with the way in which frontline workers like the wardens interact with family, friends and neighbours, it seems clear that they need active and sensitive support from their managers. There was no clear overall evidence of improved contact and liaison with family, friends and neighbours, though there were plenty of examples of it. In our examination of the work of the housing assistant we saw good examples of packages of care, including people from statutory, voluntary and informal sectors but this imaginative approach had not been communicated adequately to the wardens themselves. We underestimated how long it would take for the housing assistant herself to understand and put this approach into practice. It would probably need at least as long again for her to be able to help the wardens to adopt this approach. We think that greater support and training from management, especially the housing assistant, would be necessary to enable the warden service to reach its full potential.

The educational welfare office

The practice of the EWO did not change appreciably. We have seen already that he took part in the fortnightly fieldworkers' meetings and he played an important role in the summer schemes for children in the village. His contacts with the social workers over his cases did show an increase but the number of cases was so small (in 1981 he only had eight cases in the village – the same as in 1979) that it is hard to say anything definite. His work was also affected by a reduction in overall staff levels of EWOs, coupled with a sharp rise in truancy from the local schools. Given the potential for developing a community perspective it was a disappointment that externalities contrived to emphasize the 'school bobby' aspect of his work towards the latter stages of the project.

11   A Real Partnership?

Although we illustrated the nature and extent of informal care in Dinnington in Chapter 4, most of what we have learnt so far about the progress of the project has come from the formal services themselves. They have given us a mixed picture of the progress towards establishing a partnership in care in the community. Social workers, the nursing sister, the housing assistant and wardens have all been observed giving, or have reported themselves as giving, a significant improvement in the quality of service offered to patients and clients. As well as inter-agency co-operation and the development of a local team approach considerable emphasis was given to contacts with informal carers and the wider community. On the surface this seems a positive way to practice, but are contacts as such an indication of improvement and partnership in care? We need to look more closely at what happened, to satisfy ourselves that such contacts represent a positive step for all concerned. We must also look for evidence of a real partnership, of shared planning, as opposed to casual and merely routine contact. Finally, should we find evidence to show that there was a positive attempt to promote partnership with individual patients or clients and their networks, we need to ask whether there are any lessons to be learnt with respect to community-wide planning and intervention.

Our information in this chapter is mainly derived from two studies, one which looked at patients and clients of the various services (the user study); the other which looked at other main carers (the principal carer study). Respondents in each study took part in structured interviews.

The main evidence for improvement of services to clients has been the improved access to social services and the consequent increase in referrals. This has been sustained and suggests that people found it worthwhile calling on social service help. But is it possible to say more than this? Can we say that the users of the services were more satisfied with the new pattern? Unfortunately it is not possible to give a simple answer because the question itself is exceedingly complex.

Problems with measuring 'satisfaction'
We are dealing with a number of different services and different combinations of services which changed to varying degrees or hardly changed at all. We are not dealing with a closely controlled trial but with the interaction of a range of workers, and with the lives of several hundred

people in varying circumstances over several years. It is difficult to make generalizations about whether such a heterogeneous body of people was 'more satisfied' or not.

In addition the question of client satisfaction is a notoriously difficult area; for example, if clients express satisfaction with the service they are receiving, are they expressing satisfaction with that particular service (which may be very simple like the provision of a bath aid) or with the adequacy of that service to their overall needs? In our questionnaire we attempted to separate these two elements but whether it was really possible for them to be separated adequately in the clients' minds is another question.

Furthermore we have to recognize that the statutory services play only a very small part in most patients' lives. An old lady's sense of satisfaction is going to be far more affected by the recent death of her husband that it is by anything that is done by the health and welfare services. The effects of changes in the patient's network of family and friends or in their own health are likely to have a far more powerful effect than anything the statutory services do.

Another complication arises from our findings that the district nurse's caseload turned over quite rapidly. For example, nothing can be deduced from the fact that nursing care given by relatives average over nine visits each week to seven patients in 1980 and less than one visit each week to five patients in 1981, except that in 1981 it was a different group of patients and thus a different group of relations who visited less.

A further factor which must be considered is whether the research method was sensitive to picking up change in the quality of life. A cross-sectional method using the same questionnaire at yearly intervals for three years produced a great deal of valuable data about the nature of informal care in the village and how it related to statutory care, but it is doubtful whether it was sensitive enough to pick up the subtle changes which may be vital to assess whether a person's quality of life has changed. For this a biographical approach might have been more appropriate but it would certainly have been very time-consuming. Croft and Beresford's (1984) thoughtful essay on participatory research has some challenging things to say about the need to develop a research method which picks up the issues which are of central importance to the people in the area being served.

More fundamentally, we must ask whether it is necessarily a bad thing if, for example, the level of dissatisfaction does increase. It may indicate that the clients have acquired a better understanding of the standard of service they should be expecting and therefore are setting higher standards.

We should also mention some dissatisfaction on our part with our measures of satisfaction. This was an unfortunate consequence of the extreme pressure under which the questionnaires had to be prepared in order to 'catch' the situation before it had been altered by the project. Despite these reservations clues can be found which indicate whether, on balance, the service is better or not. But this will be a matter of judgement, not decisive proof. It is clients of social workers, together with their principal carers, who can offer us the best insights.

Views of social work clients

In the summer of 1980 we interviewed those people in the village who had been clients of social workers in summer 1979, or who approached social services in early 1980. We approached both those who were at that time either on the long-term caseload or had concluded their involvement with social workers. We repeated these sets of interviews in both 1981 and 1982.

Long-term clients

We were able to interview 15 clients who were on the long-term caseload in 1980, and 13 in 1982. The fact that three of these 1982 cases were elderly clients confirms the breakdown of traditional social work case patterns illustrated in the last chapter, and contrasts with the single elderly client on the long-term caseload in 1980. The information we gained from the study of social work clients in the caseload study complements that from the user study where respondents had seen a reduction in the level of visits by some 28 per cent as compared with 1980. This represents reducing the frequency of visiting from on average once every four weeks, to less often than once every five weeks. This would be partly due to infrequent visits made to the elderly clients.

Other important changes occurred in this long-term client group as a result of the presence of elderly clients. Needs, as defined by the social workers, had shifted to include 23 per cent with problems of physical disability – a category not identified in long-term clients in 1980. Long-term clients in 1982, who as a group were less likely to express any expectations of social work than their counterparts in 1980, shifted those expectations marginally in the area of financial and/or material help. There was a slight increase in dissatisfaction with their overall care (from 27 per cent in 1980 to 31 per cent in 1982) and more so with their care from the social worker (from 13 per cent in 1980 to 20 per cent in 1982) but once again the predominant characteristic of those that expressed any opinion about social work was that they were satisfied (80 per cent in 1982). However, it is important to note that there was an increase in the level of dissatisfaction expressed by long-term clients with social work 'within the community' as opposed to social work 'outside the community'.

We can illustrate the vagaries of 'satisfaction' by looking at three cases.

The Q Family was a lone-parent family who at the time of interview in the summer of 1982 had been on the social work caseload for nearly two-and-a-half years. The husband had been sent to prison in late 1981, leaving Mrs Q with two children under four. When asked why the social worker was involved, Mrs Q answered 'because my husband is in prison and has been a bad husband'. He had battered Mrs Q. The local health visitor, who was also caring for the client at the time of interview, had arranged for Mrs Q to go to a battered wives' hostel. Mrs Q was very happy with the care given by the health visitor – 'to get me into a refuge so quickly was really good'. Although she was 'satisfied' with the social worker, who had classified the family under 'family relationship problems', her hopes of the social work service were 'a nice three piece, to be honest'. Mrs Q considered herself to be both bored and lonely most of the time, even though she visited her mother and her grandmother daily. She listed no friends but considered the health visitor a friend – 'she's a friend now'.

Another satisfied customer was the R family. The 11-year-old boy of this family had been referred to social services in March 1981 because of delinquency. There were five children under 15 at that time, together with Mrs R, who was 33 years old, and their 36-year-old unemployed father. Three months later the 14-year-old boy was also referred to the department because of delinquency. In the summer of 1981 a locally-based social worker reported visiting the family some 15 times since that first referral. Family relationship problems had necessitated the mother, as in the last case, being given short-term refuge in a battered wives' hostel, and by the summer of 1981 the elder boy was in an assessment centre, while the younger boy and two of his younger siblings were shortly to become the subject of a juvenile liaison enquiry.

When we interviewed Mrs R in the summer of 1982 the elder boy was at a community school and the police had decided to take the younger one to court. During that twelve-month period, until the summer of 1982, the social worker had made nearly weekly visits to one or other member of the family (including visits to the detention centre, and so on) while the family had made almost fortnightly visits *into* the local office. Thirteen separate agencies had been contacted on behalf of the family while a wide range of social work skills and services had been utilized.

The family themselves were well supported by, and supportive of, their informal network. They made and received daily social visits to Mrs R's brother and mother, as well as making weekly visits to Mrs R's sister in Rotherham. Mrs R did the washing and cleaning for her brother whose wife had recently left him.

Mrs R's sole expectation of the social worker was to 'see if he could help [her] son to get straight'. That the social worker had also worked extensively with the family as a whole on a range of problems (but interestingly *not* with the extended network) was clearly something not expected. For example, the social worker had contacted specialist community health staff (sight problems), the adult literacy service, a specialist social worker, as well as a range of agencies connected with the delinquency problems. Mrs R was 'very satisfied' with her social worker and considered that she had as much 'say' in the service as she needed.

On the other hand, Mrs S was far from satisfied. A 59-year-old widow with two grown-up daughters (18 and 21 years old), Mrs S lived in a council bungalow adjoining a sheltered housing complex, and had the greatest difficulty in doing any personal or household task. Her 18-year-old daughter did the shopping, washing, ironing and cleaning, as well as helping Mrs S to bath. Other than her daughters she had no remaining relatives and only one local friend who lived up the street. This friend visited for social purposes about three times a week.

She was a long-term client of the social services department, which, until Mrs S's younger daughter left school, had also provided a home help service. From the summer of 1979 until the summer of 1981, Mrs S received visits every three or four weeks from a social worker. (It was a social work assistant until May 1980.) However, in the year prior to interview the locally-based social worker had made only three visits, although she had contacted the home help organizer, specialist social worker, DHSS offices and most significantly, Mrs S's friend during that period.

Mrs S had thought that the social worker was involved through her ill health and that she would give her advice on 'what to do on things I don't agree with the girls on'. However, she was clearly displeased at the reduction in social work visits and told our interviewer that the social worker 'says he's not going to come any more'. What Mrs S wanted was quite simple – 'only help; that's all, practical help'. It is important to note that Mrs S did not perceive any contact between the social worker and her friend. The social worker had contacted the friend as a means of secondary monitoring as the latter visited several times a week and could easily contact the social worker if something was amiss.

Of considerable significance is that, whereas in 1980 one in five of these long-term clients reported contact between their social worker and informal networks, in 1982 *none* of these clients reported such contacts. The fact that in this case there was contact, unknown to the client, raises major questions about the ethics of working with informal networks. For Mrs S, the lack of tangible practical help from the social worker was sufficient to make her 'dissatisfied' with the service.

Ex-clients
Although all these cases illustrate certain differences between the service

given to long-term clients under Stages One and Three of our model, nowhere are those changes, from the client's perspective, so dramatic as with those people who had been clients in 1981 but were no longer so in the summer of 1982.

Quite simply, while the social worker's classification of clients' needs and problems had remained more or less the same as in 1980, for this ex-client group, the clients' own expectations of the service had shifted sharply towards financial and material needs, and, as we shall show, almost as a direct consequence of this, dissatisfaction with the social work service for this group had more than doubled, from 18 per cent in 1980 to 40 per cent in 1982.

Mrs T is an illustration of a client dissatisfied with her social worker. Mrs T was an 80-year-old living with her 59-year-old daughter, also a widow. Mrs T suffered from senile dementia and was unable to perform any personal or household task without aid. She relied entirely on her daughter for her personal hygiene. Several other daughters who lived nearby visited daily for social purposes. A neighbour also visited daily, making a total of 25 visits for social purposes to Mrs T's house each week.

Due to Mrs T's ill-health her daughter had approached social services to have a telephone installed so that they could call a doctor in an emergency. The case was handled by a social work assistant based at the area office. After waiting over a year for the phone the daughter 'got fed up of waiting' and had a phone installed herself. Mrs T was far from satisfied with the service given by her social worker.

Another routine case was the U family. This family were involved with a social worker through a matrimonial supervision order. Mr U's wife had left him with a young family, and we first recorded the case in 1979 when the youngest boy was 12 years old. When we interviewed Mr U in 1982 we found him 'very satisfied' with his social worker. The original need was to check the youngest boy, but the social worker had also arranged holidays for the boy, and given a wide range of advice to Mr U.

Both these cases illustrate less complicated aspects of the social work task. They are useful in that they show us how, with relatively simple needs, some clients can be satisfied with the service, but others dissatisfied. The reasons for this difference are also simple and easy to understand. Mrs T wanted a particular aid but her family had to get it. Mr U had no choice in the matter, but ended up receiving more than he expected.

What perhaps is more worrying is that the hallmark of the practice of social work 'within the community', (that is, extensive contacts with informal networks), which we showed clearly in Chapter 9, seems to have passed by the attention of these ex-clients almost entirely. Indeed whereas, in 1980, 29 per cent of ex-clients perceived some contact between their informal networks and their social worker, by 1982 only four per cent of clients perceived such contact. Taking long-term clients and ex-clients together, the percentage reporting contacts with informal networks fell from 24 per cent in 1980 to three per cent in 1982. We shall return to this matter shortly.

The critical time for simple requests and mobilizing community resources is usually at the stage of referral and so we shall now look at those who had approached either the local or area office earlier in the year.

Clients referred in previous six months
Ninety referrals had been made to the social work area and local project offices during the five-week period of the Referral Study in early 1982. Twelve of these were (quite legitimately) multiple referrals, that is, the same person had approached the project office on different occasions. After discounting those who had died, gone away, were in hospital or had been judged by workers (not necessarily the social workers) as not physically or emotionally fit enough to be interviewed, this left 56 people, of whom we interviewed 32 (57 per cent).

When we looked at the details of those 90 referrals in the last chapter we found that elderly clients predominated and the need for aids and adaptations and financial and material aid was the major cause of referral. This was reflected in the interviews with those who had been the subject of a referral. Nearly two-thirds (66 per cent) of respondents were from elderly households and of those that expressed any expectations about social work, three- fifths did so in terms of financial and material aid (including aids for the elderly). Just over one-quarter (27 per cent) expressed hopes of the service which fell within the child care category. Among the clients and ex-clients we interviewed in 1982, dissatisfaction with social workers was high at 35 per cent, and strikingly no dissatisfaction was expressed by the respondents whose referral had been made to the area office. Significantly they were all referrals from the elderly. The percentage reporting contacts with their informal network was low at six per cent and the clients who approached the area office reported greater levels of contact than those who approached the project office. Comparisons with 1980 are difficult to make because of the low numbers involved but four of the five interviews in 1980 were with elderly respondents.

Conflicts of perspective?
Two important factors stand out from the examination of clients' views of social work. These are, first, that despite the optimistic picture of the practice of social work 'within the community' which we gave in Chapter 9, clients seemed less appreciative of this service than of the traditional approach from 'outside the community'; and second, that there appeared to be direct conflict between the social workers' and clients' perceptions

of contacts with informal networks, and that such contacts, according to the clients, occurred less frequently when social workers were at Stage Three of the model. We shall take each of these points in turn.

Greater dissatisfaction
When we looked at the levels of dissatisfaction with social workers, 19 per cent of clients were dissatisfied in 1980 compared with 31 per cent in 1982. In actual numbers there were *more* satisfied 'clients' in 1982 than in 1980; it is just that the number of dissatisfied clients rose even more sharply. When we examined dissatisfaction more closely, we found that it remained more or less constant for those areas of social work for which help is expected traditionally, that is child care and counselling. The rise in dissatisfaction was largely contained in that area related to financial and material (including furnishings) aid. Even here, satisfied customers outnumbered those who were dissatisfied in a ratio of 5:3. We have already given some examples of both those who were satisfied and dissatisfied after approaching social workers for financial and/or material aid.

At a time of increasing financial stringency we might expect an increase in this type of demand upon social workers, whether it arises from existing clients or new referrals. Demand for material aid rose consistently throughout the area, including Dinnington. However, most of this type of referral which came to the project office in Dinnington was not recorded in the official area statistics because the majority were treated as 'one-off referrals'. When we looked again at the referrals to the project office we found that the number of referrals for financial problems went up from one in 1980 to 19 in 1982. There is little doubt that the reason for it was the availability and proximity of the social workers, but the workers' availability was not matched by a similar availability of resources to meet that demand. It would seem very likely that this is related to the sharp increase in dissatisfaction. It adds weight to Pinker's warning (Barclay 1982) that social services do not have the resources to 'go looking' for need in the community.

There is another factor which may have led to increased dissatisfaction which is of special relevance to the development of locally-based work. Many doubts have been expressed about the value of long-term work with clients that is not well considered and purposeful. Goldberg and Warburton (1979, p. 135) express it colourfully:

> The model of the social worker, either in the image of a passive therapist who follows his client on a long journey of exploration, or as a universal aunt or 'nanny' forever hovering around, ready to support, prop up and 'speak for' her clients, is being superseded by more specific social work roles, both direct and indirect, linked to the network of other caregivers, both statutory and voluntary.

The queries that Goldberg and Warburton put against the style of much long-term work are supported by Sainsbury *et al.* (1982, p. 190):

> Long-term but intermittent 'support' punctuated by hectic activity at times of crises, rarely seems to have resulted in significant long-term change; and we have therefore argued for frequent, substantial, purposeful but time-limited interviewing as a more rational use of professional social workers' time. The acceptability of this approach would depend, however, upon ... greater development of other means of providing long-term 'befriending' and 'monitoring' services: for example a more integrated use of neighbourly and voluntary support-systems, more use of self-help groups, closer informal liaison between case workers and other actual or potential helpers in the local neighbourhood.

Both these quotations suggest a much more selective use of social worker time and much greater use of a wide range of other resources both statutory, voluntary and informal, especially those that are local, to maintain contact with clients. This is just what the 'within the community' approach is trying to do but the inevitable, and desirable, result of this approach is that the social worker will visit less often and frequently much less often. This is quite often a reason given for dissatisfaction with the social worker. Hadley and McGrath (1984, p. 235) concluded that generally 'those who received the most help and saw workers the most frequently were also the most likely to be satisfied'. Attempts to develop this kind of shared or indirect way of supporting or monitoring clients can anticipate that it will lead to a good deal of expressed dissatisfaction with social workers, and perhaps with other health and welfare professionals who adopt the same approach. The satisfaction or otherwise of clients is not something to be ignored, but we need to be aware of the factors that are likely to affect the expression of satisfaction or dissatisfaction with workers' performance.

Conflict over contact with informal networks
Having identified encouraging trends in the development of working with informal networks (which would include some individual volunteers), it seems at first impossible to accept that what existed in mid-1981 and early 1982 could, according to respondents, have disappeared almost entirely by mid-1982. The truth of the matter is that it did.

In order to avoid the bias caused by the disruption to the local office brought about by the loss of a member of staff in early 1982, we used the 1981 Caseload Study as a comparison to 1979 when we were looking at social work practice in Chapter 9. The disruption to the local social work service (made worse by the housing assistant's being away on extended leave) was so severe that at times the local office was closed and many cases were passed back to the area office.

To confirm that this disruption was largely the cause of the conflict, we looked back at the interviews with social work clients in 1981. We found that a quarter of those who were long-term cases of social workers at the time of interview in 1981 reported contact between their social worker and informal networks. This indicates a slight increase over 1980 when 20 per cent of long-term clients reported such contact.

The reported absence of contacts with informal networks in the 1982 interviews was largely due to the stress of staff shortages at the local office during the early part of 1982, the effects of which were not overcome until the autumn of that year. This was confirmed when we examined the pattern of contacts listed by social workers in their 1982 caseload study. The average number of contacts made per case in 1982 was the same, at 3.3, as it had been in 1979. It had, however, risen by one-third to 4.4 contacts per case between 1979 and 1981. In 1982 without exception, contacts made to informal networks had fallen below their 1981 levels, some almost back to the pre-project levels of 1979.

The vulnerability of this type of practice is something we shall consider shortly, and we must not forget the ethical questions raised about working with networks without the client's knowledge. We can, however, be reasonably satisfied that the disparity in perceptions we have discovered had valid reasons, which in themselves carry significant messages for those wishing to work 'within the community'.

Satisfaction with other workers

Levels of satisfaction with other workers changed very little; for example, the level of expressed dissatisfaction with resident wardens remained at two per cent throughout the three years 1980–2, and for home helps went down from four per cent in 1980 to three per cent in 1981, where it remained in 1982. The change was slightly greater for the visiting wardens (five per cent in 1980, vanishing in 1982), though we cannot say why. It may reflect the improvement in the clients' social life and general reduction of dissatisfaction. The figures for the district nurse varied widely from 10 per cent expressing dissatisfaction in 1980, to zero in 1981 and up to 15 per cent in 1982. Thus we found that the principal increase in dissatisfaction of the users was concentrated on the social workers, some of the reasons for which we have discussed above.

The carers' perspective

We were also interested to see how the new pattern of service affected carers. Our data are limited to principal carers (that is people who visited at least three times a week). We illustrate once again from the principal carers of social work clients. In 1980 we found that on average the 12 carers gave 3.8 hours of care each week to nine clients, seven of whom had concluded their association with the social workers. In sharp contrast to the clients (81 per cent of whom were satisfied), 67 per cent of principal carers in 1980 were dissatisfied with the support that they received, even though three-quarters of them had had contact with the social worker.

In the summer of 1982 we interviewed 21 principal carers of 15 social work clients. All but one client had concluded their association with the social worker, a situation no doubt encouraged by the shortage of staff in the local office earlier in the year. It is quite usual to find an increase in case closure at times of major review or reallocation brought about by organizational and staffing changes.

The principal difference between 1980 and 1982 was the number of elderly ex-clients being cared for, a rise from three to ten. The volume of care given to social work clients by principal carers rose from an average of 3.8 hours in a week in 1980 to 6.4 hours in a week in 1982. In addition this care was of a more intensive nature, including not only meals and laundry, but also tasks like washing the clients, or helping them to get in and out of bed.

Principal carers of (former) social work clients also seemed to be focusing their care more sharply upon those with disabilities (eight per cent in 1980 but 38 per cent in 1982 were severely disabled). Contacts with social workers had fallen marginally (as we would expect from our findings above) but principal carers reported a threefold increase in contacts with the home help. This broadening of support is again consistent with the development of 'packages of care', particularly for the elderly. In this sort of situation the social worker becomes one member of a much wider team. It is significant that for the elderly clients of the locally-based social workers, contacts between the principal carer and the home help were much more frequent than with the social worker.

Dissatisfaction with support given by health and welfare services to the principal carers of the social workers' clients fell from two-thirds in 1980 to under half (45 per cent) in 1982. However, the increase in the actual numbers of carers interviewed in 1982 meant that there were both more principal carers satisfied and dissatisfied with statutory support. Importantly, there was little difference in levels of dissatisfaction expressed by principal carers of non-elderly clients. It was the increase in carers of elderly clients, and their greater satisfaction with the support they had received, which reduced the overall level of dissatisfaction.

Even so this leaves us with a far from satisfactory picture about the development of a partnership between social workers and the community. Some of our concerns about conflicts in perspective between social workers and their clients have been explained, but others have left questions about the style of practice developed.

More qualitative evidence does exist to substantiate, at the individual case level, the *apparent* operation of partnership in care. We presented this evidence in the last chapter when we looked at the development of the work of the housing assistant. Unfortunately time and resources did not permit a truly ethnographic evaluation of the various people involved with the cases we described. Although clients and principal carers (when present) took part in planning services and constructing 'packages of care', a detailed understanding of their feelings and objectives at that time would have strengthened our understanding considerably. Nevertheless, we would argue that those case studies provide circumstantial evidence of some progress towards involving informal carers in the detailed planning of care for their dependents.

It is also useful to look at the results at the aggregate level, that is including carers of clients or patients from all the groups of workers, including those served by social workers. When we looked at the carers' views about the statutory services that the client or patient received we found that there was an increase in the dissatisfaction expressed by principal carers over the period 1980 to 1982. Although the proportion of principal carers who were friends and said they were dissatisfied with the care the client or patient received was the same in 1980 as in 1982 (20 per cent), the proportion of dissatisfied principal carers who were relatives rose from 18 per cent in 1980 to 28 per cent in 1982.

However, we also asked a more general question about the overall satisfaction of the carer with the support *they* received. In sharp contrast to our findings related to specific services, this showed a substantial increase in the satisfaction with the *overall* (that is statutory, voluntary and informal) support that the carers themselves received from 40 per cent in 1980, to 68 per cent in 1982. Although we have no evidence to substantiate the link, we might postulate that the entrepreneurial activities of statutory workers, and the increase in the caring resources of the village, contributed to this marked increase in satisfaction. At the same time the emphasis in the project on getting the workers to develop indirect work, where the workers keep in touch via a relative or friend who was in regular contact with the patient or client, may have led people to perceive that there was less contact with statutory workers and this could account for an increase in dissatisfaction with particular services.

We would point out that this evidence must be treated with care, nevertheless the apparently contradictory results of an increase in dissatisfaction on the part of carers with the care given by particular services, combined with increased satisfaction with the overall support they received themselves, is fascinating and merits further investigation. It suggests that considerable effort may be needed to enable patients and clients and their carers to understand how the service is likely to develop and why. Or, more fundamentally, that users and carers need to be involved more fully in the development of services. The increase in dissatisfaction of carers with the statutory services does suggest that the workers need to pay more attention to their links with principal carers.

An interim appraisal

We have expressed some reservations about the weight that can be put on expressions of satisfaction or dissatisfaction but it is worth looking at the overall findings from the study of users and also at the proportion expressing dissatisfaction with their total care. By total care we mean care from all sources – statutory, voluntary, friends, neighbours and family. It is impossible to claim any precise causality but the findings suggest that the project may have made some impact on the quality of life of those using the services.

Overall between 1980 and 1982 there was a drop in those patients and clients who were dissatisfied with their total care from 15 per cent in 1980 to 12 per cent in 1982.This may fit in with the finding we noted just above of the *carers'* greater satisfaction with the overall support they received. The improvement was most marked among the elderly, especially those living alone and aged 60-74, where dissatisfaction with their total care dropped from 19 per cent in 1980 to zero in 1982. The main exception was an increase in dissatisfaction amongst those living alone and aged 75 or more who were dissatisfied with their total care from four per cent to seven per cent.

In the previous chapter we noted some quite striking changes and developments towards working 'within the community' on the part of some of the workers. What modest improvements we have noted here, though worthy of attention, are indeed modest. The most that we wish to claim is that they indicate some improvement in the experience of some clients and patients. It would require a much more detailed study from a perspective that is unambiguously that of the client to establish the connection firmly. Croft and Beresford's 1984 essay on participatory research has some helpful insights into how this might be developed. Hadley and McGrath (1984, p. 236) concluded from their small-scale client study:

> These data ... provide further evidence ... that the Normanton team had built up a distinctive style of operation, even though they do not throw much more light on the question of the relative *quality* of the service produced by this method of working.

Our studies show that the new pattern of service made only limited impact on the expressed satisfaction of those using the services and, perhaps more important, we have noted that there was an *increase* in the expressed dissatisfaction of carers about the services the users received. In view of the doubts that have been expressed about the impact that caring for people in the community is likely to have on women, this is of particular importance. It is significant that the increase in dissatisfaction with the care received by the patient or client was among carers who were relatives, and therefore likely to be doing the more demanding tasks. It is right to ask questions such as whether the project had the effect of raising people's expectations, and thus their dissatisfaction, when these expectations were not met. It is also encouraging to note that carers were *more* satisfied with the overall support that they received themselves from whatever source, which suggests that the entrepreneurial activities of the workers bore fruit in the experience of the carers. Nevertheless, it is urgent to tackle the question of what gave rise to increased dissatisfaction and what adaptation or increase of the services is required.

Only a beginning

This more sobering account of the impact of working 'within the community', particularly for social work clients whom we showed to have experienced the greatest change in service, should not be a cause of pessimism in the quest to create a partnership in care. It illustrates not only the complexity of the interaction between formal and informal care which will exist in any community, but also the time-scale necessary to bring about change. We learnt this from the length of time it took to develop community-focused initiatives to overcome the barriers of distrust and ignorance between the various workers involved. If it was difficult for professionals to relate to their colleagues in the community, how much more difficult would it be to reorientate their professional perspective to think of sharing care with patients or clients and members of their informal networks. This proved particularly difficult with non-elderly patients and clients. Yet in crude numerical terms, there were more satisfied patients and clients, and more principal carers satisfied about the care they received under the 'within the community' model than there were under the 'outside the community' model. Health and welfare workers had made a beginning in the difficult task of forging a partnership with the community, but our evidence suggests that such a development is likely to take a long time.

However, the project has more to offer than this bald conclusion. We were struck by how difficult the fieldworkers found it to grapple effectively with the elusive complexities of informal care and in particular how difficult it was for them to plan their strategy towards it. This has led us to develop our earlier thinking on networks into a model applicable to fieldworkers. Four years of observation and analysis of the project in Dinnington have enabled us to develop a simple theory which lends itself readily to use as a tool for practitioners in the field. Two of the authors

(Tennant and Bayley 1985) have suggested a way of looking at informal care in a locality so that workers can decide what their strategy should be. Using the analysis of data from the study of all those aged 70–79 in the village, we argued that it was possible for fieldworkers and managers to make strategic decisions on the basis of two sets of simple information, both of which could be gathered by health and welfare workers in the course of their ordinary duties. These were:

(a) concentration – the extent of the patient or client's network of relatives, friends and neighbours and how many of them were concentrated locally; and

(b) activity – how many of them had active contact with the patient/client.

Support for this approach comes from Bulmer (1986, p. 87) who suggests that 'one can think of support networks as ranged on two criteria ... One is geographical propinquity between kin – nearness or distance – the other frequency of contact'. These are very similar to our concentration and activity. He goes on to argue that this has strategic implications for the provision of social services:

> If this sort of pattern were generalisable, it would have very significant implications for the provision of social services. For it suggests that informal care might, potentially at least, be most forthcoming for the less geographically mobile sections of the population who have kin living nearby, and least forthcoming for the mobile middle class on the one hand and the disadvantaged lower working class on the other.

Bulmer is considering the implications at a very general level. We are suggesting that these two simple pieces of data can be used both at the personal level of the client or patient and at the area level, where it is of particular value in helping fieldworkers and managers to think *strategically*.

For example, at the area level, in a situation similar to that in Dinnington where a high proportion of networks were concentrated locally and a high proportion of them were active, it would be inappropriate to consider that informal networks could take more responsibility. They are already heavily committed and thus the emphasis is likely to be on entrepreneurial activity, that is, creating new resources to supplement existing networks. We have seen that this is what happened in Dinnington, in particular VOLTAGE, RALLY and the plans for providing some voluntary day care for the elderly in the village. It is interesting to note the success of the project in this type of activity, given its appropriateness in the light of this analysis. It grew out of the workers' recognition of the extent of existing caring commitments and the need to develop support mechanisms for such carers.

By contrast, a different situation might be highly concentrated networks but with a low level of activity. Here, by definition, most of the network is local, but few if any members of the network are active. In this situation intervention strategies might broaden to consider whether informal networks could contribute more to the overall support of patients and clients and, if so, what was needed to enable them to do so. We should emphasize that this may not be appropriate, but the essential thing is to *find out*. In these circumstances the role of 'network system consultant' (Whittaker 1983) may be valid, that is, working with the members of the network to see if there were ways in which they could give help or increase the help they were giving. Often there are simple ways in which a worker can facilitate the linking of members of a network and some of these have been described earlier, in particular when discussing the care packages put together by the housing assistant in Dinnington. Hadley and McGrath (1984, p. 178) also give a nice example of this:

> A care worker described a case where she had been visiting daily to empty a commode for an elderly lady who did not like to ask her son to do it, although he also came daily. A problem arose over a bank holiday and she approached the son to see if he would take the job on temporarily. He willingly agreed and offered to take over the task permanently.

On the other hand, it might be necessary to consider broader issues which make it difficult for people in those networks to give help or support. This might involve the adequacy of bus services, or street lighting or other environmental factors.

Finally, the network may show a low level of concentration and low level of activity. Here informal care will be almost non-existent, and in these circumstances emphasis will very likely be placed upon statutory intervention, possibly with voluntary support.

The value of this model is its extreme simplicity but there are a number of ways in which it could be developed. One such way is indicated in Bulmer (1986). This book is a unified account of the work on neighbours by Philip Abrams, who died tragically at the age of 48 in 1981. It includes much of Philip Abrams's own writing. In one such section, Abrams points out that the actual *content* of the links between people cannot be ignored. It is important to recognize 'that different links can have widely different values for individuals within a network' (Bulmer 1986, p. 89). We would argue that understanding the values of the various links in a network marks the passage from working just with the patient or client and his/her immediate family to working with networks. We gave examples of this in the previous chapter though we do not have quantitative data on it from our studies. We also showed how the social workers in the local office in Dinnington learned about the variability and values of such links and adapted their working methods accordingly (see for example, pp. 110f.).

These two dimensions of concentration and activity represent information readily available to health and welfare workers. It provides a framework into which fieldworkers can incorporate their knowledge of the values of the links while giving them a simple and urgently needed model which will enable them to plan their strategy in relation to informal care. Collecting and recording such information would not require large-scale investigation, although it would require some adequate form of inter-agency record-keeping.

This personal and community-wide understanding of networks is a necessary prerequisite to developing any partnership in the community. It needs to include developing reciprocal understanding between members of informal networks and networks of statutory workers and mutual respect for the contribution each has to offer. Failure to pay attention to developing such an understanding will lead to dissatisfaction and suspicion on both sides. Health and welfare workers in Dinnington occasionally made this error, with the results we have seen above, but they also made a start in the right direction.

In the final chapter we turn to some of the wider issues.

12 Discussion and Implications

The scope of the Dinnington Project was wide. And the lessons to be learnt from it cover a wide range of issues. We start by looking at integration.

Integration
One of the basic aims of the project was to build up a comprehensive integrated service. This integration was to be both with local people, which we shall look at below, and between the various departments and workers which we shall consider now. In this respect the aim of the project was to develop closer integration at two levels, between the health and welfare services, and between manual workers (in particular home helps and workers) and professional workers.

The appointment of the housing assistant with particular responsibility for integrating the work of the wardens was an important first step in this direction, but its effect was strengthened by other innovations, in particular the fieldworkers' meeting and the use made of the project office. The local base which the project office provided proved vital. It had been made a precondition for undertaking the project and experience showed that this was fully justified. The Royal College of General Practitioners (1986), commenting on the Green Paper on *Primary Health Care* (DHSS 1986) argued that 'the basic unit of population should be determined by a practice registered list rather than geographically'. We disagree with this. Sinclair *et al.* (1984, p. 15) have shown how difficult this can make effective integration in a locality. They found 86 elderly clients in one social work area were registered with 26 different GPs. The approach advocated by the Royal College is incompatible with the development of locally-based health and welfare teams and the neighbourhood nursing service put forward by the Cumberledge Report (DHSS 1986a). A geographical area should be the basic unit and, on the evidence of the Dinnington Project, we would argue that it should be small and include a local base within it.

The accessibility and informality of the project office created a focus for the project. Above all it was an easy place for people to meet. This applied to both clients and other workers. In the first six months of 1983 other workers made 528 visits to the project office, clients 377 and volunteers and others, mostly people coming on behalf of clients, 221, making a total of 1126 visits, an average of 43 visitors a week. This was especially important for making links between the wardens, and to a lesser extent the home helps, the workers in the project office and the other workers who called in. It was one of the most important aspects of the project and served several purposes. On the one hand, it made available the extensive local knowledge of wardens and home helps to the professional workers, helping them to understand the village and facilitating the development of contacts in it. On the other hand, it enabled the professional workers to begin to view the other local workers as *colleagues* with whom they should work as members of the same team. Such co-operation was generally very informal but nevertheless regular and sustained and not inhibited by differences in status.

The network of communication created by the project was based on a combination of the local office and the regular fieldworkers' meetings. Between them they created an environment in which information could be shared when necessary. In the fieldworkers' meetings, as we pointed out in Chapter 7, the workers not only learnt about each others' roles, but also about the constraints under which they worked. As they became aware of the pressures on other workers and departments they were able to develop better relationships. The generally improved communication between workers can be seen, for example, in the contacts which took place between the district nursing sister and the assistant home help organizer once she had started spending time at the project office regularly. Relations between the home help organizer and the district nurses had been bad. Neither had understood the pressures on the other agency and tended to put the worst interpretation on things which went wrong. But issues were resolved more easily and quickly once the assistant home help organizer and the district nurses started meeting from time to time.

The fieldworkers' meeting is a good example of an interdisciplinary team at local level. Effective interdisciplinary team work of this nature is a vital part of any locally-based scheme because it enables the local knowledge of all the workers to be shared in a constructive way. At times other people, such as the local youth worker, a volunteer or community representative from the Project Management Team or the rector would be invited to the fortnightly meeting. The meeting was thus not just an interdisciplinary team, but also facilitated communication between other workers and a wide range of other people in the village.

Yet, when all that has been said, it does not really explain fully why it turned out to be so effective. It seems that the meeting gave the workers the support, sense of purpose and direction that enabled them to cope with the indifference and, as it often seemed to them, hostility of their managements. It was not always effective; sometimes the meetings covered the same ground repeatedly, for example, the summer play scheme; sometimes the person responsible for convening the meeting failed to do so; and sometimes people failed to do what they had agreed to do before the next meeting. However, despite such shortcomings and despite the length of time it took to get some things off the ground, the meeting worked.

It was helped by its basic design – it fitted the project. It was not given any fixed responsibilities and so it could develop in any direction that seemed appropriate. It was informal, though with a basic modicum of direction. It was fairly regular and its members also met quite frequently at other times and so discussion was not necessarily limited to the meeting. It was small. It was flexible and could and did include other people if it wanted to. But possibly the most important thing was that it was a *fieldworkers'* meeting, a regular meeting of workers from different disciplines who were close to the needs of those using the services and thus for whom the needs of patients or clients and/or wider needs in the community were likely to speak more loudly than purely departmental perceptions of need. It provided a setting in which the integration of the services, rather than their periodic co-operation, could develop.

Hadley *et al.* (1984, p. 140) suggest that three aspects of the programme they developed in East Sussex contributed to team-building: greater understanding of each others' roles, shared experience of working together on a common task and collective achievements. This was equally true of the fieldworkers' meeting in Dinnington and it played a key role in enabling the project to survive and develop despite the unsatisfactory management situation.

The other meeting which was important in this respect was the core team/research team meeting, especially when people from the lower layer of management became involved. This had started as a meeting roughly once every six weeks between the four members of the research team and the three members of the core team. Early in 1982 the social services team leader and the Dinnington housing manager joined; in autumn 1982 the district nursing sister was able to attend because of Joint Financing money; at the beginning of 1983 the home help organizer and one of her assistants joined; and in the summer of 1983 the deputy director of nursing services with particular responsibility for the project joined. This meeting became a setting in which ideas could be floated and genuine discussion could take place without the members' departmental responsibilities blocking it. By the middle of 1983 the meeting had become a source of creative thinking. The contrast with the formally constituted Project Management Team is instructive. Unlike the Project Management Team the core team/research team meeting had no formal constitution or agenda and the meetings themselves were very informal. It was a place where it was possible to discuss issues which elsewhere, for instance in the Project Management Team, simply led to fruitless confrontation. It offered a context within which the members of the meeting were able to explore, without being defensive, the sort of changes that might be needed in their respective organizations in order to improve their services.

It is hard to be precise about why these meetings worked. One factor is that the framework and philosophy of the project made the meetings seem eminently good sense. The project was trying to produce packages of care to meet particular people's needs, rather than trying to fit people's needs into existing departmental packages, that is, the fieldworkers were trying to develop a *corporate* approach to meeting need. The fortnightly meeting provided a focus for this at fieldworker level. This led to pressure on the first layer of management to develop a more corporate approach, too, and the core team/research team meeting provided a focus for this corporate approach at the bottom level of management. This was of particular significance in an authority such as Rotherham which had little tradition of corporate management and did not seem able to create the environment for it within the Project Management Team meetings, where departmental perspectives were so rigid.

In the core team/research team and the fieldworkers' meetings, when they were working well, real dialogue took place and clearly this is essential if integration between different workers, agencies and authorities is to take place. But during the project we were impressed both by how difficult it was for real discussion to take place within the formal decision-making machinery of large organizations, and by how powerful were the institutional forces within large organizations working against change.

Schon (1971) describes the way large organizations resist change as 'dynamic conservatism', but the strength of his analysis is that he recognizes that large organizations also fulfil important personal needs of individuals for a sense of security and identity, and so on. Given that we live in times when large organizations *must* change in order to respond to rapidly changing circumstances, this points to the acute need for what Schon calls 'learning systems'.

> These considerations set some conditions for learning systems. Social systems must learn to become capable of transforming themselves without intolerable disruption. But they will not cease to be dynamically conservative – not if dynamic conservatism is the process through which social systems keep from flying apart at the seams. A learning system, then, must be one in which dynamic conservatism operates at such a level and in such a way as to permit change of state without intolerable threat to the essential functions the system fulfils for the self. Our systems need to maintain their identity, and their ability to support the self identity of those who belong to them, but they must at the same time be capable of frequently transforming themselves (ibid., p. 60).

The fortnightly meeting of fieldworkers and the core team/research team meeting could on some occasions have been described as 'learning systems'. An understanding of the processes Schon describes and the importance he gives to 'learning systems' could help the health and welfare services to move towards genuine integration.

But the reality for the project was that the management of the different services, especially health and social services, never succeeded in providing the co-ordinated and integrated management that was needed. The problem was most evident in the Project Management Team which never had the power to manage the project as a joint undertaking. There were two aspects of this. First, the split in the workers' accountability proved to be unworkable. They were accountable to their departments for departmental and professional matters and to the Project Management Team for project matters (see also Payne 1982, p. 21). In practice the two were so closely linked that conflict was inevitable. Second, this problem would not have been as severe if the Project Management Team had been given the power to manage, but when it came to confrontations with senior departmental management its lack of power was evident. The departments did not delegate any of their powers to the Project Management Team. The progress that was made in the core team/research team meeting indicates the progress that *might* have been made if there had been some real devolution of powers.

The weakness of the Project Management Team reflected a similar weakness in its senior committee (that is the Chief Officers' meeting, the Neighbourhood Services Unit or its variants and successors, some of which included members). It met spasmodically at long intervals, rarely discussed and never dealt with any of the management problems and at no time got anywhere close to providing strong, united, co-ordinated local authority/health authority support and control of the project. Indeed the project was attacked frequently at these meetings. This meant that there was no imaginative delegation of responsibilities, no supportive understanding of the problems they were facing, and no sense of the fieldworkers and management developing an exciting new project together. The tension between the workers' accountability to their own departments and to the project was frustrating, at times disheartening, and was a major blockage in the attempt to provide a better-integrated service.

Participation

The involvement of local people in the planning and running of the project proved to be the most difficult and least successful part of it. In the earliest discussion paper the first characteristic of the pattern of service which was to be developed was that 'the involvement of members of the community, not just professionals, will be a fundamental aspect of the approach adopted'. The original project proposal, put forward by Bayley and his research assistant in January 1977 (see pp. 23f.) had the potential for including local people, especially those involved in caring, in developing a pattern of service based on families' own perceptions of needs and how those needs could be met in ways that took full cognizance of the local culture. Administratively it would have been a difficult scheme to run but it would have enabled effective and realistic involvement of local people at a point when they could have had a major influence on the shape of the service.

The failure of either the health or local authority to respond to this proposal led to the project being taken up again at the end of 1977 on terms which were laid down by them and which undermined the community emphasis. From the point at which it was decided to do a survey based on workers (which led to the report of June 1978) the main thrust of the project was centred on how statutory workers should be deployed, not on how members of the community could be fully involved in the thinking, planning and execution of the project. This change in the orientation of the project was more fundamental than was realized at the time and its effects were far-reaching.

Once the project was under way, efforts were made to remedy this by the inclusion of seven community representatives on the Project Management Team. However, they found it difficult to take a constructive part in proceedings. They felt that the meetings were dominated by the professionals and they found the formal bureaucratic style of the meetings alien and frustrating. In part this may have been due to lack of community work skills either within the core team or available to it, but, more fundamentally, it reflected an inherent weakness in the project. We have seen already that there were a number of unsatisfactory features about the Project Management Team and that its powers were severely limited. For these reasons it was not a satisfactory body on which to ask the community representatives to sit. It demonstrated in stark form the difficulties of relating formal bureaucratic structures and methods to forms of organization which make lay participation effective.

The project has shown how difficult it is to build in genuine participation by local people, especially if it is not done at an early stage. We should point out that the community representatives were appointed, not elected. The failure to thrive of the neighbourhood council movement serves to underline that there are many unresolved and intractable questions to be tackled in order to make the rhetoric of local participation a reality. The Hyde Park Project in Sheffield represents the radical approach that appears to be needed to make local representation in management a reality. Hyde Park is a huge multi-story housing complex with deck access to the flats or maisonettes. It is an estate with a high proportion of single-parent families and unemployed people. In the scheme the tenants' organization, Hyde Park Community Action, has *control* over the workers. Some workers from the local authority may attend meetings of the management committee but do not have voting rights. The two workers, a community worker and a social worker, were appointed in 1984. However, they are not part of the social services department although they have close links with it. It is true that there are certain statutory duties which only social workers employed by the local authority can carry out, and it is also true that this project does not include local control of such workers, but the links with social services are close and the department will be involved with and affected by the project. This imaginative scheme is tackling one of the key issues in the development of locally-based work. There is a profound challenge here both to politicians and managers about how far they are prepared to go in devolving power to localities and giving local people a real say in how local services are planned, managed and delivered.

It has to be recognized that there are likely to be many people who have deeply entrenched attitudes that are strongly opposed to participation for professional, practical and political reasons. Such attitudes, combined with large-scale and inflexible organizations dominated by professionals, make the issue of participation by local people in the health and welfare services possibly the most intractable problem these services face.

In the face of such gloom, we would like to finish this section by offering a glimmer of hope. At the end of the previous section we referred to the importance of 'learning systems'. If it is possible to locate, encourage or create 'learning systems' in the health and welfare services, this may offer an opportunity from which genuine participation can develop.

Partnership
We have seen above how some local fieldworkers from the different worker groups in Dinnington came to work more in partnership with one another. In this section we are concerned with how far the workers managed to develop a partnership with their patients or clients, and those who cared for them.

It had been hoped that the workers would develop a partnership style of practice and that one of the distinctive aspects of this would be that they would work more closely with the social care and support networks of their patients or clients. While the details of what the project achieved in working to networks are complex, the overall position is quite clear. Those workers who were involved centrally and were committed to the project, the two social workers, the housing assistant and the district nurse made limited but appreciable progress in seeing their patients or clients as living within networks and so contacted a wider range of people and resources about their care. However, overall, the difference in approach was not noticed or valued to any great extent by their clients or their carers, whatever may have happened in the case of some individuals. Other workers, such as the home helps and wardens, were not so directly involved with the development of the project. It was hoped that their practice would be influenced by their contact with the core members of the project. In practice we found little to suggest that they were more aware of or sensitive to the needs of carers.

This might indicate that the project has little to say about working with networks. This is not the case. Although there has been little impact overall, some workers did make progress in developing their practice. It was evident to the research team that as the project developed these workers were finding imaginative ways of working with networks. Examples of these can be found, especially for the district nurse in Chapter 8, the social workers in Chapter 9, and the home helps and wardens in Chapter 10. The way in which the social workers worked with some of their long-term family cases through their rather tangled networks, which were at some times supportive and at other times anything but, was probably the most sophisticated use of this method.

The workers gained a realistic view of what could and could not be expected of informal care. The importance of this is obvious in the light of the variability, vulnerability and volatility of informal care, discussed in Chapter 4. It was evident that there was not a vast reservoir of informal care in Dinnington waiting to be tapped. It was much more a question of providing better support to existing networks and in some cases enabling people who had ceased to be carers because the burden had become too great, to return to a supportive or helping role but almost invariably at a less intense level.

It is obviously important for workers to be realistic about how much potential support there is likely to be available in the locality in which they are working. With this in mind, in Chapter 11 we developed a simple model of networks which indicates how those who wish to work in with informal networks can consider what their *strategy* should be (see pp. 160-161).

Everything that we have discussed about working with informal networks shows that there are no easy or slick answers and the method requires detailed and specific training with workers at every level. However, the analysis we have given above should make it easier for agencies to decide what their basic strategy should be. The major lesson for the formal services about informal care is that *they must take the trouble to find out what is happening.* Reid and Smith (1981, p. 13) put the issue well: 'We cannot help people use their strengths if our knowledge is limited to their weaknesses.'

Professionalism

From one point of view it might seem that the locally-based approach undervalues professionalism. There is some evidence of this in the writing of Cooper, formerly area officer of the Normanton team, as Bennett (1983, pp. 53f.) points out. It could be argued that the emphasis on informal care and the competence of the people carrying it out, coupled with a similar emphasis on volunteers and the important role of people like the home helps and wardens, leaves little space for professionals. Much depends on what is meant by professionalism. If it means that skills are the sole province of certain professionals and that ordinary people have no part to play, then that is indeed a type of professionalism for which the locally-based approach has no time at all.

If, on the other hand, it is a form of professionalism which sees itself as having certain skills to offer and, where appropriate, to share with local people then it is highly relevant and we would argue that the locally-based approach makes more demands on workers' professionalism not less. As an example let us consider accountability. This normally implies the workers' accountability to their clients, to their professional bodies and to their departments, but the locally-based approach also implies accountability to the locality and this would make considerable additional demands on the workers.

The greater demand on workers' professionalism is perhaps best illustrated by considering confidentiality. Leighton (1983, p. 51) is critical of patch-based social work in this respect.

> Another example of values embedded in the advocacy of patch may be illustrated by just one example from *Going Local*. It is said to be a strength of the patch system that the corner shop is willing to inform the workers that a certain old lady is buying 'far too much Guinness and not "enough" food'. Here we have the fulfilment of everyone's fears about 'Big Brother' social services of 'The Welfare'. A criticism of a lifestyle is implied, a lifestyle which involves no lawbreaking or injury to any other party and no self referral of a perceived problem. Would the 'patch' worker pick on you or me for our deviance from 'healthy' patterns of behaviour, would they carry out a friendly neighbourhood visit on the local magistrate who may also be a heavy drinker? When does 'patch' become a gross invasion of privacy?

He is quite right to ask when patch does become a gross invasion of privacy, but he shows little faith in the sensitivity and professionalism of social workers if he assumes that in the case he mentions the social worker will stamp in and make the old lady conform. Yes, that would be an invasion of privacy. But a visit by a social worker who will respect her right to make choices about how she lives, while also being alert to ways in which she can be helped, could be an opportunity to do something valuable for a lonely old person. Locally-based work may confront social workers with situations which will challenge their professional judgement, but this is a test of their training, professionalism and proper understanding of accountability, not a sign that Big Brother is with us. The locally-based approach does imply open and probably more complex relationships with people in the localities that the workers are serving. It is part of the price of treating clients and those amongst whom they live as fellow citizens with whom a partnership has to be forged. This involves awkward decisions, for example, about what to do in response to gossip, which cannot be escaped by a high-minded refusal to have anything to do with it because it is such an integral part of daily living. Confidentiality in a locally-based setting cannot be a refuge to hide behind. It has to be a living principle which the worker applies with sensitivity and discrimination.

The locally-based approach raises a number of similarly difficult ethical and professional issues, for example a locally-based worker may acquire more information than it is comfortable for her officially to have. How does she deal with it? How far must the worker let her client or patient know when she is maintaining contact via someone else? One presumes she should, but it is a reminder that a different style of work requires alertness to a different range of issues and that both initial and in-service professional training should address them.

Another issue is how methods of record-keeping need to be adapted to enable the worker, and her employer, to keep a reasonable track of what she is doing without overburdening the worker. If the worker is likely to meet patients or clients frequently in a variety of settings and as part of an interdisciplinary locality team, there is a professional task to be done to develop a form of record-keeping which is more appropriate and done on an inter-agency basis.

Relationships between manual workers, paraprofessionals and professionals is another important area. First, it requires a recognition by professionals of the competence of people like home helps and wardens and their right to be treated as colleagues. This, as we have seen, is an area in which the Dinnington Project did make progress. Second, it requires a careful judgement by a professional about how much responsibility it is appropriate to ask a manual worker to take on when this is not reflected in their level of pay. There is a danger that the locally-based approach, with its emphasis on informal care, will lead to the exploitation of both families, especially women, and also low-paid female manual workers. A major responsibility falls on the professionals to prevent this. This will not be easy. This was a considerable problem in Normanton where a salary differential of £1000 a year opened up between the social work assistants and the care workers as a result of salary negotiations following the social workers' strike in 1979. Although the two groups of workers were doing very similar jobs in practice, though not formally, the Normanton team could do little about it despite vigorous efforts (Hadley and McGrath 1984, p. 170). A similar problem arose in the Dinnington Project. The housing assistant felt that she was being transformed into a pseudo-social work assistant, carrying a similar caseload but without the same salary.

The trade unions representing low-paid workers will face similar problems in relation to locally-based work. How can volunteering be encouraged without endangering members' jobs? How can flexibility in working be encouraged without low-paid workers being exploited? Does more integrated work mean that job descriptions need to be renegotiated? The trade unions face a particularly delicate task in negotiating with management a satisfactory outcome for their members.

Generalism and specialism

This is one of the most pressing questions in the debate about locally-based work. There is an inherent logic in a locally-based worker being able to cover as wide a range of tasks as possible in order to avoid constant referral of clients or patients to other workers outside the area. Thus the generalist worker has been a normal characteristic of locally based-work.

This issue was faced by the Cumberledge Committee in its report on neighbourhood nursing (DHSS 1986a). They recommended that district nurses, health visitors and school nurses should work together as an integrated neighbourhood local nursing team and that there should be 'a common training course for all first level nurses wishing to work outside hospital in what are now the fields of health visiting, district nursing and school nursing' (ibid., p. 42). There would be specialist modules which would cover one of several options such as maternal and child health, home nursing, health care of adolescents and young children, mental health care, health education, nurse practitioner work or occupational health, (ibid., p. 43). But they went on to say:

> We must emphasise that we are not proposing the introduction of a generic nurse, but we do see common training as the one way to break down the rigid roles these nurses have at present. We are seeking to preserve the type of skills possessed by the health visitor and to create more scope for her to practise them. We are also seeking to heighten and widen opportunities for district nurses and school nurses. At last, they would be able, individually and as team members, to take a far more flexible approach to their clients and patients and to treat them not as so many separate parts but as whole people – in whole neighbourhoods (ibid., p. 44).

The committee had, however, to consider three broad groups of specialist nurses also working in the community – community midwives, community psychiatric nurses and community mental handicap nurses, and other specialist nurses. These latter 'include stoma care nurses, diabetic nurse specialists, continence advisers, nurses for terminally ill people, and health visitors for elderly people' (ibid., p. 29).

The committee recommended that these nurses should not become 'core members of the neighbourhood nursing service nor accountable to neighbourhood nursing managers' (ibid., p. 27) but they did recommend that 'Community midwives, community psychiatric nurses and community mental handicap nurses should ensure, through their respective managers and the neighbourhood nursing manager, that their specialist contributions are fully co-ordinated with the work of the neighbourhood nursing service' (ibid., p.29). and that

> All other specialist nurses who work outside hospital should be based in the community and managed as part of the neighbourhood nursing service. Each specialist nurse should be assigned to one or more neighbourhood services and have the commitment of her time to each service specified, (ibid., p. 29f.).

They also suggested that:

> If a family already has regular contact with a community nurse, the specialist nurse should aim to work through her. She should help her at the same time to develop her skills: it is a waste of valuable resources if specialised nurses work exclusively to particular patients in the community rather than transfer at least some of their skills to nurses already working in the community (ibid., p. 30).

Thus this model envisages a core team of nurses who would have a common training plus specialist modules which would enable them to cover the great majority of local cases and situations. In addition, and co-ordinated with them, there would be some specialist nurses. The centre of gravity of the community nursing service would be the neighbourhood and the specialist services would have to relate to that, although it is acknowledged that it is sensible for community psychiatric nurses and community mental handicap nurses to continue to work in multi-disciplinary specialist teams (ibid., p. 28).

The Cumberledge Report is an entirely theoretical model at the time of writing (late 1986) but it mirrors many of the questions that have been raised with regard to social work. It is important because it suggests an organizational framework for resolving problems of co-ordination that would facilitate joint working between nursing and other locally-based services. The model is not unlike that developed in Dinnington in which one social worker in the local office was authorized under the mental health acts and the local social workers carried out the full range of tasks with help from specialist workers for blind and deaf people and some people with physical handicaps. These specialists were based at the area office. On the face of it Dinnington does not have a great deal to contribute to the debate because no serious problems arose over the need for specialist help, but that very lack of problems may be one of the most important lessons the project has to offer.

Pinker, in his note of dissent to the Barclay Report (1982, p. 249), was very concerned that 'The community social work model might well strengthen links with the informal networks, but only at the expense of co-operation with the other formal services and efficient discharge of statutory responsibilities'. We have shown that in Dinnington there was no evidence to support this concern. In fact, contacts and co-operation with other workers and agencies improved greatly and access to specialist help and advice did not appear to be a problem. It could be argued, however, that the demand for specialist help was not heavy and that in many areas the need for specialist help would be much greater and therefore the Dinnington model is not typical of many urban environments. But our findings are similar to those of Black *et al.* (1983) and the conclusion they reached from their study of three teams which had varying degrees of generalism and specialism.

> The generic and specialist team approaches made little difference ... to the form that practice took, so we were left wondering why this question about labour division has been so much debated when there remain important contextual organisational problems to sort out (ibid., p. 215).

In Dinnington there did remain 'important contextual organizational problems to sort out' and these were far more pressing than any questions of specialization. However, it can be argued that specialization and the locally-based approach must be treated as alternatives as there are unlikely to be sufficient personnel to have teams of specialists *and* locally-based teams. But there are other models, in particular, locally-based teams supported by a limited number of specialist workers acting as consultants. The disadvantage of this model is, as Stevenson and Parsloe (1978) have shown, that such consultants are rarely consulted. However, in Dinnington contacts with specialist workers went *up* during the period of the study and the workers appeared to have good working relationships with such specialists as the educational psychologist and the community psychiatric nurses. If there had been a social worker specializing in mental handicap, would he or she have been used as well? It seems likely and for two simple reasons. First, the workers in the project office took trouble to get to know a wide range of specialist workers. Second, they maintained these relationships by making the office a welcoming place to call into. This is evident from the sheer number of workers who did so. We would suggest that there is potential in the 'General Practitioner Model', that is, locally-based teams with specialist consultant back-up, provided both sides are prepared to work at the relationship. This appears to be the model that the Cumberledge Review Team have suggested for neighbourhood nursing.

The model which Olive Stevenson (1981) puts forward of an area team with a number of different units is attractive in many ways, especially her insistence that the community needs and resources unit must feed all the others. 'The idea is thus to link the strengths of the patch system with the specialist expertise which it is argued is essential also' (ibid., p. 134). However, we would argue that an area team of this size would have to serve too large a population to enable the workers to know their areas with the intimacy that is needed. We think it would be difficult for the community needs and resources unit to act as an adequate substitute for the local base in terms of its impact on the workers. The danger is that the existence of a community worker in the area team would be taken as the justification for social wokers to ignore the community dimensions of their work.

However, we should make clear that the specialization issue was not addressed specifically in our study and that our arguments here stem from our belief that the case for locally-based teams is very strong and that some means need to be found of making special expertise available to them. In view of the increasing complexity of child care legislation, ready access to expertise in that area is likely to be especially important. We are not saying special knowledge and expertise are unimportant. We are saying that really strong links with a local area are more important in organizational terms, and that special knowledge needs to support a locally-based service, rather than local contacts being built in to support area teams with specialists. Furthermore we have shown that a locally-based approach can improve interdisciplinary co-operation, but effective interdisciplinary work at the local level requires as much devolution of authority as possible. It hinders interdisciplinary work if workers are continually having to contact their superiors.

The size of the local team is an important factor in whether there is sufficient expertise to deal with most situations. For purely practical reasons like covering holidays and sickness the social work team in Dinnington of just two workers was too small and we would advocate a *minimum* social work team size of three. It will always be difficult to create teams that are large enough to provide the minimum size of team needed, yet small enough for the team to know the area and be known by it.

We would argue that it is vital that this question should not be considered in relation to one individual worker group, department or authority alone. The major question to be addressed is *not* specialization versus generalism, important though that is, as we have recognized above, but the 'contextual organizational problems' to which Black *et al.* (1983) referred. We need to consider the skills and expertise that a team of workers can offer. A home help cannot give an injection but can she give welfare rights advice or, at least, suggest that a client should seek such advice and tell him/her where to go? Can a home help organizer deal with a simple request about aids and should social workers make assessments for the provision of home helps? Would it be possible to develop a joint assessment form covering social work, home help, warden service and district nursing?

Nor should this be confined to statutory services. There is great potential for the involvement of voluntary groups and agencies, for example, Citizens' Advice Bureaux, Age Concern, Mind, MENCAP as well as voluntary bodies set up to meet the needs of that particular locality. VOLTAGE and RALLY became an important part of the local scene in Dinnington and the social work co-ordinator was planning to bring together a wider group of voluntary bodies involved in similar activities. Could such bodies form an integral part of the complex of services that any area needs? A good example of what can be done is the work of the Huntley Patch Team serving a predominantly rural area of the Grampian Region (Watts 1984). The first step in this scheme was a local information and advice centre, but through this they discovered that there were many unmet needs and a community development function was added. 'Initial projects included a single parent family group, women's opportunity course, luncheon club, a craft co-operative and the provision of a jobs' board' (ibid., p. 56). Eventually this expanded to become the Gordon Rural Action and Information Network (GRAIN).

Is this just development gone wild? The social workers involved would not agree.

> Through the creation of a new organisation, GRAIN, we as social workers have available to us *locally* a variety of new resources to satisfy individual clients' needs without the necessity to become a 'social worker' client. In exchange for the creation of the resources the social work department offers support and advice or a social work input to both the agency project committees and individual workers involved in the organisation.
>
> As individual workers or even as a team we feel that it would have been impossible with our individual case loads and other responsibilities to have created so many useful resources in such a comparatively short time without the involvement of other organisations in the community, especially the Information Centre, which genuinely identifies Community Needs.

This goes a long way towards answering a question which was raised in Chapter 9 about whether it was appropriate for trained social workers to be doing some Citizens' Advice Bureau-type work. In the first place we should note that the workers in a CAB are not untrained and that they are generally well supervised. In view of this it may be entirely appropriate for a trained social worker to deal with a problem which might otherwise have gone to a CAB, had one been available. But that does not apply to all enquiries, and while there is real value in establishing contacts and being aware of problems early on, it is not necessarily the most appropriate way to use trained workers. GRAIN appears to incorporate a CAB-type role and the Honor Oak team in Lewisham included a CAB worker. This really is the ideal solution – to include CAB-type workers within a widely conceived interdisciplinary locality team.

The mutual gains that there had been for the voluntary bodies and the social workers in GRAIN matches what was found in Dinnington. A somewhat similar enterprise was undertaken in Normanton called the Social Care Assembly Normanton (SCAN) which was a town-wide community care council (Hadley and McGrath 1984, pp. 183f.). Such an approach makes it clear that some means need to be found to make community work/community development skills available to the local team. This might be by having a community worker as a member of the team, as was the case in the team that Bennett (1980) describes, or it could be by having the help of consultants.

The message for the statutory agencies is that they must stop thinking, planning and acting in a departmentally restricted way and join forces with other bodies, whether statutory or voluntary. This could well make possible a far better service and quality of individual and corporate life in the locality than could traditional compartmentalized services, however difficult this is for those who value neat and tidy organization.

We do not wish to devalue the importance of patients or clients receiving the skilled help they need, but we have shown that it is far more difficult to make strong links with informal care in a locality than it is to build up good links with other professional workers. The emphasis therefore needs to be placed on a form of organization which facilitates forging strong links with the locality rather than seeing specialist teams as the top priority. The case for this is all the stronger because we have shown that the Dinnington model encouraged excellent interdisciplinary working.

Resources

Locally-based work requires resources, especially time and money. At one time it was thought that there was scope for considerable savings to be made by an approach which was able to make more extensive use of voluntary and informal sources of care in the community. If it is a matter of just thrusting responsibility for care back on families and volunteers unaided then it is a cheap option. However, if we are concerned about providing as good a quality of life as possible for patients and clients and their families, the indications are that the costs are going to be comparable with good high-quality residential care, and, in the sort term, there will be additional costs in setting up the new pattern of service. Furthermore, it is unrealistic to think that there will not be a continuing need for residential care for some people. The main argument is not that a locally-based pattern of care will save money but that for a similar level of expenditure it will provide a more satisfactory quality of life to more people, because it should make it easier to avoid the admission to institutional care of people who neither need it nor want it and whose families do not want it either.

We were always aware of the ideological knife edge between saving money and exploiting people, especially women, which we were walking on this issue, but our position was and is very clear. We wanted to develop a pattern of service which would provide the help and support that was needed to enable families and others to do the caring they wanted to do. Our evidence, along with that of many other studies, is that overall families do *not* neglect their dependent members but often continue caring under great stress. We would argue that a locally-based approach has greater potential for providing effective support for such caring than do traditional area-based services. In relation to this the 1986 judgement of the European Court which will make the invalid care allowance available to married and cohabiting women is very welcome. It illustrates well how local resources are affected by national and international decisions and policies. This is not an argument for centralized decision-making, merely a recognition of the close relationship between national policies and what happens at the local level.

The resources that are required extend beyond the need for money. There is also a need for time (and thus, of course, more money). Time is needed to train people for change; to train people to manage change; and time is needed for the changes to take place. It requires a consistent policy over a number of years supported by a well-thought-out plan of training for locally based services to take root. This requires real commitment from managers to the objectives of locally-based services. The managers then need to learn the skills to enable changes to take place; fieldworkers need the time to work out how their practice should change; and ordinary people need to be involved in consultation and planning to ensure that change takes place in accordance with community-defined needs. This all takes time and needs to be recognized and budgeted for at the outset.

Conclusion

Have we been too optimistic? Are the blocks to real participation so formidable that it is unrealistic to expect slow incremental change to be sufficient? Is a more radical reorientation needed? We cannot give a definite answer to those questions but when we look back at the project it was the small-scale bottom-up initiatives, like the splendid RALLY scheme, which worked and the top-down organization like the Project Management Team which did not. It takes longer to encourage growth from below but, in the long run, it is likely to be more effective.

It would be idle and improper to assume that the movement towards more local, smaller-scale, more accessible health and welfare services is based purely on the belief that such services will be more efficient and will meet people's needs better. It is worth mentioning briefly some of the beliefs that we think underlie the decision to develop the health and welfare services in this way.

1. We talk about *personal* health and welfare services. One of the hopes is that by organizing the services on a small-scale local basis, the *scale* of the services can be more human and more manageable. It therefore gives the services a much better chance of being personal.
2. The small scale and, we hope, their increasing local involvement, gives people, especially those who are vulnerable, a better chance of exerting more control over their lives and over those, especially professionals, who are there theoretically to *serve* them.
3. The emphasis on an integrated service reflects a concern that people should be treated as whole people, valuable in their own right as persons, not as a collection of symptoms or problems.
4. The emphasis on seeing people in their social context reflects a desire to treat them not just as separate individuals but recognizes that it is as social beings that we attain our human identity.
5. The emphasis on the social context also reflects a belief that the environment can be a contributor to the social problems that clients may manifest; and we need to move away from focusing purely on individual or family failure as an explanation of their problems.
6. Perhaps the most important belief underlying the project is the notion of reciprocity, that it is important to give all people, including clients or patients, the opportunity to give as well as to receive. Richard Titmuss (1970, p. 255) wrote :

The ways in which society organises and structures its social institutions – and particularly its health and welfare systems – can encourage or discourage the altruistic in man. Some systems can foster integration or alienation; they can allow the 'theme of the gift' – of generosity towards strangers – to spread among and between social groups and generations. It is an aspect of freedom in the 20th century which, compared with the emphasis on consumer choice in material acquisitiveness, is insufficiently recognised. It is indeed little understood how modern society, technical, professional, large-scale organised society, allows few opportunities for ordinary people to articulate giving in morally practical terms outside their own network of family and personal relationships.

Thus at the heart of this project was the question, which we discussed earlier, about what the relationship should be between services and served, between society and those whom society pays and authorizes to act on its behalf for some of its members. It is an important question which does not just affect those working in the health and welfare services, but the whole of society. We would claim that a society in which the health and welfare services are so organized that they encourage reciprocity will be a healthier one. Indeed we would hope that any crude distinction between givers and receivers will become blurred and disappear because at different times we are all both. A recognition of our mutual interdependence may make us a saner society.

Of course the Dinnington Project has not lived up to all its hopes. We have catalogued its failures and successes in exhaustive (and probably exhausting) detail, but we have no doubt that the project was an honest step in the right direction, that is to organize the health and welfare services, in Schumacher's words, 'as if people mattered'.

Bibliography

Abrams, M. (1978), *Beyond Three Score and Ten: A First Report on a Survey of the Elderly*, Mitcham, Surrey, Age Concern Publications.

Abrams, P. (1978), 'Community care: some research problems and priorities' in Barnes, J. and Connelly, M. (eds), *Social Care Research*, London, Bedford Square Press.

Allibone, A. and Coles, R. (1982), '*A study of the cost-effectiveness of a community caring scheme providing medical services for the patients of a primary health care team in a rural area — England — UK*' Department of Economic & Social Studies, University of East Anglia.

Aves, G.M. (Chairman) (1969), *The Voluntary Worker in the Social Services*, London, Allen & Unwin.

Baldock, P. (1983), 'Patch systems: a radical change for the better?' in Sinclair, I. and Thomas, D. (eds), *Perspectives on Patch*, London, National Institute for Social Work, pp. 38–45.

Baldwin, S. (1977), *Disabled Children — Counting the Costs*, London, Disability Alliance.

Ball, C. and Ball, M. (1982), *What the Neighbours Say: A Report on a Study of Neighbours*, Berkhamsted, The Volunteer Centre.

Barclay Report (1982), *Social Workers, their Role and Tasks*, London, Bedford Square Press.

Barker, J. (1980), 'The relationship of "informal" care to "formal" social services' in Lonsdale, S., Webb, A. and Briggs, T. (eds), *Teamwork in the Personal Social Services and Health Care*, London, Croom Helm.

Bartlett, H.M. (1970),*The Common Base of Social Work Practice*, New York, National Association of Social Workers.

Bayley, M.J. (1973), *Mental Handicap and Community Care*, London, Routledge and Kegan Paul.

Bayley, M.J. (1978), *Community Oriented Systems of Care*, Berkhamsted, The Volunteer Centre.

Bayley, M.J. and Parker, P. (1978), 'Use of Assets and Development of Social Services Project: a report on services in Dinnington', report to Rotherham MBC, July, unpublished.

Bayley, M.J., Parker, P., Seyd, R. and Tennant, A. (1981), *Origins, Strategy and Proposed Evaluation*, Neighbourhood Services Project, Dinnington, Paper No. 1., Department of Sociological Studies, University of Sheffield.

Bennett, B. (1980), 'The Sub-office: a team approach to local authority fieldwork practice', in Brake, M. and Bailey, R. (eds), *Radical Social Work and Practice*, London, Arnold.

Bennett, B. (1983), 'A View from the Field', in Sinclair, I. and Thomas, D. (eds), *Perspectives on Patch*, London, National Institute for Social Work, pp.52-64.

Beresford, P. and Croft, S. (1981), *Community Control of Social Services Departments: a discussion document*, London, Battersea Community Action.

Beresford, P. (1984), *Patch in Perspective: Decentralising and Democratising Social Services*, London, Battersea Community Action.

Beresford, P. and Croft, S. (1986), *Whose Welfare: Private Care and Public Services?*, Brighton, Lewis Cohen Urban Studies Centre.

Black, J., Bowl, R., Burns, D., Critcher, C., Grant, G. and Stockford, D. (1983), *Social work in Context*, London, Tavistock.

Boldy, D. (1976), 'A Study of the Wardens of Grouped Dwellings for the Elderly', *Social and Economic Administration*, Vol. 10, No. 1, pp.59-67.

Bowling, A. and Cartwright, A. (1982), *Life after Death: A study of the elderly widowed*, London, Tavistock.

Brake, M. and Bailey, R. (eds) (1980), *Radical Social Work and Practice*, London, Arnold.

Bristow, A.K. (1981), *Crossroads Care Attendant Schemes*, Rugby, Association of Crossroads Care Attendant Schemes.

Bulmer, M. (1986), *Neighbours: The work of Philip Abrams*, Cambridge, Cambridge University Press.

Butcher, H. and Crosbie, D. (1977), *Pensioned off: A study of the needs of elderly people in Cleator Moor*, University of York Papers in Community Studies, No. 15, CDP Unit, Department of Social Administration, University of York.

Cantor, M. (1975), 'Life Space and the Social Support System of the Inner City Elderly of New York', *Gerontologist*, No. 15, pp. 23-26.

Cantor, M. (1980), 'The informal support system: its relevance in the lives of the elderly' in Bergatta, E.F. and McClusky, M.G. (eds), *Aging and Society*, London, Sage.

Cartwright, A., Hockey, L. and Anderson, J.L. (1973), *Life before Death*, London, Routledge & Kegan Paul.

Challis, D. and Davies, B. (1980), 'A new approach to community care for the elderly', *British Journal of Social Work*, vol.10, no.1.

Challis, D. (1983), 'A new life at home', *Community Care*, 24 March.

CIPFA (1981), *Personal Social Services Statistics 1979–80 Actuals*, London, CIPFA.

Collins, A.H. and Pancoast, D.L. (1977), *'Applying social work skill to natural networks'*, paper presented at National Association of Social Workers Symposium, San Diego, California, 21 November.

Cooper, M. (1983), 'Community social work', in Jordan, B. and Parton, N. (eds), *The Political Dimension of Social Work*, Oxford, Blackwell.

Craig, J. (1985), *A 1981 Socio-economic classification of Local and Health Authorities of Great Britain*, London, HMSO.

Craven, E., Rimmer, L. and Wicks, M. (1982), *Family Issues and Public Policy*, London, Study Commission on the Family.

Crawford, L., Smith, P. and Taylor, L. (1978), *It Makes Good Sense: A Handbook for Working with Natural Helpers*, Portland, Oregon, Portland State University Graduate School of Social Work.

Croft, S. and Beresford, P. (1984), 'Patch and participation: the case for citizen research', *Social Work Today*, 17 September.

Curle, A. (1949), 'A theoretical approach to action research', *Human Relations*, no.2, pp.269–80.

Currie, R. and Parrott, B. (1981), *A Unitary Approach to Social Work – Applications in Practice*, Birmingham, British Association of Social Workers Publications.

Davies, B., Barton, A. and McMillan, I. (1973), 'The silting of unadjustable resources and the planning of personal social services', *Policy and Politics*, vol.1, no.4, pp.341–55.

Department of Health and Social Security (1981a), *Care in the Community: A*

Consultative Document on Moving Resources for Care in England, London, DHSS.

Department of Health and Social Security (1981b), *Growing Older*, Cmnd 8173, London, HMSO.

Department of Health and Social Security (1986a), *Neighbourhood Nursing – A Focus for Care: Report of the Community Nursing Review* (Chair: Julia Cumberledge), London, HMSO.

Department of Health and Social Security (1986b), *Primary Health Care: An Agenda for Discussion*, Cmnd 9771, London, HMSO.

Dexter, M. and Harbert, W. (1983), *The Home Help Service*, London, Tavistock.

Dimond, E.(1984), *'An alternative to residential care? The evaluation of a community care initiative for the rural elderly in Gwynedd'*, unpublished MA thesis, University College of North Wales.

Durie, A. and Wilkin, D. (1982), 'Gender and the care of dependent elderly people', Paper presented to the British Sociological Association Conference, Manchester.

Equal Opportunities Commission (1980), *The Experience of Caring for Elderly and Handicapped Dependents: Survey Report*, Manchester, EOC.

Equal Opportunities Commission, (1982), *Caring for the Elderly and Handicapped: Community Care Policies and Women's Lives*, Manchester, EOC.

Evans, R.J. (1978), 'Unitary models of practice and the social work team' in Olsen, M.R. (ed.), *The Unitary Model*, London, British Association of Social Workers.

Fahsbeck, D.F. and Jones, A.M. (1973), *Progress on Family Problems: A Natural Study of Clients' and Counsellors' Views on Family Agency Services*, New York, Family Service Association of America.

Finch, J. and Groves, D. (1980), 'Community care and the family: a case for equal opportunities?, *Journal of Social Policy*, vol.9, no. 4, pp.487–511.

Fischer, C.S. (1982), *To Dwell Among Friends: Personal Networks in Town and City*, Chicago, University of Chicago Press.

Ford, G. and Taylor, R. (1985), 'The elderly as underconsulters: a critical reappraisal', *Journal of the Royal College of General Practitioners*, vol.35, pp.244–7.

Frankenberg, R. (1966), *Communities in Britain*, Harmondsworth, Penguin Books.

Froland, C., Pancoast, D., Chapman, N. and Kimboko, P. (1981), *Helping Networks and Human Services*, London, Sage.

Fry, J. (1977), 'The control of practice' in *Trends in General Practice*, Royal College of General Practitioners.

Glennerster, H. (1982), 'Barter and bargains', *Health and Social Services Journal*, 24 June.

Goldberg, E., Mortimer, A. and Williams, B. (1970), *Helping the Aged*, London, Allen & Unwin.

Goldberg, E.M. and Connelly, N. (1982), *The Effectiveness of Social Care for the Elderly*, London, Policy Studies Institute/Heinemann.

Goldberg, E.M. and Warburton, R.C. (1979), *Ends and Means in Social Work*, London, Allen & Unwin.

Gottlieb, B.H. (ed.,) (1981), *Social Networks and Social Support*, London, Sage.

Hadley, R., Dale, P. and Sills, P. (1984), *Decentralising Social Services: A Model for Change*, London, Bedford Square Press.

Hadley, R. and McGrath, M. (eds) (1980), *Going Local: Neighbourhood Social Services*, NCVO Occasional Paper no.1, London, Bedford Square Press.

Hadley, R. and McGrath, M. (1981), 'Patch systems in SSDs: more than a passing fashion', *Social Work Service*, no.26, May.

Hadley, R. and McGrath, M. (1984), *When Social Services are Local: the Normanton*

Experience, London, Allen & Unwin.

Haines, J. (1975), *Skills and Methods in Social Work,* London, Constable.

Hedley, R. and Norman, A. (1982), *Home Help: Key Issues in Service Provision,* London, Centre for Policy on Ageing.

Henwood, M. and Wicks, M. (1984), *The Forgotten Army: Family Care and Elderly People,* London, Family Policy Studies Centre.

Hillingdon, London Borough of (1977), *Domiciliary Services Evaluation, Part III, the Home Help Services,* Social Services Research.

Holder, D. and Wardle, M. (1981), *Teamwork and the Development of the Unitary Approach,* London, Routledge & Kegan Paul.

Holme, A. and Maizels, J. (1978), *Social Workers and Volunteers,* London, Allen & Unwin.

Hughes, N.J. (1986), *'Ideology, social work and the politics of patch',* unpublished MA thesis, Department of Sociological Studies, University of Sheffield.

Hunt, A. (1978), *The Elderly at Home: A Study of People aged Sixty-five and over Living in the Community in England in 1976,* London, HMSO.

Illing, M. and Donovan, B. (1981), *District Nursing,* London, Baillière Tindall.

Isaacs, B. and Neville, Y. (1976), 'The measurement of need in old people', *Scottish Home and Health Studies,* no.34.

Johnson, M.L., Di Gregorio, S. and Harrison, B. (1981), *Ageing, Needs and Nutrition: A Study of Voluntary and Statutory Collaboration in Community Care for Elderly People,* London, Policy Studies Institute, Research Paper, 82/1.

Knight, B. and Hayes R. (1981), *Self Help in the Inner City,* London, London Voluntary Service Council.

Kratz, C.R. (ed.) (1979), *The Nursing Process,* London, Baillière Tindall.

Kushlick, A. (1970), 'Residential care for the mentally subnormal', *Royal Society of Health Journal,* vol.90, no.5, pp.255–61.

Kushlick, A. and Blunden, R. (1974), *Proposals for the Setting Up and Evaluation of an Experimental Service for the Elderly,* Health Care Evaluation Research Team, Wessex Regional Health Authority.

Land, H. (1978), 'Who cares for the family?', *Journal of Social Policy,* vol.7, no.3, pp.257–84.

Leat, D. (1979), *Limited Liability? A Report on Some Good Neighbour Schemes,* Berkhamsted, The Volunteer Centre.

Leat, D. (1983), *Getting to Know the Neighbours: A Pilot Study of the Elderly and Neighbourly Helping,* London, Policy Studies Institute.

Leighton, N. (1983), 'Patch in perspective' in Sinclair, I. and Thomas, D.N. (eds), *Perspectives on Patch,* London, National Institute for Social Work.

Litwak, E. and Szelenyi, I. (1969), 'Primary group structures and their functioning: kin, neighbours and friends', *American Sociological Review,* vol.34, pp.465–81.

MacDonald, R., Qureshi, H. and Walker, A. (1984), 'Sheffield shows the way', *Community Care,* 18 October.

MacMillan, K. (1977), *Education Welfare: Strategy and Structure,* London, Longman.

Marshall, M. (1983), *Social Work with Old People,* London, Macmillan.

McIntosh, J.B. (1979), 'Decision making on the district', *Nursing Times,* 19 July.

Mocroft, I. (1981), 'The Milson Road Project' in *Volunteers in Primary Health Care: Two Case Studies,* Berkhamsted, The Volunteer Centre.

Moroney, R.M. (1980), *Families, Social Services and Social Policy,* Washington, DC, US Department of Health and Human Services.

Munday, B. and Turner, S. (1981), *Partnership or Take Over? A Study of*

Professional–Volunteer Collaboration in Social Care, University of Kent at Canterbury.

Nissel, M. and Bonnerjea, L. (1982), *Family Care of the Handicapped Elderly: Who Pays?*, London, Policy Studies Institute, No.602.

Office of Population Censuses and Surveys (1981), *Access to Primary Health Care*, London, HMSO.

Office of Population Censuses and Surveys (1982), *General Household Survey 1980*, London, HMSO.

Office of Population Censuses and Surveys (1984), *Social Trends 14*, London, HMSO.

Pancoast, D. and Collins, A.H. (1976), *Natural Helping Networks: A Strategy for Prevention*, Washington, DC, National Association of Social Workers.

Parker, R. (1981), 'Tending and social policy' in Goldberg, E.M. and Hatch, S. (eds), *A New Look at the Personal Social Services*, Discussion Paper no.4, London, Policy Studies Institute.

Parsloe, P. (1981), *Social Services Area Teams*, London, Allen & Unwin.

Payne, M. (1982), *Working in Teams*, London, Macmillan.

Pendleton, D., Schofield, T., Tate, P. and Havelock, P. (1984), *The Consultation: An Approach to Learning and Teaching*, Oxford General Practice Series 6, Oxford, Oxford University Press.

Pincus, A. and Minahan, A. (1973), *Social Work Practice: Model and Method*, Itaska, Illinois, Peacock Publications.

Plank, D. (1977), *'Caring for the elderly: a report of a study of various means of caring for dependent elderly people in eight London Boroughs'*, Greater London Council research memorandum, July 1977.

Pritchard, P. (1981), *Patient Participation in General Practice*, Occasional Paper 17, London, Royal College of General Practitioners.

Qureshi, H., Challis, D. and Davies, B. (1981), *Motivations and Rewards of Helpers in the Kent Community Care Scheme*, Discussion Paper No.202, University of Kent Personal Social Services Research Unit.

Rapoport, R.N. (1970), 'Three dilemmas in action research', *Human Relations*, vol.23, no.6, pp.499–511.

Reid, W.J. and Smith, H.D. (1981), *Research in Social Work*, New York, Columbia University Press.

Ridgwick, J.H. (Chairman of Working Party) (1981), *Strategic Planning of Services for the Mentally Handicapped*, Sheffield Area Health Authority.

Riverside Child Health Project (1983), *Annual Report, May 1983*, Newcastle-upon-Tyne.

Robinson, M. (1978), *Schools and Social Work*, London, Routledge & Kegan Paul.

Rossiter, L. and Wicks, M. (1982), *Crisis or Challenge? Family Care of Elderly People and Social Policy*, Occasional Paper No.8, London, Study Commission of the Family.

Royal College of General Practitioners (1986), *Quality in Practice Bulletin*, no. 29, October.

Sainsbury, E., Nixon, S. and Phillips, D. (1982), *Social Work in Focus: Clients' and Social Workers' Perceptions of Long-term Social Work*, London, Routledge & Kegan Paul.

Schlotfeldt, R.M. (1975), 'The need for a conceptual framework' in Verhonick, P.J. (ed.), *Nursing Research*, Boston, Little, Brown & Co.

Schon, D.A. (1971), *Beyond the Stable State*, London, Temple Smith.

Seebohm Report (1968), *Report of the Committee on Local Authority and Allied*

Personal Social Services, Cmnd 3702, London, HMSO.

Shanas, E., Townsend, P., Wedderburn, D., Friis, H., Milhoj, P. and Stenhouwer, J. (1968), *Old People in Three Industrial Countries,* London, Routledge & Kegan Paul.

Sharron, H. (1982), 'A stitch in time', *Social Work Today,* vol.13,no.18, 12 January.

Sinclair, I., Crosbie, D., O'Connor, P., Stanforth, L. and Vickery, A. (1984), *Networks Project: A Study of Informal Care, Services and Social Work for Elderly Clients Living Alone,* London, National Institute for Social Work Research Unit.

Skeffington Report (1969), *People and Planning: Report of the Committee on Public Participation in Planning,* London, HMSO.

Smith, Gilbert (1978), *Social Work, Community Work and Society. Block 2, The Organizational and Legal Context,* The Open University, Milton Keynes, Open University Press.

Smith, G. and Ames, J. (1976), 'Area teams in social work practice', *British Journal of Social Work,* vol.6, no.1.

Stevenson, O. (1980), 'Social service teams in the United Kingdom', in Lonsdale, S., Webb, A. and Briggs, T. (eds), *Teamwork in the Personal Social Services and Health Care,* London, Croom Helm.

Stevenson, O. (1981), *Specialisation in Social Service Teams,* London, Allen & Unwin.

Stevenson, O. and Parsloe, P. (1978), *Social Service Teams: The Practitioner's View,* London, HMSO.

Stott, N.C.H. and Davis, R.H. (1979), 'The exceptional potential in each primary case consultation', *Journal of Royal College of General Practitioners,* vol.29, pp.201–5.

Study Commission on the Family (1980), *Happy Families : A Discussion Paper on Families in Britain,* London.

Tennant, A. and Bayley, M. (1985) 'The eighth decade: family structure and support networks in the community' in Yoder, J.A. (ed.), *Support Networks in a Caring Community,* Dordrecht, Martinus Nijhoff.

Thatcher, M. (1981), Speech to the Women's Royal Voluntary Service, 19 January.

Thomas, D. and Shaftoe, H. (1983), 'Does casework need a neighbourhood orientation?' in Sinclair, I. and Thomas, D. (eds), *Perspectives on Patch,* London , National Institute for Social Work, pp.31–7.

Titmuss, R.M. (1970), *The Gift Relationship: From Human Blood to Social Policy,* London, Allen & Unwin.

Tizard, J. (1964), *Community Services for the Mentally Handicapped,* London, Oxford University Press.

Townsend, P. (1963), *The Family Life of Old People,* Harmondsworth, Penguin Books.

Vickery, A. (1982), 'Settling into patch ways', *Community Care,* 14 January.

Walker, A. (1981), 'When there is someone to help you, there's no place like home', *Social Work Today,* vol.12, no.20.

Walker, A. (ed.) (1982), *Community Care: the Family, the State and Social Policy,* Oxford, Basil Blackwell and Martin Robertson.

Walker, G. (1975), 'Social networks in rural space: a comparison of two Southern Ontario Localities', *East Lakes Geographer,* vol.10, pp.68–77.

Warburton, W.R. (1982), *What Social Workers Do,* Cambridgeshire County Council Social Services Department.

Warren, D.I. (1981), *Helping Networks: How People Cope with Problems in the Urban Community,* Notre Dame, Indiana, University of Notre Dame Press.

Watts, S. (1984), 'The development of the Huntley patch system' in Hadley, R. and Cooper, M. (eds), *Patch Based Social Services Teams, Bulletin No. 3,* Department of Social Administration, Fylde College, University of Lancaster.

Webb, R. and Craig, J. (1978), 'Socio-economic classification of Local Authority Areas' in *OPCS Studies on Medical and Population Subjects,* no.35, London, HMSO.

Wells, K. (1980), *Social Care for the Terminally Ill at Home and the Bereaved,* Kent Voluntary Service Council.

Welsh Office (1982), *Report of the All-Wales Working Party on Services for Mentally Handicapped People,* Cardiff.

Wenger, G.C. (1984), *The Supportive Network,* London, Allen & Unwin.

Whitehouse, A. (1982), 'The integration of a community', *Community Care,* 26 August.

Whittaker, J.K. (1983), 'Mutual helping in human service practice', in Whittaker, J.K. and Garbarino, J. (eds), *Social Support Networks: Informal Helping in the Human Services,* New York, Aldine Publishing Company.

Wilkin, D. (1979), *Caring for the Mentally Handicapped Child,* London, Croom Helm.

Williamson, J., Stokoe, I.H. and Gray, S. (1964), 'Old people at home: their unreported needs'. *Lancet,* no.1, pp.1117–20.

Willcocks, A.J. (Chairman) (1972), *Role of the Warden in Grouped Housing,* Report to Age Concern of the Working Party set up to consider the role of the grouped (sheltered) housing schemes for the elderly, Age Concern.

Wilson, E. (1982), 'Women, the "Community" and the "Family" in Walker, A. (ed.) *Community Care, the Family, the State and Social Policy,* Oxford, Basil Blackwell and Martin Robertson.

Wolfenden Report (1978), *The Future of Voluntary Organisations,* London, Croom Helm.

Young, K. (1982), 'Changing social services in East Sussex', *Local Government Studies,* March–April, pp. 18–22.

Younghusband, E. (1973), 'The future of social work', *Social Work Today,* vol.4, no.2, pp.33–7.

Index

'Aber' study, 68
Abrams, Mark, 36
Abrams, Philip, 33, 162
accessibility (of staff), 88, 102, 106
accountability, 9 -10, 26, 88-9, 156, 160
Activities of Daily Living scales, 38
activity levels, 161-2
Age Concern, 75-6, 178
aids and adaptations officer, 134, 135, 139
Allibone, A., 11
alongside the community (development model), 51, 54
Ames, J., 65
Anglesey scheme, 13
assessments (joint), 178
attitudinal change, 21, 51-52, 54
Aves Report (1969), 5

Bailey, R., 14
Baldock, Peter, 18
Barclay Report (1982), 5, 54, 77, 115, 154, 176
Barker, J., 33
basic nursing care, 42-3
battered wives hostel, 150
Bayley, M., 1, 3, 5-6, 22 ,23, 28, 41, 128, 144, 161, 168
Bennett, B., 14, 65, 172, 179
Beresford, P., 7, 20, 148, 159
Beveridge Report (1942), 17
Black, J., 8-9, 65, 68, 176
Blunden, R., 12
Blunkett, David, 18
Boldy, Duncan, 137
Bonnerjea, L., 33, 43, 45
Brake, M., 14
Bristow, A.K., 33, 45

Bulmer, M., 161, 162
Butcher, H., 36, 48

Cantor, Marjorie, 35, 42, 44
care
    formal (before project), 56-77
    hierarchy, 42-4
    informal, see informal care
    packages of, 12, 13, 157, 158
Care Co-ordinator, 22
Care in the Community (DHSS), 5
carers' perspective, 156-9
carer study, 29-30, 147
Cartwright, A., 44
caseloads, 8, 96-107
caseload study, 28, 84, 144, 149, 155
Census (1981), 31
Central Index on Request, 129
centralization, 10, 19
Challis, D., 12
Chief Officers' meeting, 27, 167
child abuse, 98, 103, 117, 118
Citizens' Advice Bureau, 112, 178
Cleator Moor study, 36
'client model', 79
clients
    satisfaction, 147-9, 152-6, 159-60
    user study, 29, 147-9
    views of, 149-53
Coles, R., 11
Collins, A.H., 15, 16, 79
Combined Care Team, 22
Community Care, 14, 113
community care
    assumptions/premises, 1-3
    development of notion, 5
Community Development Projects, 7

community health councils, 10
community practice model, 51-55
community social workers
    (viability), 115-19
community support worker, 13
concentration levels, 161-62
confidentiality, 172-3
Connelly, N., 64
Conservative Party, 17
consultation, 6-7
    rates, 56-9, 83, 85
contextual organizational problems,
    176, 177
control, 7
Cooper, M., 172
co-operation, 11, 18, 21
core team, 26, 113
    induction course, 78, 79-80
    - research team meeting, 166,
    167-8
Craig, John, 31
Crawford, L., 15
crisis intervention theory, 118
Croft, S., 7, 20, 148, 159
Crosbie, D., 36, 48
Crossroads study, 45
Cumberledge Report (1986), 60, 91,
    164, 174, 175
Currie, R., 14, 114

Davies, B., 12
Davis, R.H., 57
decentralization, 19-20, 51-52, 103,
    114, 115-16, 117, 128
decision-making, 95
democratization, 18
demographic developments, 16
depression, 19
Dexter, M., 70
DHSS, 11, 27, 70, 98, 139, 164
Diary Study, 135
Dimond, E., 12
Dinnington
    characteristics, 31-2
    informal care in, 32-49
Dinnington Comprehensive School,
    98
Dinnington Project
    aims and scope, 164-82
    assumptions and premises, 1-3
    community practice model, 51-55
    context (informal care), 4-20
    formal care before, 56-77
    health service, 83-93
    influence of, 78-82
    local services, 123-46
    real partnership (evidence), 147-
    63
    setting up, 21-30
    social workers, 94-122
district nurses, 59-63, 86-91, 92
Dobbs, 59-60
domestic setting (care), 12-13
Dunnell, 59-60
Durie, A., 45
dynamic conservatism, 167

education welfare officer, 26, 76, 99,
    103, 146
elderly
    demographic developments, 16
    hospital-at-home scheme, 11, 12-
    13
    housing assistant (role), 130-33
Elderly Persons' Support Unit, 13
Employment, Department of, 98
'encapsulated case-load' model, 8
energy problems, 117
entrepreneurial activities, 158, 161
Equal Opportunities Commission,
    33, 45
ex-clients, 151-53
exploitation, 173, 174, 180

Fahsbeck, D.F., 118
family care, 1-2
family-centred intervention, 119,
    121
family problems, 117, 150
Family Service Unit, 14
fieldworkers' meeting, 78, 81,
    165-8

Fischer, C.S., 15, 49
flexibility, 9, 13, 107, 174
Ford, G., 57
formal care (before project)
  district nurses, 59-63
  educational welfare officer, 76
  general practitioners, 56-9
  health visitor, 63-4
  home helps, 71-74
  social workers, 64-71
  wardens, 74-6
four-to-six-month cases, 106
Frankenberg, R., 33
free market system, 17
friends (role), 34-9, 41-4
Froland, C., 15
from-the-bottom-up approach, 22, 23
Fry, J., 57
full employment, 19

Garbarino, J., 15
Gateshead scheme, 12
Gemeinschaft settings, 33
general care, 41, 42, 43
General Household Survey, 34, 38,
  48, 56, 85
generalism (and specialism), 174-9
'general practitioner model', 176
general practitioners, 11, 12, 56-9,
  164
  changes, 83-6
  study, 28-9
geographical factors (Dinnington),
  48-9
Glennerster, H., 11
Goldberg, E., 10, 65, 67, 69, 97, 154
Gordon Rural Action and
  Information Network, 178-9
gossip networks, 144, 173
Gottlieb, B.H., 15
GRAIN, 178-9
group-centred intervention, 119, 121
Growing Older (White Paper), 6

Hadley, R., 7, 79, 155, 159, 162, 166
  174, 179

Harbert, W., 71
Hayes, R., 33
health service, 83-93
  developments, 10-12
  welfare and, 2-3
Health Services and Public Health
  Act (1968), 139
health visitor, 63-4, 91, 93
Hedley, R., 73
Henwood, M., 16
'hierarchical compensatory model',
  44
Hillingdon study, 72
Holder, D., 13-14
Holme, A., 65
home helps, 24, 25, 26, 71-74, 99,
  102, 123-8
Honor Oak team, 179
hospital-at-home schemes, 11, 12-13
household care, 42, 43
Housewives Register, 105
housing, 114, 117
  sheltered, 134-9
  assistant, 26, 95, 128-31
  case studies, 131-34
Hughes, N.J., 19, 20
Hunt, A., 31, 34, 36, 45
Huntley Patch Team, 178
Hyde Park Project, 169-70

induction course, 78, 79-80
informal care
  assumptions and premises, 1-3
  political interest in, 17-20
  professional interest in, 4-16
  variability, 50, 83, 171
  volatility, 50, 83, 103-4, 118, 171
  vulnerability, 50, 117, 171
informal care (Dinnington)
  extent and source, 34-5
  geographical factors, 48-9
  making visits, 38-9
  network size, 39-41
  relatives/friends/neighbours, 41-4
  research evidence, 32-4
  responsiveness to need, 37-8

sex roles in caring, 44-8
visiting frequency, 35-6
'integrating methods' phase, 13
integration, 11-12, 164-8, 181
interdisciplinary approach, 11, 177, 179
intervention levels, 119-22
political interest, 17-20
invalid care allowance, 180
Isaacs, B., 47

Jenkin, Patrick, 6, 17
job satisfaction, 9
Johnson, M.L., 37-8, 48
joint financing, 11, 166
Jones, A.M., 118

Kent scheme, 12
key figures, 80
Knight, B., 33
Kratz, C.R., 10
Kushlick, A., 12

Labour Party, 18
Land, H., 47
'lay referral network', 70
learning systems, 167-8, 170
Leighton, N., 172
Litwak, E., 44
local authority services
education welfare office, 146
health services, 83-93
Home help service, 123-8
housing assistant, 128-34
reorganization, 4, 10, 21
social workers, 94-122
warden service, 134-46
localization, 94
locally-based approach, 13, 20
patch system, 7, 14, 18, 79, 117, 172, 177-8
theoretical model, 119-22
local participation, 168-70
long-term cases, 98-104, 117-18
long-term clients, 149-51

MacDonald, R., 13
McGrath, M., 7, 14, 79, 155, 159, 162, 174, 179
MacMillan, K., 76
Maizels, J., 65
marital problems, 117
meals-on-wheels (Leeds), 37-8
medium-term cases, 100-101, 104-6, 118-19
meetings
core team-research team, 166-8,
fieldworkers', 78, 81, 165-6, 167
MENCAP, 7, 178
mental handicap, 1-2, 12, 13
Milson Road Project, 11
Minahan, A., 13, 14
Mind, 178
Mocroft, I., 11
morbidity patterns, 84
'multi-method phase', 13
Munday, B., 112
mutual help groups, 5, 6

natural helping networks, 15-16
needs, responsiveness to, 37-8
neighbourhood care schemes, 11
neighbourhood-centred care, 119, 121
neighbourhood nursing services, 11, 91, 175
Neighbourhood Services Unit, 25, 27, 168
neighbours
natural helping networks, 15-16
role, 34-9, 41-4
network-centred intervention, 119, 121
'network dimension', 69
networks
characteristics (Dinnington), 32-50
informal (contact with), 153, 155-6
natural helping, 15-16
partnership within, 170-71

size (Dinnington), 39-41
strategy planning, 160-63, 171
network system consultant, 90, 92, 118, 161
Neville, Y., 47
Nissel, M., 33, 43, 45
non-accidental injury, 103, 116
non-user study, 30, 41
Norman, A., 73
Normanton team, 172, 173, 179
nurses, 59-63, 86-91, 92
nursing auxiliaries, 59, 60
nursing officer, 26
nursing process, 10-12

Office of Population Census and Surveys, 31, 82
General Household Survey, 34, 38, 48, 56, 85
one-off referrals, 113, 154
organization (community practice), 51-55
organizational changes, 21
organizational problems, 176, 178
outside the community (development model), 51, 52-3

packages of care, 12, 13, 157, 158
Pancoast, D.L., 15, 16, 79
parents' groups, 6
Parker, Paul, 24, 25, 27, 28, 79, 80, 144
Parker, Roy, 47
Parrott, B., 14, 114
Parsloe, P., 8-9, 176
participation, 6-7, 168-70
partnership, 3, 170-71
evidence of improvement, 147-63
patch system, 7, 14, 18-19, 79, 118, 172, 177, 178
paternalism, 17
patient associations, 11
Payne, M., 54, 168
Pendleton, D., 58
peripatetic wardens, 139-45
personal services, 181

person-centred intervention, 119, 121
Pincus, A., 13, 14
Pinker, Professor, 115, 154
Plank, D., 138
political interest (in informal care), 17-20
Poulton, 60
pressure groups, 6
preventive social work, 116, 118
Primary Health Care (Green Paper), 164
principal carers, 29-30, 147, 156-9
Pritchard, P., 11
professional interest (in informal care), 4-16
professionalism, 7, 10, 172-74
project (evidence of improvement)
carers' perspective, 156-9
conflicts of perspective, 153-6
interim appraisal, 159-60
Project Management
Committee, 95
Team, 27, 123, 165-9, 181
project office, 78-9, 91, 120, 145, 164
referrals to, 107-15, 130
public expenditure, 16

RALLY, 82, 92, 121, 136, 161, 178, 181
reciprocity, 181-82
record-keeping, 173
referrals
to district nurse, 88
general practitioners, 83
home help, 124
project office, 107-15, 130
social work, 14, 64-71
referral study, 28, 62, 70, 113, 153
Reid, W.J., 171
relatives (role), 34-9, 41-4
rent arrears, 129, 133
Report of the All-Wales Working Party on Services for Mentally Handicapped People (Welsh

Office), 7
research programme, 27-30
residential wardens, 134-9
resources, 9, 179-80
    access to, 84, 86, 90, 91
    additional (creation), 78, 81-82
'review' system, 97
Richards, Margaret, 14
Ridgwick, J.H., 13
Riverside Child Health Project, 11
Robinson, M., 76
Rotherham Metropolitan District
    Council, 3, 21-2
Chief Executive, 21-2, 23, 25, 26
Royal College of General
    Practitioners, 164

Sainsbury, E., 8-9, 65, 155
satisfaction
    conflicts of perspective, 153-6
    development model, 160-63
    interim appraisal, 159-60
    measurement, 147-9
    principal carers' perspective, 156-9
    views of clients, 149-53
SCAN, 179
Schon, D.A., 167
'Seatown' study, 10, 68, 69
Seebohm Report (1968), 4, 5, 7, 8
self-help, 4, 6, 19, 94
self-referrals, 108, 110, 114
'service orientation', 9, 10
seven-to-eleven-month cases, 104-6
sexual roles (in caring), 44-8
Seyd, Rosalind, 27
Shaftoe, H., 94
Shanas, E., 48
Sharron, H., 116, 118
sheltered accommodation, 134-9
short-term cases, 98, 100-101, 106-7,
    118
short-term clients, 152
Sinclair, I., 9, 14, 56, 163
Skeffington Report (1969), 6
skills, professionalism and, 172-74
Smith, Gilbert, 64, 65, 70

Smith, H.D., 171
social care, 42, 43
Social Care Assembly Normanton,
    179
social class, 18
social service departments
    (developments), 7-10
Social Trends, 83
social work
    client views, 149-53
    community (viability), 115-19
    developments, 13-15
    preventive, 116, 118
social workers
    accessibility, 94, 110, 114
    before project, 64-71
    caseloads, 96-107
    conflicts of perspective, 153-6
    referrals to project office, 107-15
    theoretical model for locally-
        based work, 119-22
    viability of community social
        work, 115-19
specialization, 7
specialism, generalism and, 174-9
State Enrolled Nurse, 59-60
State Registered Nurse, 59-60
Stevenson, Olive, 8, 65, 176-7
Stott, N.C.H., 57
study of process, 30
supervision (one-to-one style), 8
Szelenyi, I., 44

Taylor, R., 57
tending, 47
Tennant, Alan, 27, 41, 161
Thatcher, M., 17
Thomas, D., 94
Titmuss, Richard, 181
Tizard, J., 12
Toc H group, 105
Townsend, P., 33, 45
trade unions, 174
training, 174, 178-9, 180
    induction, 78, 79-80
truancy levels, 146

Turner, S., 112

unitary approach, 13-15
Urban Aid, 25-6, 27
user study, 29, 147-9

variability (informal care), 49, 83,
    171
Vickery, Anne, 14
visits
    inward, 35-6, 37, 42, 45, 46
    outward, 38-9
volatility, 49, 83, 103-4, 118,171
VOLTAGE, 81, 88, 92, 121, 132,
    135-6, 144, 161, 178
voluntary bodies, 4, 6, 7, 19
    RALLY, 82, 92, 121, 136, 161,
        178, 181
    VOLTAGE, 81, 88, 92, 121, 132,
        135-6, 144, 161, 178
vulnerability, 49, 118, 171

wages, 18, 173-4
Walker, A., 44
Warburton, R.C., 10, 65, 67, 68,
    108, 154
wardens, 24-6, 74-6, 99-100

peripatetic, 139-45
residential, 134-9
Wardle, M., 13-14
Warren, D.I., 15
wartime conditions, 19
Watts, S., 178
Webb, Richard, 31
welfare, health and, 2-3
welfare state, 4
    political interests, 17-20
Wells, K., 11
Welsh Office, 7
Wenger, G.C., 33-4, 40, 48-9
Whitehouse, Anne, 114, 115
Whittaker, J.K., 15, 90, 119, 162
Wicks, M., 16
Wilkin, D., 45
Willcocks, A.J., 75-6
Williamson, J., 57
Wilson, E., 47
within the community
    (development model), 51, 53,
        54-5
    theoretical model, 119-22
Wolfenden Report (1978), 5
worker study, 30, 137
working parties, 21-2, 25-7